NOT IN KANSAS ANYMORE

A catalogue record for this
book is available from the
National Library of Australia

NOT IN KANSAS ANYMORE

Christian Faith in a Post-Christian World

Edited by Michael Frost, Darrell Jackson
& David Starling

Not in Kansas Anymore: Christian Faith in a Post-Christian World
© Michael Frost, Darrell Jackson & David Starling 2020

Paperback ISBN: 978-1-5326-7787-8
Hardcover ISBN: 978-1-5326-7788-5

© **Morling Press and Wipf and Stock Publishers 2020**

First Published in Australia in 2020

Morling Press
122 Herring Rd Macquarie Park NSW 2113 Australia
Phone: +61 2 9878 0201
Email: enquiries@morling.edu.au
www.morlingcollege.com/morlingpress

Wipf and Stock Publishers
199 W. 8th Ave., Suite 3
Eugene, OR 97401 United States of America
www.wipfandstock.com

The publication is copyright. Other than for the purposes of study and subject to the conditions of the Copyright Act, no part of this book in any form or by any means (electronic, mechanical, micro-copying, photocopying or otherwise) may be reproduced, stored in a retrieval system, communicated or transmitted without prior written permission.

All Scripture quotations, unless otherwise indicated, are taken from the Holy Bible, New International Version® Anglicised (NIVUK), NIV®. Copyright ©1979, 1984, 2011 by Biblica, Inc.™ Used by permission. All rights reserved worldwide.

Scripture quotations marked 'NRSV-A' are from the New Revised Standard Version Bible: Anglicised Edition, copyright © 1989, 1995 National Council of the Churches of Christ in the United States of America. Used by permission. All rights reserved worldwide.

Designed by: Impressum www.impressum.com.au

CONTENTS

Foreword ix
Michael Frost

Introduction xiii

1
The Beguiling Technicolour of Oz 1
Steve McAlpine

2
Diaspora as Means of Grace: 20
Matthew Anslow

3
No Place for Exile 46
Kate Harrison Brennan

4
The Weapons of our Warfare: 60
David Starling

5
To Aliens and Strangers: 73
Tim MacBride

6
Stooping to Conquer: 87
Edwina Murphy

7
Why We Need the World: 99
Dave Benson

8
Christian School Communities 128
James Dalziel

9
Humility, Embodiment and Contextualisation: 145
Karina Kreminski

10
Dangerous Memories 159
Brooke Prentis

11
Re-placing Mission: 180
Darrell Jackson

12
An Endlessly Cunning, Risky Process of Negotiation 194
Michael Frost
Bibliography 211
Not In Kansas Anymore

FOREWORD
Michael Frost

Given the remarkable cultural shifts that have occurred in the West over the past fifty years, it's tempting for Christians to want to close their eyes, click the heels of their shiny red shoes, and repeat, 'There's no place like home', over and over. But we're not in Kansas anymore. Whether we call it the secular age, the post-Enlightenment era or post-Christendom, Christians are struggling to find ways to make sense of their faith in this strange new terrain. This leads to difficult questions about our identity, our place and how we should respond to the world around us.

One of those people trying to develop a road map for the church in a new era is Stephen McAlpine. In 2015, he wrote a blog post entitled, *Christian: Are You Ready For Exile Stage Two?*, in which he said the church's increasing exile from society was occurring in two stages. Exile Stage One, he declared, had occurred around the turn of the century as the church came to terms with cultural shifts that left it feeling overlooked and out of step. He wrote,

> *In Exile Stage One the prevailing narrative was that the Christian church was being marginalised, Christendom was over; the church needed to come up with better strategies; to strip away the dross, and all in order to reconnect Jesus with a lost world.*[1]

---

[1] https://stephenmcalpine.com/christian-are-you-ready-for-exile-stage-two/

He went on to describe Exile Stage One with facetious references to pub churches, MacBooks, coffee snobbery, candle lighting and being able to quote a single line of Lesslie Newbigin.

His sarcasm aside, the gist of his post was to inform his readers that all the old discussions about the collapse of Christendom hadn't prepared the church for what McAlpine was now designating as Exile Stage Two.

According to McAlpine, in Exile Stage Two the world isn't merely disinterested in the church, it is hostile toward us. The point of his post was to prepare Australian Christians for the fact that we're not in Athens, debating respectfully with intrigued listeners at the Areopagus. We're in Babylon. And Babylon is very unfriendly territory.

A couple of years later, Rod Dreher would publish *The Benedict Option* which appealed strongly to those who agreed with McApline's anxieties about Exile Stage Two. Dreher's vision for the future of the church was to toughen up in order to survive a coming Dark Age of secularism. Similarly, McAlpine sees Exile Stage Two as a time for fighting words:

> *A personalised, pietistic 'Jesus is my homeboy' theology-lite simply will not stand up in the face of a public reshaping of language. Exile Stage One proponents must unlock the armoury door, whet the stone and sharpen the tools of language once more, not in order to slay people, but in order 'to contend for the faith once for all entrusted to the saints' (Jude 1:3).*

Maybe it's because I was one of those writers disdained by McAlpine as a promoter of the 'theology-lite' Exile Stage One, but I wasn't entirely convinced by his analysis. He dismisses the work of Newbigin, and presumably the American Newbiginians like George Hunsberger, Alan Roxburgh and Darrell Guder, too readily by mere caricature. When I wrote, *Exiles: Living Missionally in a Post-Christian Culture* (2006), influenced as I was by those writers, as well as Walter Brueggemann, Stanley Hauerwas and Stuart Murray, I didn't think any of us were fostering

FOREWORD

complacency about secular culture. Neither could we be construed as presenting a personalised, pietistic Jesus-is-my-homeboy vision of Christ. Rather, we were exploring what it would look like for the gospel to help shape culture without the church resorting to the old Christendom categories of domination and control.

But I wasn't the only one not entirely buying McAlpine's approach. In 2016, David Starling interrogated the question of whether Christians could legitimately refer to themselves as exiles in the West, acknowledging that times had changed and the church was being increasingly marginalised.[2] But Starling was a little more circumspect than McAlpine about the metaphor of exile, pointing out that our sense of post-Christendom 'exile' should be tempered by our knowledge that the early church also saw exile as a metaphor for life *before* they came to know Jesus, and that all Christians (not just inhabitants of the post-Christendom West) are, in another sense of the metaphor, exiles awaiting a future homecoming.

But later that year, Kate Harrison Brennan went further. She published a retort to McAlpine's exile language, *No Place for Exile: How Christians Should (Not) Make Sense of their Place in the World*, in which she pointed out that the church still enjoys a privileged position in Australian society and that referring to itself as being in exile represents a collapse in sense-making. The uncritical adoption of the posture of exile, she wrote, is an unimaginative option at best, and a disastrous one for Christian witness at worst.

When Christians invoke 'exile' as the way to make sense of who they are, where we are and how we are to respond, a state of emergency is being invoked, and a rationale is created for the use of extraordinary powers.[3]

---

2 https://www.eternitynews.com.au/opinion/are-christians-in-exile/
3 https://www.abc.net.au/religion/no-place-for-exile-how-christians-should-not-make-sense-of-their/10096264

MICHAEL FROST

Harrison Brennan's criticism, while couched as a response to exile language generally, is really more directed to McAlpine's Exile Stage Two approach. Her concern is that McAlpine appears to be sounding a retreat from secular society when what we need is engagement, to sink roots into the Babylonian soil, seek the good of the city, and reveal an alternate way, the way of the cross. In fact, where Harrison Brennan ends up in *No Place for Exile* is exactly what us old proponents of Exile Stage One were advocating. As the author of a book called *Exiles*, I found myself in the strange position of disagreeing with a brother who was embracing exile and agreeing with a sister who said there is no place for exile.

And so, I decided we should all have it out. In August 2017, I got Stephen McAlpine, Kate Harrison Brennan, David Starling and myself into a room together, and invited some other scholars and practitioners to help us reflect on the church's status in the secular age. We called the symposium, *Not in Kansas Anymore*, because the one thing we all agree on is the fact that Western culture is going through continuous and accelerated change. Like Dorothy and Toto, we are not in black-and-white Kansas anymore; we're in what Stephen McAlpine calls the 'beguiling technicolour of Oz'. In making sense of our identity, our mission, and our posture in society, is it dangerous or useful to adopt the language and framework of exile? The papers collected here are the presentations made at that symposium. It is our hope and desire that they will stimulate your thinking and help shape your practice as you seek to faithfully witness to Christ in our current age.

Michael Frost
Morling College

INTRODUCTION

The essays in this volume all originated as papers presented at a symposium hosted by Morling College in August 2017. The symposium, organised by Michael Frost, addressed the theme of the church's place in the strange, new post-Christendom world of the twenty-first-century West. It drew together a cast of presenters from within and beyond the Morling faculty, who addressed the theme from a variety of disciplines and perspectives.

The aim of the day was not to offer a single, consistent vision or manifesto, but rather to spark thought by juxtaposing diverse, complementary, and at times contradictory proposals for discussion. There was, nonetheless, a certain degree of coherence to the day; as in any good conversation, we didn't all think the same as each other, but we were all talking about the same thing. The coherence of the day derived partly from the care with which the various presentations were grouped into smaller, thematic clusters, to facilitate interaction and mutual engagement. It was also manifested in a cluster of recurring metaphors that resonated throughout the day in multiple papers. A number of these took their inspiration directly from the symposium title's reference to *The Wizard of Oz*, appropriating it as an imaginative language with which to describe the landscape of our contemporary culture and the inward resources that will be required to traverse it. Others took the 'not in Kansas' reference as an invitation to explore the contemporary application of the Bible's language of exile, diaspora, pilgrimage and homemaking. Perhaps the deepest level of the day's coherence, however, was in the seriousness with which all of the presenters took the task of the symposium, approaching the topic not as an exercise in dispassionate, descriptive social commentary but as an exercise in practical theology and an invitation to deliberate on how the church should respond to its changed (and ever-changing) situation.

The first three chapters of the book belong together and originated as the three papers that were presented in the day's first plenary session. Stephen McAlpine's paper, 'The Beguiling Technicolour of Oz', offers an interpretation of the cultural landscape in which we find ourselves in early twenty-first-century Australia and the future into which we are headed: are we, he asks, headed for a 'zombie apocalypse', in which the church is confronted by a hostile and controlling secularism intent on enforcing compliance with the ethics and beliefs of a post-Christian culture, or a 'beautiful apocalypse' that glitters, entices, defangs and domesticates? The most likely answer, he suggests, is a combination of the two, in which the coercive power of legislative enforcement is legitimised and enhanced by the aesthetic power of the artists and advertisers. If the church is to remain faithful as it negotiates this terrain, it will need, like the scarecrow, the 'brain' of a smarter apologetic (one that does not assume cultural neutrality, and therefore a common place to converse, but cultural hostility, and therefore presents a contrasting worldview and practices that reject domestication), like the tin man, the 'heart' of a stronger desire (embedded practices and desires that trump those offered by the beautiful apocalypse) and, like the lion, the 'courage' to persevere in bold and public proclamation (gospel resilience in the face of increasing cultural hostility).

Matthew Anslow's paper, 'Diaspora as a Means of Grace', draws on the way in which notions of exile and dispersion have been appropriated and applied within the Anabaptist tradition, seeking to find within them

INTRODUCTION

a resource for the Western church to assist it in understanding its nature and vocation in the new situation created by the demise of Christendom and the emergence of a post-Christian cultural context. Without wanting to minimise the elements of trauma and oppression involved in the experiences of exile and dispersion that stand behind the metaphorical use of such concepts within the Scriptures, Anslow highlights the 'new way of being Israel' that these experiences made possible, and the further extension of these developments within the New Testament, opening up a way for the experience of dispersion to be embraced as a divine gift and vocation. The remainder of the paper offers examples of the way in which a 'diaspora' ecclesiology of this sort has been understood and practised within the Anabaptist tradition, and concludes with some implications for the church in the post-Christian West.

If Matthew Anslow's paper offers a fresh proposal for how exile image might be appropriated by the post-Christendom church and expresses a mild preference for 'diaspora' over 'exile' as a category less susceptible to confusion and misuse, the third paper, 'No Place for Exile', by Kate Harrison Brennan, tackles the exilic premise head-on, arguing that 'the adoption of an exilic mindset by the contemporary, post-Christendom church is not only bad biblical theology [but] can also be disingenuous and profoundly hazardous to the Church and its mission'. Although Harrison Brennan is vigorous in the attack that she mounts on the tendency of contemporary Western Christians to invoke the metaphor of exile as a way of making sense of our place in the world, and the 'oddly literal' reading of texts such as Jeremiah 29 that she sees as being implied by such interpretive strategies, she still sees value in the use of Jeremiah's letter to the exiles as a tool for interpreting our current reality—a strategy she goes on to employ in the second half of her paper. If due allowance is made for the differences between the situation of the Babylonian exiles and our own, Harrison Brennan argues, there is much for us to learn from Jeremiah's sober realism, his encouragement to the people of God to work collaboratively toward the welfare of the city in which they find themselves, and his renewal of their vision so that they can anticipate, in the midst of their present reality, the future that God has promised.

In chapters four and five, the focus shifts to the New Testament. David Starling's paper, 'The Weapons of our Warfare: Culture, Conflict and Character in 2 Corinthians', examines the warfare metaphors that the apostle Paul employs in 2 Cor 6:3–10 and 10:1–5 and their function within the wider context of the letter, reflecting on their significance for the contemporary Western church as it struggles to understand its place within the increasingly bitter culture wars of our time and responds to the growing perception that the church is out of step with the values of mainstream society. In the face of the intense pressures that we feel within that context to assimilate to the surrounding culture, or to allow ourselves to be co-opted into fighting the wrong battles with the wrong weapons, Starling finds within Paul's paradoxical uses of the warfare metaphor a wisdom that is strikingly pertinent to our contemporary cultural moment.

Tim MacBride's paper, 'To Aliens and Strangers: Preaching the New Testament as Minority Group Rhetoric', focuses on the rhetorical strategies employed in 1 Peter, Hebrews, 1 John and Revelation to address the situation of the audience as a minority group within a hostile social environment. Drawing on the insights of biblical scholars who have employed theories from the social sciences to analyse the minority group rhetoric of the New Testament, MacBride surveys the strategies employed by the writers of these texts, highlighting ways in which they might serve as a model for preachers in the contemporary Western context.

Chapter six, 'Stooping to Conquer: The Gentleness and Generosity of the Early Church', by Edwina Murphy surveys the history of the early church for examples of how they responded to a social context in which the Christian faith was accorded no special political privileges and the

INTRODUCTION

governing authorities were frequently hostile toward it. Drawing on the work of Alan Kreider and Rodney Stark and illustrating her claims from the story of the second-century martyrs of Lyons and the writings of Justin Martyr, Tertullian and Cyprian, she highlights the way in which believers in the pre-Constantinian era sought to imitate Christ's gentleness and generosity, exhibiting a 'strength of hope and firmness of faith' in an anxious and uncertain age.

Chapters seven and eight share a common focus on school education as a sphere of ministry and witness within our contemporary social context. Dave Benson's paper, 'Why We Need the World: Musings from the Interface of Theology and Education', draws on H. Richard Niebuhr's classic typology of the various modes in which Christians have typically engaged with culture, to offer a critical analysis of the ways in which conservative Christians in our contemporary context tend to interact with the public education system. He goes on to argue for a larger, more coherent way of serving our neighbours within the public education system, which is informed by the grand narrative of Scripture and not reducible to any one of the four models of engagement that Niebuhr described.

James Dalziel's paper, 'Christian School Communities as a Twenty-First-Century Benedict Option', takes as its starting point the call issued by conservative American pundit, Rod Dreher, for Christians to imitate the strategy adopted by the sixth-century Benedict of Nursia, acknowledging the reality that conservative Christians have been defeated (at least for the time being) in their attempts to retain their control of the political order and shifting their focus toward building robust, formative Christian communities that can shape believers to survive and flourish as a minority presence in a post-Christian culture. Whilst Dalziel acknowledges the elements of overstatement and oversimplification in Dreher's manifesto, he sees much that is of value within the program that Dreher advocates, and argues that Christian schools which go beyond a merely 'transactional' relationship with their stakeholders to pursue a genuinely formative, authentically Christian community, can be a powerful example of the Benedict Option in action. The second half of the paper offers seven suggestions for furthering and deepening the implementation of that vision within the context of a local Christian school.

In chapter nine, 'Humility and Embodiment: Missional Opportunities for the Exiled Church in a Post-Christendom Context', Karina Kreminski embraces the exilic metaphors of Scripture and the sense they convey that Christians are 'not meant to be quite at home in the world where we live', but rejects two common postures that Christians adopt in response to that reality: a posture of withdrawal, that retreats from the world in search of a safe place of refuge, and a posture of militancy, that wages war against a post-Christian culture in a quest to 'reclaim' the lost privileges of Christendom. In place of these postures, Kreminski advocates an approach that seeks to make a home within the place of exile, 'work[ing] with God to grow his reign until the return of Jesus, for a restored universe when this world will be our ultimate dwelling place'.

In chapter ten, Darrell Jackson explores exile in the context of cross-cultural mission. In 'Re-placing Mission: Exilic Options Considered', he considers the legacy of missionaries, including William Carey, as figures of exile who were simultaneously civilisers of empire and evangelisers of the gospel. Enlightenment and Christendom assumptions appear throughout Carey's work. Surprisingly, little attention has been paid to cross-cultural mission in missional writings. Michael Stroope's critique of the Enlightenment and Christendom assumptions of the modern missionary movement, including the use of the compromised terminology of 'mission', expresses concerns that overlap with those of Frost and other missional writers. Jackson adopts the work of John Flett to offer an alternative, suggesting instead that a better way to describe contemporary

INTRODUCTION

cross-cultural mission might be to use the language of 'loving apostolic practices'.

Brooke Prentis's chapter, 'Dangerous Memories in the Land We Now Call Australia: Do the Exiles Hear the Call to Country Today?', speaks a word to the non-Aboriginal 'fellow exiles' who live in this country, on behalf of the Aboriginal peoples whose relationship with the land includes both the thousands of years before the European invasion and colonisation of this continent and the more recent history of exile and dispossession that have resulted from it. She brings to the conversation at least two kinds of 'dangerous memory'—the memory of that history and the shadow it continues to cast over this land, and the memory of the prophets, whose words about bloodshed, stolen land and unjust gain are clear and confronting. Her paper ends with a gracious invitation: 'We know two are better than one, so, may we, both Aboriginal and non-Aboriginal exiles, join Creator, Holy Spirit, Jesus, and hear the call to country— the new dangerous memories in the land we now call Australia'.

Finally, in chapter twelve, 'Exile: The Endless, Cunning Process of Risky Negotiation', Michael Frost revisits the call that he issued in his 2006 book, *Exiles,* for Christians to find hope and purpose in a post-Christendom context by appropriating the framework in which the biblical prophets encouraged the Hebrew exiles to sustain their faith through their time in Babylon. Responding to the various ways in which the language and imagery of exile have been used and criticised in the years since then, Frost argues for its continuing validity and helpfulness, but insists that when rightly understood it should not be taken as a warrant for nostalgia, fear or self-preoccupation. In place of those responses, Frost advocates a response to exile that understands the church's post-Christendom situation as a reminder of what we were always called to be: a people on the move, formed and re-formed in each new context by the story of Jesus that we recount to one another. His paper concludes with an allusion (following

MICHAEL FROST

Stanley Hauerwas's lead) to the exiled rabbits of Richard Adams's novel, Watership Down, that forms a fitting conclusion to this book:

> *Our all-too-human impulses work towards being untroubled. We build houses, embrace respectability and try not to stand out. We want to escape into the cool, cool earth rather than to cut out across the open fields, courting danger and negotiating challenges. So, what will get us up and out of our safe warrens? What will continue to foster unease about being exiled in a post-Christendom world? Surely, it will be the radical stories of Jesus, the prince with a thousand enemies.*

1

THE BEGUILING TECHNICOLOUR OF OZ

Steve McAlpine

If Facebook did family status updates ours would say, 'It's complicated'. I have three brothers and two half-brothers. Some incommunicado. Others on good speaking terms. Two mums between the six of us. And a just-dead dad to all the brothers, who was also ex-husband to both now-single mums. Got it? Despite that, the recent wedding of one of my half-brothers to the mother of his young daughter was a joyous and raucous occasion, albeit *sans* two brothers, yet with both mums there. Go figure!

It was also attended by my newly appointed sister-in-law's (or is that half-sister-in-law's, or sister-in-half-law's?) brother, his husband, and their two-year-old daughter; new arrivals in Australia from South Africa, where same-sex marriage has been legal since 2006. I was asked to conduct my half-brother's ceremony but as pastor of an independent church plant that does not yet give me the right to bestow rites, I had to settle for the more relaxing role of master of ceremonies.

With our kids ensconced at a table with other kids, my wife Jill and I grabbed a drink and sat down opposite my sister-in-law's brother, Leonard, and his husband Beyers. After the obligatory 'how are you' and 'I'm so and so' and 'this is such and such', Leonard asked me the one question that I refuse to ask people within the first five minutes of meeting them: 'So what do you do?' I wondered if it was too much to think that I could have a couple of glasses of red, a good meal, and a bit of a dance. I took a deep breath and committed myself to say: 'I'm in sales'.

What came out of my mouth was, 'I'm a pastor of a church'. Leonard didn't blink. Within a second, he pushed back, 'So can gay people come to your church or what?' I didn't blink when I replied, 'Anyone can come to our church', although I might have blinked if he hadn't left it at that. Beyers didn't blink either. Smoothly, and ironically, he started chatting about his experience of Perth so far. Beyers is driving an Uber while he waits for his real estate licence.

'You know what astounds me?' he remarked as we started our entrée. 'The fact that no one talks about God here. Hardly anyone goes to church.'

'You've noticed!'

'Religion is a no-go area. And believe me, I've tried, especially when driving people around. We've signed our daughter up for a local Catholic school because the state school won't teach her anything.'

'What else do you notice?' I asked. As a recent arrival, Beyers had a window into our culture that those who are local cannot see through. Culture junkie that I am, I was interested.

'What's with alcohol here?' he went on. 'Everyone just wants to party all of the time. I drive to pick up people in Fremantle on a Friday and Saturday night and the streets are literally lined with drunk young women lying there in skimpy clothes waiting for a cab. I've never seen anything like it.'

The rest of the evening was great; a healing event for our family after our loss earlier in the year. I even danced for a bit, or at least stood and swayed from side to side as my rhythmically confident Capetonian wife carved it up. Leonard chilled and we chatted more. Beyers had to head off to drive for Uber and friended me on Facebook the next day.

And it struck me. Between them, Leonard and Beyers referenced the two sides of the contested narrative that the church in Australia faces—or believes it faces—as we head into this 'not-Kansas' era. Is the future aligned with Leonard's questioning? A secular frame exemplified by an alternate sexual culture championed by global corporate giants and legislated by politicians? A brittle, yet brutal secularism that stares down the church's ethic and shuts down dissenting voices? A zombie apocalypse, so to speak?

Or is Beyers's observation more on the money? Is the Oz we land in more likely to be, as Mark Sayers puts it, a 'beautiful apocalypse';[1] a future of rampant individualism in which everything glitters and entices, but is ultimately hollow? A world in which no-one is angry about Christianity, because Christianity is too weightless, hollow, and toothless to get angry about? A future in which the church has been defanged and domesticated by ease and the lure of personal fulfilment?

Choose Your Apocalypse Now! Which Is It To Be?

This is no abstract question for me as a pastor. Sydney writer Tim Adeney makes this prescient observation: 'All action embeds a hypothesis about the future. Whether I'm ordering a coffee, pressing a space bar, shopping for a week, selecting a school for my children, taking out a 30-year mortgage, selecting a bin to put my rubbish in, or invading a country, I do so with a view of the future'.[2] Hence, I pastor in the present with a particular future in mind. This is true on a macro level, the eschatological 'now/not yet'. The resurrection has ushered in the age of the Spirit, drawing us towards a

---

1 Sayers, *Disappearing Church*, §5, Kindle.
2 Adeney, 'Predicting Benedict', lines 38–41.

glorious emancipation (Rom 8:18–25). I prepare our congregation for that eschatological future.

Yet it is also true on a micro level. I make choices based on the micro-futures I hypothesise, the cultural 'now/not yet'. I must wisely chart a course for God's people living in a rapidly changing secular frame, and that micro-future is as contested as the macro-future is decided.

So, do we rent a public building *now* assuming a beautiful apocalypse in which we will never be required to sign off on undertakings as part of the rental agreement that may challenge our liberty of conscience? Do we construct a compound in the hills *now* with cyclone fencing, and stock up on beans, spam and shotguns in light of the coming zombies? Our actions reveal a hypothesis about the future, whether we fully articulate this or not.

My hypothesis is that both are the future. Indeed, they are two sides of the same apocalypse. The zombie apocalypse of increased hostility towards the Christian frame *is* beautiful on the surface. Has the recent 'No' campaign on same-sex marriage come close to capturing the colour, vibrancy and narrative longing of the 'Yes'? Not even close. The gay community is a creative minority *par excellence* and, as all creative minorities do, has successfully engaged the resources of the cultural centre.

And a key reason the 'No' campaign has lost this argument is that the zombie so loathed by the church was embedded within the beautiful apocalypse that the church itself has often fallen for. We baptise the beautiful on the surface, never realising it means communion with the zombie lurking beneath. You can't argue in one breath for the good life for oneself and in the next deny it to others—not with any integrity at least.

So how do we navigate this potholed, slightly jaundiced brick road? Indulge me as I push the Oz theme farther than it may have been intended to go, by offering the following motifs as our solution. Firstly, the church-scarecrow will need a brain—a smarter public apologetic in the face of increasing secular incredulity. Secondly, the church-tinman requires a heart—a community shaped by stronger desires than the beguiling world can offer. And finally, the church-lion requires courage—a gospel resilience in the face of increasing cultural hostility.

A Brain: A Smarter Apologetic

The 'not-in-Kansas' church will require a brain—a smarter apologetic that engages the world primarily from the point of sharp difference.

By that I do not simply mean more convincing arguments that prove the resurrection, or that demonstrate Christianity's intellectual credentials. These methods have been coming under increasing pressure for the past two decades, falling victim to the law of diminishing returns. A smarter apologetic is one that does not assume cultural neutrality, and therefore a common place to converse, but cultural hostility, and therefore presents a contrasting worldview and practices that reject domestication.

So, a Christian identity announces on Facebook or Twitter that they have been invited as a guest on to next week's *QandA* program on the ABC. They ask, 'What topics would you like to see me discuss on next week's program?' The online Christian community then goes into overdrive. Up to a point, their helpful suggestions and strategies do not matter. What matters most is the hope that lies behind them: that the Christian panellist will, under the hot glare of the studio lights, and the even hotter glare of the studio audience, acquit themselves and the church well.

What do we mean by 'well'? On *QandA*, the Christian guest has done well if the gospel and the church come out of it all looking sensible, or at least not stupid, bigoted, sexist, or dumb. If the Christian identity proves that we can mix it with the big boys and girls we can all rest easy, and we offer our congratulations or commiserations. Our efforts to achieve at least an honourable draw, assume an Athenian situation in which our acceptance, or otherwise, is not so much based on the force of our moral argument, but the presence of our intellectual prowess. We long to hear, 'Underneath it all, you're just like us'.

Yet the problem of the hardening secular frame is that the wiggle room is steadily shrinking. Increasingly less and less of what we consider acceptable as a public apologetic is accepted by the public. And increasingly the orthodox Christian frame is seen not only as odd but as bad. This is especially so in the hot button topics of sexual ethics that so dominate programs such as *QandA*. To say on such a show that 'I am an advocate for the traditional view of marriage, but I am not a bigot', is akin to saying 'I believe in the right for Deep South landowners to have kept African slaves, but I am not a racist'.

Of course, it's not simply about sex, but our current apologetic stresses that if we as religious people can demonstrate that our goals, values and frame are not all that different from those of the secular frame we've somehow succeeded. Our goal is to stress similarity, not difference. 'We're all looking for a good fulfilling relationship, right? Here's how our approach is better.' Better by degree, not different in essence.

Canadian philosopher Charles Taylor believes this accommodationist approach cedes far too much ground.[3] The premise, on the surface at least, is that we are equal players on a level playing field. But secularisation has set the rules of engagement, whereby ground zero is what Taylor calls a 'subtraction story', a firm *a priori* bedrock which assumes unbelief as a starting point after dogma has been sloughed away, notably religious belief and any notion of the transcendent. The believer, whoever she is, must argue from the bedrock of the immanent frame.

Taylor rejects this assumption. 'But this very idea is absurd, since what we have is not a playing field at all, but a very accidented terrain: there are lots of tilts, but they don't all slide in the same direction. The tilt

---

[3] Taylor, *Secular Age*, §12, Kindle.

of the Bible Belt is not that of the urban university.' To which we might add, the tilt of the national broadcaster's micro-levelled live studio.

Here is where 'zombie' meets 'beautiful', and here is where the church's capitulation is revealed. Our apologetic strategy has been to stress sameness in order to receive secularism's approval and a place at its table because at an unspoken level we value the same things it does—'the hearth gods of ease and comfort,' as R. R. Reno puts it.[4]

Why have we not stressed dissonance and difference in our public apologetic? It is, after all, a long-term strategy with proven benefits. The Jewish community in the West is a vibrant, creative minority that punches above its weight in terms of talent and influence. When a Jewish father prepares his child to go out into the world his message is: 'We're different, so off you go, be different'. Contrast this to the Christian parent: 'It's a tough world out there, kid; here's how to fit in'. The Jewish child goes into the world expecting pushback and the Christian child looks for a safe space to settle.

This may be as simple and as confronting as turning up to *QandA* and announcing that we play by a different set of rules, that we do not recognize your gods and that nothing about us makes sense outside of belief in the resurrection of Jesus. But it's deeper than that. It's not merely about our public face towards the sexual revolution. It's about how we as a church have unwittingly been lured in by the beguiling beauty and glitter of late modernity and its hollow promises. Our corporate apologetic as a church must increasingly stress dissonance and difference.

Miroslav Volf memorably states, 'The idea of flourishing as a human being has shrivelled to meaning no more than leading an experientially satisfying life. The sources of satisfaction may vary: power, possessions, love, religion, sex, food, drugs—whatever. What matters the most is not the source of satisfaction but the experience of it—my satisfaction.

---

4   Reno, *Resurrecting the Idea*, §6, Kindle.

Our satisfied self is our best hope'.[5] That idea is not confined to godless moderns. When newcomers arrive at our church, however orthodox they present initially, I simply assume they have drunk this cultural Kool-Aid. My premise is that they too believe that their satisfied self is their best hope, and that we may be a convenient way to experience that. No matter how much they affirm orthopraxy in all things sexual, I assume the factory setting of 'consumer' until time proves otherwise.

And it *will* take time to prove otherwise. Our *modus operandi* is now to play hard to get. Attend, watch, learn, take part in liturgical Sundays, hang out with other Christians, have a meal with them. But don't expect us to chase you up or sign you up and hand you a 'how to give or how to serve' card by next week. We certainly don't have any programs you can join, and we're not taking ideas from you as to what programs we should start. Our primary aim is to provide a stronger liturgy than that shrivelled idea of flourishing espoused by the beautiful apocalypse—an alternative plausibility that will weather the coming storm.

That all sounds sparse and not a little harsh. But it is foundational work. The leader of our church network, in commenting on the number of 'second service' Christians we attract from other churches puts it like this: 'In reality all of our people are "second service" people. They have all been discipled somewhere else Monday through Saturday. And that discipleship program has proven extremely effective'. Millennials are our largest cohort. We are not concerned to badge their ministries and vocations with our Providence Church label. We aim to love them in Christ and equip them to be a creative minority in an increasingly hostile culture. They're under no illusions about how much pressure this blend of the 'zombie' and the 'beautiful' will place them under. Perhaps it's a mini version of the Benedict Option, a weekly strategic withdrawal to re-equip for the Babylon of the coming week.

---

5   Volf, *Against the Tide*, 108.

THE BEGUILING TECHNICOLOUR OF OZ

In that context, six sermons on financial freedom or a church service strained of the gristle of communion, confession, repentance, responsive prayer, and praise won't cut it, yet this is exactly the approach taken up by mainstream evangelicalism in the past generation. In the face of innovative, plausible seductions, what we offer is not a lack of innovation, but a conscious rejection of it as the grounds of a smarter apologetic.

In his book, *Antifragile: Things That Gain From Disorder*, Nassim Nicholas Taleb comments on the scourge of 'neomania'—an over-reliance and hope in 'the new', which results in fragility, rather than avoids it.[6] Taleb observes that when we think of our future needs we believe that the future will require additions: 'innovations, improvements, killer technologies'.[7] But counterintuitively it is the exact opposite of what we will need. Antifragility calls for us to take things away, to reduce from the future in order to be prepared for it. But do not expect instant results or to be liked for it. Taleb observes:

> *As shown from the track record of the prophets: before you are proven right you will be reviled; after you are proven right you will be hated for a while, or, what's worse, your ideas will appear to be 'trivial' thanks to retrospective distortion.*[8]

Fifteen years ago, we wondered how small our mobile phones could get. Our phones today are not small. Steve Jobs did not ask us fifteen years ago how small we wanted our phones. He gave us something counterintuitive: a larger phone, even though we assumed smaller was the future. The iPhone was a smarter apologetic.

---

6   Taleb, *Antifragile*, §20, Kindle.
7   Taleb, *Antifragile*, §20, Kindle.
8   Taleb, *Antifragile*, §20, Kindle.

A Heart: Stronger Desires

The church in this iteration of Oz will require a stronger heart: embedded practices and desires that trump those offered by the beautiful apocalypse.

I was standing in the check-out line at Target when I saw the writing on the wall. A piece of liturgy in huge black letters—Target's vision statement: *Every Australian has the right to look good and feel good about the way they dress and live.* If we were looking for a preamble to the Australian constitution that would fit nicely. It's a rights-based statement of extraordinary power and reach. The success of Target's vision statement is not dependent on your ability or otherwise to recite it. Its strength lies in an unarticulated growing desire for such a vision as you enact it. Target's liturgical statement is embedded through liturgical practice.

When we think about liturgy, we think of religious words being said in church but, as Calvin College's Jamie Smith points out, it's far more than that. He describes liturgies as ritual practices that form our identity and inculcate into us a vision of the good life. They are identity forming in such a way that they mean to trump other liturgies.[9]

We jokingly refer to shopping as retail therapy. But if our neural pathways are forged through practices that, over time, become our unspoken defaults, you can see how effective liturgical practices are. We are shaped more by what we love than by what we know. In speaking of his own children, Smith observes that the mall has a pull on them and their hearts. Its intention is to inscribe on their hearts a vision of the good life, one that becomes more embedded each time the practice of the mall (shopping) is enacted.[10] The liturgical practices of the mall disciple them. As all liturgical practices do to all of us, transparently religious or otherwise. The mall—or whatever our vision of the good life

---

9   Smith, *Desiring the Kingdom*, 86.
10   Smith, *Desiring the Kingdom*, 93–103.

is—becomes our second service, the place or activity that once embedded through practice, becomes the thing that we love and that shapes us.

Think of how this works in sport. I am fifty. I run between sixty and one hundred kilometres a week. This was off a zero base at the age of forty-three. I love running. I run six days per week, and only take one day off because I know I should. But how did that happen? Why do I love running? I certainly didn't before I started running. And I most certainly did not buy a year's subscription to *Runner's World* on the off-chance that as I read the articles and bought the products, I might grow to love running.

The answer is simple. I love running because I run. Because I started to run and kept running (shout-outs to Forrest Gump). The liturgical practice of running has embedded itself and shaped me in more ways than physically. I spend discretionary income on items I would have ignored ten years ago. I get up at five o'clock to run. It has overtaken other practices that could have lured me.

The most embedded practice of our culture is the practice of bedding someone. Sexual autonomy is fast becoming the bedrock human right, replacing, emotionally to begin with, but culturally, politically—and soon legally—the old-world rights such as religious freedom in the public square. The multi-hued liturgical statement, 'Love is Love', is a self-justifying moebius strip, hermetically sealed from critique, pitching a vision of the good life implicit in practices unfettered from any biblical ideas of what love and human flourishing actually are.

In the beautiful apocalypse, sex is used to sell everything. In the zombie apocalypse, everything is used to sell sex. Whether it be the fear of bullying, or the promise of a utopian ideal of deep autonomy, sexual autonomy is an embedded practice that is self-confirming. Dale Kuehne notes in his book *Sex and the iWorld* how all-pervasive and persuasive it is to us: 'One of the hallmarks of the iWorld is the optimism that a society of extreme individualism is not only possible, but good'.[11]

Yet, for all our efforts to prop this up and celebrate it, the culture is, as Dale Kuehne observes, increasingly lonely and atomistic. Something is not working. The promise of autonomy at a deep level is not delivering, at least not without major caveats. A brilliant and wrenching example is the movie *Her*, in which Joachim Phoenix's character falls in love with his personalised operating system, a system that grows in depth and complexity the more he engages with it. In his beautiful apocalyptic world of pastel and high-tech employment where he works writing actual letters for those who can no longer word the tomes of forgiveness, love, explanation, etc. that we once took for granted, his own relationship has crumbled. The joy—real joy—he discovers in Scarlet Johansson's seductively-voiced OS is both touching and fleeting. But when the facade collapses it crashes through the floor, exposing the grimacing skull behind the smiling face. There is no redemption there. And if you cannot find it in your innermost being, where can you find it?

This is where the church must hold its nerve by not simply disappearing into its own virtual world, or co-opting the apocalyptic liturgies in a vain attempt at chasing relevance. This is where we rediscover and re-embed our own cultural liturgies, both in word and practice.

Liturgical Word

Our own church practice is to embed a thicker liturgical frame into our weekly gatherings. Our aim is to ensure our language drips heavy with theological meaning at a time when language is fast becoming a husk, captive to the will of Image Almighty. This is largely remedial work. We have gathered a group of people, churched, de-churched, and

---

[11] Kuehne, *Sex and the iWorld*, 65.

previously unchurched, who are either suspicious of a liturgical past, have never experienced it in the present, or cannot perceive its worth going into the future.

We have thickened up word-liturgy for a decidedly non-liturgical crowd. We have longer prayers that walk our congregation through praise, confession, repentance, and request. We have weekly communion, longer and varied Scripture readings (though shorter, sharper preaching), songs that gather and that send out. Our kids' program is opt-in and 'lite'. We unashamedly say to those who are hell-bent on the culture's liturgical practices that the sheer discipline of turning up will grow your love. Our aim is to embed word-liturgy as an ongoing practice.

We are, in the process, countering the unfortunate conclusion that since everything is worship (a noble idea), then nothing really is, at least not in terms of being more worthwhile as a practice that shapes us. This is proving patently untrue. The sheer discipline of turning up week in, week out is liturgical, and all the more so as the liturgical practices of the culture expand to fill every nook and cranny that we afford them. I recognise the enervating genius behind Syndrome's attempts in the classic Pixar movie *The Incredibles* to make everyone super, because *'when everyone is super, no one will be'*.

Liturgical Practice

This leads us inevitably to our commitment to liturgical practices that do what Smith says they do on the packet; that is, to embed a vision of the good life that trumps other alternative visions.[12] For us that means doing what Nassim Taleb says will make us 'antifragile' going into the future:[13]

---

12 Smith, *Desiring the Kingdom*, §3.
13 Taleb, *Antifragile*, §20, Kindle.

our practice involves a reduction of the culture to highlight the practices that will matter most going into the future.

When Jørn Utzon was designing the global icon that is the Sydney Opera House, he was urged to surround his project with other buildings, the idea being that the world's truly great buildings found their greatness in their proximity to lesser constructions. He strongly resisted that urge, believing that the beauty of his idea would be realised standing alone. We recently holidayed in Sydney. Utzon's point is proved. The large expanse of concourse and steps leading up to that dazzling building truly serves to enhance it. The growing excitement I saw in my nine-year-old son as we left behind the bustle of Circular Quay and traipsed around to the Opera House was palpable. The open space both shrank us and enlarged the vision Utzon had for the building. There is something of the pilgrimage in visiting the Opera House. The surrounding open space does not give the building its worth, it merely evidences it.

In an ecclesiastical culture justified by busyness, the church must learn to leave empty space. It must learn to clear the ground in order to give significance to liturgical practices that must be embedded in this new world. To be a regular at Providence Midland Church means to attend church weekly, attend a community meal with fifteen to twenty others monthly, and to pray together once a month. And that's it. The rest we let people figure out. Our aim is to leave people wanting more. Many of our people serve and help in our local community. We don't sign people up to weekly small groups or for any other ministry. We don't have the financial or time resources to start programs, nor would we direct financial and time resources to those things if we did. We do need some rosters filled in, but they too are fairly light.

When we see the puzzled looks of newcomers who want to know what we do we simply tell them to practice this with us first for some time before commenting on it. Our experience is that when we fill up the church calendar the practice that falls away is the least embedded practice: meeting in homes to eat food and share life. What others are viewing as the trim on the dashboard we view as the steering wheel. This important practice feels, in our busy world, the most expendable after everything else has been done. We want to create space for it because we know that over time it will embed itself and surpass other atomising and individualistic practices. It will become what we love.

This is increasingly important in a world that placards 'Love is Love', but increasingly fails to experience love as a costly embedded liturgical practice in community. And as the sexual and relational confusion builds in our culture it is imperative that we do the important work of creating space for it. Rosaria Butterfield notes that when she left behind the lesbian community and joined the church, she was initially dismayed at how thin the church version of community was. What the church presented as a thick expression of life together seemed anemic. She observes:

> *When I was in the LGBT community, someone's house was open every night, for food, fellowship, and advice. I presumed that that is how a community works: people have open availability with each other, and you are valued and remembered ... in a community when you return from a long trip and your plane lands, you send a one-word text message to someone who cares that you made it home safe. You text 'safe' not because you need a ride home, but just because you are safe and home again. Your safety and the fact that you are home again matters to someone.*[14]

When we offer a better community of love to the sexually broken or the relationally confused in our culture, we'd better give them what's on the packet. Church has too often outsourced that role to the traditional family unit. But the traditional family unit is increasingly broken or non-existent for so many. We prove what we love by what we do. And what we do

---

14   Butterfield, *Openness Unhindered*, §7.

embeds what we love as what we love. The liturgical practice of doing life together in light of what liturgical words lay claim to will ensure an anti-fragility, whatever this 'not-in-Kansas' world throws at us.

Courage: Gospel Resilience

The church going into the future will require courage; a gospel resilience that refuses to blink in the face of a culture that demands uniformity even whilst declaring diversity.

On many a drive to school last year I discipled my teenage daughter in the art of extremophilia. In his book *Disappearing Church: From Cultural Relevance to Gospel Resilience,* Mark Sayers explains how extremophiles are creatures that not only survive, but thrive in hostile conditions, such as deep, cold oceans or arid deserts. These creatures don't escape the condition; they can't. But they don't give in to its demands either. They flourish.

Sayers believes that the drive to be relevant will leave Christians further and further exposed to the fault lines of the disintegrating cultural narrative in the West, the result being a Christianity that is always reactive and never proactive, and which has proven in the US mainline denominations to be a complete disaster. A reactive theology won the politics and lost the church.

Gospel resilience, on the other hand, will lead to extremophile disciples who are relevant precisely because they are resilient, a resilience that comes from being a creative minority whose 'ability to thrive in a caustic environment [is] linked to an ability to find a sense of meaning outside of their environment'.[15]

My daughter is under no illusions as to how caustic her environment is becoming. Her orthodox Christian frame, still young and forming,

---

15   Sayers, *Disappearing Church*, §5, Kindle.

is even yet under attack from her school friends; friends who, as they grow older, are aligning their values even more strongly with the post-Christian ethical frame. Her chosen career path is media and film. Her school friends will seem lightweight compared to the pushback she gets there.

My role on those school journeys has not been to maintain or rebuild an illusion in my daughter that it will all be fine. But that it won't be fine. And also, that it's okay if it's not. We worship a sovereign God who kept a creative minority secure in Babylon. We worship a God who will ensure that we don't need to be tucked away in a cultural backwater, stagnating and increasingly lifeless in order to survive. 'Dad, you make me feel a bit nervous!' my daughter occasionally says during these conversations. 'Nervous is okay', I reply. 'The point is what the nervousness drives you to.'

So, I've finally used the oft-pilloried Babylon motif. But Babylon is a city that gives off mixed signals. We hear Babylon and think of Biff's World, the seedy, dark version of Hill Valley that Biff Tannen establishes in the alt-universe of *Back to the Future II*, once he gets his hands on to the almanac.

But Babylon is not as straightforward as that. Such things seldom are. Babylon captures both the brutality and beauty of the approaching apocalypse. The fiery furnace is reserved only for those who do not bow down to the gold and glitter. For those who do? Well, *that* Babylon is so breathtaking that even its architect and ruler cannot stop popping his head over the parapet to admire it: 'Is not this the great Babylon I have built as the royal residence, by my mighty power and for the glory of my majesty?' (Dan 4:30).

Make no mistake, Babylon has a plausibility structure which it will gift to those who seek its reward. Babylon is scrupulously fair: it plays a *quid pro quo* game. For every denounced Jew thrown to the furnace there were doubtless dozens more who found a *via media* that satisfied Babylon. And there's a reason we don't know their names.

Therein lies the struggle for the creative minority. For it threatens to be a minority within a minority. What will enervate my daughter's faith is less likely to be the Babylonian nationals who ignore or deride her, but those within the faith community who, over time, fail to do what Sayers speaks of: 'find a sense of meaning outside of their environment',[16] and who either drift slowly away, beguiled by the beautiful apocalypse and its promises, or make an abrupt U-turn through fear of the zombies and their threats.

Extremophiles are like Daniel. Daniel can open his window in prayer towards a heap of rubble called Jerusalem some seven hundred miles away and *still* consider it to be the location of future hope. Babylon had present plausibility. Jerusalem did not. But Daniel perceived that, though he could serve the king and flourish in Babylon, it had no future and that Jerusalem did. Sadly, many a Jew lost their patience, their identity, and their faith because Babylon simply waited them out.

Gospel resilience is about waiting Babylon out. The courage we require is not the *faux* courage of the angry blog post or a placard protest, or even the political push to recover whatever it is that we think we have lost. The courage we require is the God-given ability to read the Scriptures as a text written for perceived cultural losers and yet remain committed to loving and serving our culture as best we can as we go about our daily lives.

Our role as pastors and leaders among God's people is to disciple them into finding that sense of meaning outside of their environment, even as the rest of the week disciples them to finding meaning merely within the immanent frame. As I say to our people when reinforcing the notion that the future of our church is to 'run lean': 'My role is not to get you to help me to do my job in here, it's to equip you to flourish tomorrow morning in Babylon'.

---

16   Sayers, *Disappearing Church*, §5, Kindle.

THE BEGUILING TECHNICOLOUR OF OZ

Rory Shiner, writing for The Gospel Coalition Australia, ponders what we might wish we had done, if in ten years' time we look back. He observes that, first and foremost, we will regret not doubling down on the discipleship of the next generation:

> *Being a Christian will be harder for my children than it has been for me. We need to disciple the next generation for challenges that mine did not face. We won't be able to get away with a lite, ill-disciplined programme of Christian entertainment. They will need a thick, rich, deep and compelling vision of the Christian life and of Christian thought. I'm pretty sure this will also involve a stronger sense of Christian history than was typically imparted to my generation. People will need to know they are part of something bigger. The years ahead are surely the years for our best possible teaching and instruction. If we skimp now on deep thought and a vision of Christianity that is true, good and beautiful we will leave the next generation hopelessly vulnerable.*[17]
>
> *True, good, and beautiful. Currently those are all contested categories. Indeed, what was once thought to be so is increasingly being cast aside. Yet the meaning of those terms will one day be realised well beyond our capacity to imagine. Their locus, while yet still outside of our environment, will one day come and inhabit them, primarily in the person of Jesus and the kingdom he ushers in.*

Hebrews tells us not that we are building a kingdom but that we are receiving one, to be fully realised when the new Jerusalem comes down from heaven. The true and final apocalypse will occur—the appearance of the resilient one whose patient endurance in the face of extreme hostility was both salvific and exemplary. On that day, he will banish the hostile and arid conditions of this fallen age and usher in a kingdom of peace and flourishing. And when that happens, there will be no place like home.

---

17   Shiner, 'What Will We Wish?'

2
DIASPORA AS MEANS OF GRACE: A NEO-ANABAPTIST('S) PERSPECTIVE ON THE CHURCH, 'EXILE' AND POST-CHRISTIAN CULTURE

Matthew Anslow

> *Thus says the Lord:*
> *Stand at the crossroads, and look,*
> *and ask for the ancient paths*
> *where the good way lies; and walk in it,*
> *and find rest for your souls.*
>
> Jeremiah 6:16[1]

Is the church in 'exile', or is it not? It certainly seems that 'exile' is becoming an increasingly prevalent diagnosis of the Western church's current situation. Moreover, synchronously, and in proportion to its ascent, this diagnosis is being debated as a theological and missiological framework.

---

[1] Except where otherwise indicated, biblical quotations within this chapter are from the NRSV translation.

No doubt the collapse of Christendom, as well as the numerical decline of the Western church and its gradual marginalisation from Western democratic politics, plays a significant role in the emergence of 'exile' as a theme. What is at stake in debates about exile is no less than the church's perception of its relationship to the world, and thus its understanding of certain dimensions of its mission.

It ought to be unsurprising that Anabaptists—throughout their history no strangers to exile—have a special interest in this debate. Indeed, some Anabaptist scholars have made use of the theme of exile to articulate their distinct theological and ecclesiological emphases. By exploring such expositions of 'exile', I hope to draw attention to new possibilities for our understanding of that theme and, more importantly, for the nature and vocation of the church at the end of Christendom and the beginnings of a post-Christian culture in the West.

I should be clear from the outset that I am not seeking to write for or on behalf of the whole church, including Anabaptists. While the ongoing conversation about exile is by no means exclusively relevant to Christians in Western nations—for whom the emergence of a post-Christian culture has been an ongoing experience for some time—my contribution here is aimed specifically at them. No doubt, non-Western perspectives bring untold wisdom to the table, and we ought to be attending to such witness.

What Are We Talking About Again?

A key problem with talk of 'exile' is that proponents (and detractors) are often awfully vague regarding the sense in which they use the term. This is no doubt exacerbated by the fact that much of the conversation about the church-in-exile has occurred at a popular rather than scholarly level.[2]

---

2   Here I am by no means disparaging the popular in favour of the academic, so much as pointing out that academic discourse tends to demand greater precision of language.

There tends to be confusion, for example, about how literally we ought to understand and use the language of exile. It is perhaps for this reason that some have tended to appropriate the identity of Israel in exile.[3] In short, I agree with Brueggemann's assertion that exile is a *metaphor*, one that is not easy, obvious or compelling for all.[4]

More definitive for making sense of 'exile'—even before we approach how literally we ought to use the term—is the social phenomenon to which our notions of exile point. One of the most consistent assumptions about exile is that it simply describes a lack of adjacency to power.[5] The result is that discussions of whether the church is in exile or not tend to be debates about the church's proximity to worldly power. As such, these frequently tedious discussions are often mired in competing evaluations of the church's societal position—what do we make of tax exemptions for churches; church schools; the entrenched privilege of clergy; declining church attendance in the West versus the growth of the worldwide church; the church's position in the culture wars, and so forth. Marginalisation from power is no doubt a significant aspect of exilic experience, whether Israelite or otherwise, but we should be wary of simply assuming it is the determinative feature of exile, at least in a theological sense.

A problem is that, for many proponents and detractors of the use of 'exile' language, Constantinianism—the waning alliance between church

---

3   Here I am in some agreement with Kate Harrison Brennan's diagnosis that, 'The strong tendency in the Church is to go even further than our general historical amnesia by adopting, directly, the identity of the Israelites. The Church is tempted to inhabit an identity other than our own, and to claim a position of exile'. Harrison Brennan, 'No Place for Exile'. I disagree, however, with Harrison Brennan's application of this charge to most, if not all, Western uses of exile in describing the church's current position.

4   Brueggemann, *Cadences of Home*, 1.

5   So Harrison Brennan when she states that, 'When Christians believe that they are in exile in Western societies, *contrary to the evidence of our position and power*, it points to the fact that Christians are experiencing a collapse in sense-making' (emphasis mine). Harrison Brennan, 'No Place for Exile'.

and state, and the identification of church with society—continues to set the terms of the conversation.[6] Judgements as to whether the church is in exile are determined according to the church's esteem in the world. For some, we are in exile because we have been defeated in the culture wars, a sign of having lost a previously held power. But this is an ecclesiological frame that gives precedence to the agenda of the world, even while proclaiming our remoteness from it. For others, we are not in exile because the church is still remarkably powerful in the world. Again, this judgement follows from an assumption that the world's estimation of the church is in some way determinative for our identity and approach to the world.[7] We are—or are not—in exile, not because God has or has not called us there, but because the world tells us that we are or are not.

In recent decades, Anabaptist authors have begun to explore the theological theme of exile in ways that highlight their characteristic approach to church and mission. Chief among them is the provisional but

---

[6] It is important to note here the tendency of many Anabaptists to display no small degree of sanctimoniousness regarding Constantinianism and Christendom. This, I suspect, is the fruit of cursory readers too loosely wielding anti-Constantinian authors such as Yoder and Hauerwas. Yoder was, after all, careful to note that, though it ought to be rejected overall, there were undoubted benefits of the Christendom arrangement, which, as distinct from Constantinianism, was a historical phenomenon beginning in the Middle Ages. Yoder was, however, insistent that the theological phenomenon of Constantinianism—namely, the fourth-century reorientation of the relationship between church and world—be rejected as heresy. See Yoder, 'Otherness of the Church', 57; Nikolajsen, *Distinctive Identity*, 98–101. Yoder, 'Constantinian Sources', 135–47 is a good example of Yoder's non-synonymous use of 'Christendom' and 'Constantinian'. See also Hauerwas, 'Can Democracy Be Christian?' Related to this is David Bentley Hart's insistence on 'the need for a generously indeterminate trust in the mysterious workings of God's will *sub contrario*', which is important in any discussion of Christendom/Constantinianism. Hart, 'No Enduring City', 216.

[7] I mean this in a prescriptive rather than descriptive sense. There is no doubt that the world's estimation of the church has been formative for the church, not least in terms of the church's quests for power—such is, after all, an aspect of Constantinianism. However, it is problematic to view the results of the church's pathologies as theologically decisive.

influential work on exilic theology by John Howard Yoder,[8] as well as the more recent and developed work of Daniel Smith-Christopher.

An Anabaptist Perspective on Israel's Exile

Yoder's contribution to exilic theology is most comprehensively seen in his essay 'See How They Go With Their Face to the Sun'.[9] Here Yoder paints a picture of exile as a transformative moment in Israel's history in which the vocation of YHWH's people undergoes a fundamental shift whereby 'dispersion shall be the calling of the Jewish faith community'.[10] Yoder calls into question the Palestinocentrism that makes the 'Land of Israel', particularly Jerusalem, the centre of world Jewry. Instead, he notes that this centre was, in fact, historically found in Babylon, from the time of Jeremiah through to the Middle Ages.[11]

Babylon's centrality to the Jewish story is encapsulated in the primeval story and symbol of Babel (Gen 11). 'The first meaning of Babel in the Genesis legend', says Yoder, 'is the effort of a human community to absolutize itself'.[12] If the Genesis story overall depicts the spreading out of Noah's descendants according to the will of the Creator, Babel represents rebellious humankind's attempt to resist such spreading out and its consequent diversification of human culture. In other words, Babel

---

[8] In making use of Yoder's work, it would be remiss of me not to draw attention to the issues involved in doing so. There is an inherent tension between, on the one hand, the prolificacy of his writing on reconciliation, nonviolence and ethics, and, on the other hand, his acts of sexual abuse. By utilising Yoder, I do not wish to dismiss the complexity of these issues, nor overlook his abusive legacy, especially given that the journey of healing and reconciliation continues for many of Yoder's victims. While Yoder's behaviour ought to be unqualifiedly condemned, it is difficult to speak of exile from an Anabaptist perspective without referencing his work, simply because it has been so influential for subsequent Anabaptist thought on the subject.

[9] Yoder, 'Face to the Sun', 51–78.

[10] Yoder, 'Face to the Sun', 52.

[11] Yoder, 'Face to the Sun', 57.

[12] Yoder, 'Face to the Sun', 62.

is an attempt to centralise and amalgamate human society and culture. According to Yoder, God responds graciously to humankind's defensive attempt by dispersing all peoples, 'restoring the centripetal motion'.[13] Yoder proceeds:

> *It is 'confusion' only when measured against the simplicity of imperially enforced uniformity. It is narrated as a gracious and creative intervention of God, reinforcing the process of dispersion and diversification which had already begun and which God intended as a good thing. Thus the 'confusion of tongues' is not a punishment or a tragedy but the gift of new beginnings, liberation from a blind alley.*[14]

Far from being a wrathful or destructive act, God's dispersion of the peoples at Babel sets the stage for the call of Abraham. The lexical relationship between Babel and Babylon is obvious,[15] and suggests that the rhetoric of Genesis 11–12, at least in its final form, was forged in the context of the Babylonian exile.[16] Such rhetoric, according to Yoder, contrasts with the promises of false prophets, described in Jeremiah, that the captivity will soon end and that triumph still awaits the house of David.[17] The Babel

---

13　Yoder, 'Face to the Sun', 63.

14　Yoder, 'Face to the Sun'.

15　The same Hebrew word, *Bābel*, is used for both Babel in Genesis 11 and Babylon throughout the OT.

16　The dating of Genesis is contested and is, for some, sensitive. Nonetheless, I follow Brueggemann: 'It is now increasingly agreed that the Old Testament in its final form is a product of and response to the Babylonian exile. This premise needs to be stated more precisely. The Torah (Pentateuch) was likely completed in response to the exile... This suggests that by their intention, these materials are ... an intentional and coherent response to a particular circumstance of crisis ... Whatever older materials may have been utilized (and the use of old materials can hardly be doubted), the exilic and/or postexilic location of the final form of the text suggests that the Old Testament materials, understood normatively, are to be taken precisely in an acute crisis of displacement, when old certitudes—sociopolitical as well as theological—had failed'. Brueggemann, *Theology of the Old Testament*, 74–75. See also Middleton and Walsh, *Truth is Stranger*, 223, n. 9.

17　Yoder, 'Face to the Sun', 65.

story, however, reflects that some within the exilic community embraced their dispersed existence as, hereafter, the context for their divinely willed vocation.

None of this detracts from the traumatic and often oppressive nature of Israel's exile. Those who promote an 'exilic theology' ought to be cautious of minimising such negative aspects of literal exile.[18] Israel, after all, continued to believe that it had been exiled due to its sin.[19] Isaiah's description of exile as imprisonment (61:1–3) should warn us against addressing the theme flippantly.[20]

Still, in the midst of monumental trauma, Israel's prophets were envisaging a new way of being Israel. Jeremiah 29 previews a significant shift in Israel's vocational orientation. Jeremiah's letter to the exiles includes the well-known message, 'Seek the *shalom* of the city where I have sent you into exile, and pray to the LORD on its behalf, for in its *shalom* you will find your *shalom*' (Jer 29:7). For Yoder, this suggests that the real mission of the scattered Jews is to settle into Babylon and to be God's people there. Though Yoder does not directly address the fact that Jeremiah, in his letter to the exiles, does in fact promise some kind of return to the land of Israel (Jer 29:10–14),[21] he does go on to point out

---

18 Edward Said, Palestinian-US American academic in postcolonial studies, notes that, 'Exile is the unhealable rift forced between a human being and a native place, between the self and its true home. The essential sadness of the break can never be surmounted'. He goes on: 'Exile is fundamentally a discontinuous state of being. Exiles are cut off from their roots, their land, their past'. Said, 'Mind of Winter', 49, 51.

19 On seeing exile as the result of one's own sin, rather than the power of foreign powers, as a coping strategy for exiled people, see Smith-Christopher, *Biblical Theology of Exile*, 80–81.

20 Also, for example, Isa 52:2; Jer 39:7; Lam 3:7; Nah 3:10. See Smith-Christopher, *Biblical Theology of Exile*, 65–73.

21 Smith-Christopher suggests that a Deuteronomic editor could be behind these verses, a case of *ex eventu* prophecy. Smith-Christopher, *Religion of the Landless*, 135–36. I would suggest that Jeremiah's 'seventy years' might not represent a concrete time period at all, but rather an indefinite period, the announcement of which would be designed to quell expectations of imminent return to Judah.

that, whatever Jeremiah's promises, the epicentre of Jewish mission in subsequent centuries was Babylon.[22] This mission consisted, for example, not in attempting to teach the Babylonians Hebrew, but rather in learning local languages.

> *Jews will not only learn the local languages; they will in a few generations (and for a millennium and a half) be serving the entire ancient Near Eastern world as expert translators, scribes, diplomats, sages, merchants, astronomers. They will make a virtue and a cultural advantage of their being resident aliens, not spending their substance in fighting over civil sovereignty. Their conviction that there is but one God—creator, sovereign, anikonic, historically active, able to speak—enhances their cultural creativity over against the polytheistic, superstitious, tribally structured, fertility-focused popular religions of their neighbors.*[23]

This, for Yoder, contrasts with those who eventually returned to Jerusalem. Ezra, Nehemiah and their cohort sought to rebuild the temple and the city, and to re-establish Israel to its former glory. The later Maccabees would attempt to re-establish native kingship itself. Both nationalistic projects were doomed to failure. Diaspora Jews, on the other hand, had moved beyond such forms of nationalism, participating 'creatively, reliably, but not coercively in the welfare' of their host culture.[24] Unlike those who returned to Jerusalem, the ability of diaspora Jews to fulfil their obligations to YHWH was not dependant on the decrees of an imperial power. In fact, diaspora Jews could make themselves necessary to the natives of their new homelands through their multilingual expertise in

---

22 See, for example, Bird, *Crossing Over Sea and Land*, 55-132. In sum, Bird argues that there is no evidence of missionary activity in Palestinian literature, but some evidence in diaspora literature. In this context, missionary activity refers only to seeking out converts. Note Bird concludes that, overall, Judaism in the Second Temple period was not a missionary religion (again, in the sense of seeking out converts).

23 Yoder, 'Face to the Sun', 71.

24 Yoder, 'Face to the Sun', 72.

a range of fields, a reality reflected in numerous biblical and extrabiblical stories of the Persian and Hellenistic periods. This they could accomplish without the kind of bubbling nationalism of their Palestinian counterparts.

All of this is despite the ongoing portrayal of Babylon as the epitome of God's imperial enemies in subsequent biblical tradition. It is tempting to assume that, in making their homes in Babylon, some diaspora Jews came to live there without tension. But the biblical narratives of the period deny this. Biblical figures frequently endure persecution, even while they serve their host culture in significant ways. There was a reason that at least some exiles wanted to return to their land and a reason why, according to Jeremiah 29, prophets continued to promise that this would occur.

In this context of domination, the prophet Hananiah proclaims that YHWH had broken the power of the king of Babylon and that Judah's king would be brought back, and the exiles and temple vessels returned to Jerusalem. Daniel Smith-Christopher notes the martial language of Hananiah who, having physically destroyed the yoke that was over Jeremiah's neck, says, 'Thus says the LORD: This is how I will break the yoke of King Nebuchadnezzar of Babylon from the neck of all the nations within two years' (Jer 28:11).[25] He suggests these are the words of a violent revolutionary calling the people to draw their swords to end Babylon's rule over them.[26] In contrast, says Smith-Christopher, is the message of Jeremiah: 'Build houses and live in them; plant gardens and eat what they produce. Take wives and have sons and daughters; take wives for your sons, and give your daughters in marriage, that they may bear sons and daughters; multiply there, and do not decrease' (Jer 29:5–6). Far from being a general symbol of permanence, 'build, plant, and marry' constitutes a composite image that finds its literary context in

---

[25] Smith-Christopher, *Religion of the Landless*, 135.
[26] Smith-Christopher, *Religion of the Landless*, 135–36.

commands about warfare.[27] Specifically, the three images combined form a summary of exemptions from warfare (cf. Deut 20:1–9). According to Smith-Christopher, Jeremiah's use of this image amounts to his declaration of an armistice on the exile community vis-a-vis Hananiah's call for armed resistance.[28] In other words, Jeremiah calls for limited cooperation rather than open rebellion.[29] It is in this context that Jeremiah calls for the seeking of the *shalom* of the city (Jer 29:7).

The implications of this are not minor. Hananiah's and Jeremiah's calls represent conflicting strategic advice about how to live in exile. Jeremiah rejects violent resistance, and its undergirding nationalism, entirely. Gone is the Israel of nostalgic pining. A new reality is upon the people of God, and they must embrace it, conforming not to some past identity—one about which, given their exile, they should have some sense of shame[30]—but to a renewed sense of their calling by YHWH.

Not that this means unquestioning cooperation with Babylon. The call to 'build, plant, and marry'—in part a call to enjoy YHWH's blessings even in difficult times—ends with the imperative, 'multiply there, and do not decrease'. In other words, retain your Jewish identity and be faithful to YHWH. Such 'spiritual' resistance became a major theme in later Jewish history, and could be traced back to Jeremiah's influence.[31] But such resistance could not come at the cost of Israel's call to be a light to the nations (to borrow imagery characteristic of Isaiah). Jeremiah's strategy in exile was to resist being conformed to the idolatrous culture in which the exiles found themselves whilst

---

27　Smith-Christopher, *Religion of the Landless*, 133–34.
28　Smith-Christopher, *Religion of the Landless*, 134–35.
29　Smith-Christopher, *Religion of the Landless*, 135.
30　Smith-Christopher, *Biblical Theology*, 120–23 (esp. 121).
31　Smith-Christopher, *Biblical Theology*, 137. See also Davidson, *Empire and Exile*, 117–128. It is also worth remembering that Nabonidus, king of Babylon, attempted to draft Jews into the army, and Jeremiah's armistice, read in the face of such an attempt, may well take on further dimensions of resistance.

simultaneously seeking the wellbeing of the city. This is well captured in Yoder's summary:

> *When Jews in Babylon participated creatively, reliably, but not coercively in the welfare of that host culture, their contribution was more serious than 'bricolage'. There was no problem of shared meanings, since they had accepted their host culture and become fluent in it. Their own loyalty to their own culture (kashrut, anikonic monotheism, honoring parents, truth telling, work ethic, circumcision) was not dependent on whether the Babylonians accepted it, yet much of it was not only transparent but even attractive to Gentiles. Living in Babylon, then ... was not a problem for them. The surrounding Gentile culture had become their element. The polyglot Jews were more at home in any imperial capital, more creative and more needed, than were the monolingual native peasants and proletarians (and priests and princes) in that same city.*[32]

Exile, then, is hardly a place of violent resistance or conformity, much less withdrawal.

Smith-Christopher points to subsequent Hebrew narratives that reflect similar perspectives on exile. Jonah, for instance, read allegorically, symbolises the notion of exile as vocation:

- Jonah/Israel is called on a 'mission'
- Jonah/Israel turns away from God's call
- Jonah/Israel goes into darkness/exile
- Through this experience, Jonah/Israel can embody their mission to a foreign city.[33]

Jonah may protest, but this only shows that the transformation resulting from his mission is brought about by God, and not by the brilliance of the agent. Even despite Jonah's disobedience—in fact, because of it—YHWH

---

32 Yoder, 'Face to the Sun', 72–73.
33 Smith-Christopher, *Biblical Theology of Exile*, 132–33.

will graciously upend Jonah's plans and expectations in order that he might fulfil his vocation as a 'light to the nations'.

Daniel 1–6 highlights a different aspect of exile, but likewise one consistent with Jeremiah. Daniel makes clear the form Hebrew nonviolence takes, namely the kind of diaspora existence under imperial rule described by Yoder. Daniel will serve in Babylon's court, but also tells Nebuchadnezzar that his rule will come to an end (Daniel 2). Smith-Christopher describes Daniel's nonviolence as 'radical doubt and irreverence to the self-proclaimed state power and piety, a nonviolence based on the fact that God's plans are centered on the people of God primarily, and the nation-state is not the center of the universe'.[34]

There are numerous additional examples of such themes in the OT and intertestamental literature, but these few are sufficient to make the point that, despite the trauma of exile, Israel's prophets shed new light on their experience, such that exile became a door to a new way of being God's people and a new way of Israel understanding its own vocation. Exile could be perceived as simply the loss of power and land, but a thoroughly theological and prophetic lens offers the hue of exile as a radical reorientation of Israel's mission from being nationalistic, geographical, and a matter of statecraft to being universalistic, transnational—even cosmic—and a matter of communal identity. To be 'not at home' is to be so, at least in part, in relation to the nationalistic politics of the world.

This exilic transition is still a matter of conflict in the NT period. Jesus is born into a situation where Sadducees, Pharisees, revolutionaries, Essenes, Herodians and other groups are all responding, in diverse ways, to the challenges of gentile domination. Even in the land of Palestine, they were exiles, and not by choice. The NT suggests, however, that the Jesus movement embraced its exilic status, following its master in living in a kingdom without a land, one 'not of this world', as 'citizens of heaven'.

---

34   Smith-Christopher, *Biblical Theology of Exile*, 187.

First Peter is addressed to 'exiles' (1 Pet 1:1, 17; 2:11), and while this no doubt refers to those living in literal dispersion, commentators are quick to point out that, as the letter progresses, its use of the term develops a metaphorical sense (note also the reference to Rome as 'Babylon'; 5:13).[35] N. T. Wright's well-known judgement that most Jews of the Second Temple period believed themselves still to be in exile,[36] and that Jesus brought about an end to exile, could be correct, but even so the question would remain: in what sense did exile end? The dispersion of the early Jesus followers 'to the ends of the earth' suggests that exile had ended because the church had embraced exile as its vocation. In other words, Jesus had delivered Israel from exile by inaugurating an exilic kingdom 'not of this world'.

It is here, I think—with dispersion viewed as God's gracious vocational gift—that any exilic theology ought to begin. The generation of such an understanding of the theme of exile is, of course, possible within numerous theological traditions. I would, however, wager that it is not only characteristically—even predictably—generated from a distinctively Anabaptist ecclesiology, but is more likely to be so than in other Western traditions.

Radical Reformers as Exiles

The Radical Reformers were, after all, no strangers to being strangers. Exile (banishment) was a well-trodden path for the early 'Anabaptists', in the most literal sense. Though there was significant variation amongst them—far too much to offer a nuanced account here—the Radical

---

35 See for example, Richard, *Reading 1 Peter*, 30; Senior, *1 Peter*, 7–10; Jobes, *1 Peter*, 61–66.

36 Wright, NTPG, 268–72; JVG, 126–27, 203–4, 248–50. Wright's judgement here is not decisive for my argument. It is quite possible that Palestinian Jews did not view themselves as being in exile. See Pitre, *Jesus, The Tribulation, and the End of Exile*, 31–40. But even so, exile would have continued to be an operative theme given the non-return of the ten tribes, and the ongoing Diaspora. It would not be surprising for the church, as it was dispersed around the empire over time, to have embraced a diasporic identity like that found in 1 Peter.

DIASPORA AS MEANS OF GRACE

Reformers shared at least one thing in common: detestation and the threat of punishment from both the Reformers and Catholic hierarchy, as well as the various civil authorities with whom these ecclesial powers were allied.

The Radical Reformers did not begin with any kind of comprehensive theology of exile; in fact, far from it. For example, the Radical Reformers in Zurich were initially allied with Huldrych Zwingli in his attempts to reform the church there from 1522.[37] But Zwingli's compromises with the civil authorities caused some of his supporters—among them Conrad Grebel, Felix Manz, and Simon Stumpf—to push for a new, independent church.[38] At this early stage, they sought to elect a new, reform-minded city council; they, like Zwingli, continued to hope for the approval of the civil authorities.

Though these earliest Radical Reformers began to develop a hermeneutic that privileged the gathered community over-against the educated elite, it took some time for them to invest authority for church reform in something other than civil authorities. It was their failure to influence the direction of Zwingli's reformation, rather than some theological epiphany, that produced the first separatist critiques.[39] The first rebaptisms of adults—severely controversial at the time—were responses to the Zurich city council's ruling of a requirement to baptise infants, despite the Radical Reformers' opposition to the practice.

The separatist critique of the Radical Reformers eventually led to the composition of the Schleitheim Confession, most probably by early Radical Reformer and martyr Michael Sattler.[40] Article IV of the Confession, which details the Radical Reformers' notion of separation, says:

---

37 Weaver, *Becoming Anabaptist*, 33–37.
38 Weaver, *Becoming Anabaptist*, 36–37.
39 Weaver, *Becoming Anabaptist*, 43–44.
40 Wenger and Snyder, 'Schleitheim Confession'.

> *We have been united concerning the separation that shall take place from the evil and the wickedness which the devil planted in the world ... To us, then, the commandment of the Lord is also obvious, whereby He orders us to be and to become separate from the evil one, and thus He will be our God and we shall be His sons and daughters. Further, He admonishes us therefore to go out from Babylon and from the earthly Egypt, that we may not be partakers in their torment and suffering, which the Lord will bring upon them.*[41]

The caustic language, with its dualism and concern for purity, is odd to us moderns. It is no doubt a reflection of its time, but is also characteristic of diaspora communities more generally; in situations where it is impossible to be physically separated from a social order that is deemed evil, the marginalised must separate themselves in terms of identity and practice.[42] For the Radical Reformers, unable as they were to physically separate themselves in any meaningful sense from the civil, Catholic and Protestant authorities, separation from 'Babylon' needed to occur even while they were in Babylon. This is why the Schleitheim Confession is focused on ecclesiology—Articles I–III deal with baptism, church discipline, and communion, and Articles V–VII deal with pastors, the sword, and oaths, in a fashion distinct from that of civil society. The separation sought by the Radical Reformers is to be understood in this context, namely as the early

---

41   Yoder, *Schleitheim Confession*, 11–12.
42   Smith-Christopher, *Biblical Theology of Exile*, 137–62. Of the Hebrew concept of purity expressed in Ezra-Nehemiah, Smith-Christopher says: 'The diasporic Hebrew language of "purity" and "separation" needs to be read within the social context of minority existence in diaspora, and as such, takes on important social implications of definition and social identity ... While one may agree with the dangers of isolationist stances in relation to the world, in the ancient Hebrew context such separation was not an option. It is precisely because actual physical isolation is not an option that attention to identity and social integrity become essential to survival'. I would argue that the same applies to the Radical Reformers and the Schleitheim Confession.

stages of a diasporic movement that sought to live in nonconformity with the world, even while it was in the world.

The result of all of this was an increasingly marginal movement of people who sought to follow Jesus faithfully without the aid of government authorities, and who paved the way for later free church and congregational movements in Europe and North America. Though the language of exilic theology was not employed at the time, we can observe its contours, even at this early, undeveloped stage. The point is not that the early Anabaptists are unique in such an exilic existence—they clearly are not. Rather, the point is that in the contingent factors that gradually produced this diasporic movement we can discern commonalities with the Hebrew experience, and from both we can learn a renewed way of being God's people. We can go even further and suggest that the painful experience of physical exile was necessary for God's people to recognise—even in their midst of their trauma—the grace of God in renewing their vocation. For Israel, this meant a reimagining of its existence as something other than a nation, much less a monarchy. For the Radical Reformers, it meant reimagining their existence as a church not hypnotised by the heretical ecclesiological commitments of Constantinianism. Through exile they learned to be exilic in a much deeper, ecclesiological sense—a sense that has continued until today in a great variety of ways amongst contemporary Anabaptists. In this way, exile itself takes on a sacramental character inasmuch as it, in both its physical and theological forms, dispenses God's grace on the church and the world by empowering, in the words of Stanley Hauerwas, the church to be the church.[43]

---

43   Hauerwas, 'Servant Community', 375. In this sense, such sacramental character is not dissimilar to that of baptism and communion.

One Option Among Many

What, then, might the implications of this be for us in an increasingly post-Christian age of Western society?[44] An exilic theology offers a distinctive path amid post-Christian societies, as well as potential dangers. But, of course, there are various exilic theologies. Perhaps the current moment's most prominent such work is Rod Dreher's *The Benedict Option*. The book is one useful conversation partner, since it so encapsulates the current mood in much of Western Christianity, and it is representative of a major strand of exilic thought. Although it is not possible in this context to offer a deservedly thorough analysis of Dreher's work—besides, there has been a torrent of commentary on it already—some comments are in order.

Dreher presents the Benedict Option (BenOp) as a strategy in the midst of the ongoing marginalisation of Christianity in the West. It is, in essence, an embrace of 'exile in place' in the form of a vibrant Christian counterculture based on the example and teaching of Benedict of Nursia.[45] 'Benedict Option Christians look to Scripture and to Benedict's Rule for ways to cultivate practices and communities' in the face of the church's decline and cultural marginalisation.[46] Benedict's Rule is beyond meaningful description in this context, though in Dreher's rendering it calls for a highly disciplined life, in contrast to the consumerism, hedonism and technologism of our modern world.

There is much to be gleaned from Dreher's account of the BenOp, even if one disagrees with any number of its particulars. Nonetheless, the book is not without issues, at least from an Anabaptist perspective. Though Dreher claims several times that the BenOp is 'worth doing'

---

44 Anabaptist experience might caution against the use of a label like 'post-Christian' since, in their historical experience, Constantinianism hardly qualifies as thoroughly 'Christian'. Perhaps it is more accurate to talk about an age that is post-Christendom.
45 Dreher, *Benedict Option*, 18.
46 Dreher, *Benedict Option*.

whether or not it has any discernible effect on society,[47] a number of his comments tend against such a sentiment. For example, Dreher laments over the 'political homelessness' of conservative Christians in light of the fate of the Republican Party;[48] he insists that, 'Without a robust and successful defense of First Amendment protections, Christians will not be able to build the communal institutions that are vital to maintaining our identity and values';[49] and he muses that faithful orthodox Christians in the US are now in exile 'from a country we thought was our own'.[50] Such comments, in addition to the book's saturation with commentary on the culture wars in the US, give the impression that the BenOp's 'strategic withdrawal' constitutes a strategy, even if unconsciously, to eventually wrest back political clout for conservative Christians in the future. This, it goes without saying, is not cohesive with the neo-Anabaptistic notion of exile explored above, being more reminiscent of Israelites in Babylon dreaming of Jerusalem than of Israelites imbibing a new vocational trajectory.

Even if this evaluation of Dreher's perspective was off the mark, and his vision for BenOp communities was not concerned to eventually regain political influence, the BenOp would remain a reaction to perceived cultural demise and 'the light of Christianity ... flickering out all over the West'.[51] Dreher's recurrent image of building an ark—while not intended to imply a 'run for the hills' approach unjustly alleged by some

---

47   Dreher, *Benedict Option*, 54: 'We are not looking to create heaven on earth; we are simply looking for a way to be strong in faith through a time of great testing.' See also, 97: 'Building Benedict Option communities may not turn our nation around, but it's still worth doing'.
48   Dreher, *Benedict Option*, 80.
49   Dreher, *Benedict Option*, 84.
50   Dreher, *Benedict Option*, 99.
51   Dreher, *Benedict Option*, 8.

of his critics[52]—nevertheless reflects a missiology overly defined by the perceived darkness of the current age.[53] No doubt, points of crisis offer distinct opportunities for ecclesiological epiphanies, such as occurred with the Radical Reformers in the sixteenth century. However, a danger of being reactive to such crises is that the ecclesiological path taken is led not by an understanding of the church's character and mission as defined in Christ, but by the contingencies of culture and history.[54] This is the problem of being 'strategic'. Some Radical Reformers, for example, fell into this trap. For others among them, however, ecclesiology was not overly dictated by historical circumstances, though such contingencies provided moments of gracious clarity that helped in the formation of an ongoing approach to faith, life and the church. Such moments did not amount to 'exile' in any new sense, but rather to a reminder of the exile in which the church always exists.

From an Anabaptist perspective, the formation and cultivation of faithful communities of practice requires no particular historical or sociological impetus, except that we live in an unredeemed world generally; it is always our vocation to exist as alternative communities to the world.

---

[52] It is clear in *The Benedict Option* that Dreher expects BenOp communities to continue to serve those outside, though some of the book's content does confuse this point, not least the nature of the ark analogy. See, for example, Dreher, *Benedict Option*, 71–75.

[53] A comment here is necessary. We may indeed live in a cultural moment that is largely incompatible with Christian life and ethics and, in many ways, is becoming more so. However, it is not clear that such moments prior to the 1960s (the beginning of Dreher's 'turning point') were vastly more compatible. The Sexual Revolution—among Dreher's main subjects of antagonism—may not yet have occurred, but the subjugation of women and non-whites, two examples among others incalculable, testify to a less sanctified past than Christian nostalgia might recall. And besides, it is questionable for Anabaptists, considering their history, whether this age is much darker than others—Michael Sattler testifies to us from the cloud of witnesses, although not verbally since his tongue was torn out.

[54] I do not mean to imply that history has no bearing on the church. However, there is only one historical contingency that defines the essence and mission of the church, namely, that God became a man, lived, died, was resurrected, and ascended to heaven.

Hauerwas and Willimon, in the expanded edition of their classic *Resident Aliens*, say it well:

> [*In* Resident Aliens *we*] *may have given the impression that the position we were trying to develop depended on the inevitable loss of Christendom. In other words, what we were about may have seemed to be a way to suggest how the church might be repositioned in the face of loss of membership, social status, and political power. We do think, of course, that the loss of Christendom is inevitable, but we also were arguing that loss is a providential sign to make possible a church capable of challenging the powers.*[55]

In other words, the loss of Christendom *points towards* the church's identity—even apart from the historical incidence of Christendom's decline—rather than *defining* that identity.[56]

Diaspora Now

What does any of this mean for us? In a sense, we must continue to discern this together since, as Smith-Christopher notes, there is no single, timeless

---

[55] Hauerwas and Willimon, *Resident Aliens*, 176.

[56] Christendom was, according to David Bentley Hart, always destined for collapse anyhow: 'Christian culture could never generate any political and social order that, insofar as it employed the mechanisms of state power, would not inevitably bring about its own dissolution. Again, the translation of Christianity's original apocalyptic ferment into a cultural logic and social order produced a powerful but necessarily unstable alloy. For all the good that it produced in the shaping of Western civilization, it also encumbered the faith with a weight of historical and cultural expectation often incompatible with the Gospel it proclaimed ... Christendom could not indefinitely survive the corrosive power of the revelation that Christianity itself had introduced into Western culture. Christian culture's often misunderstood but ultimately irrepressible consciousness of the judgment that was passed upon civil violence at Easter, by God, was always the secret antagonist of Christendom as a political order'. In other words, the collapse of Christendom not only points toward, but is a result of, the church's identity. Hart, 'No Enduring City', 224–25.

exilic model; it must be worked out distinctly in all new contexts.[57] But if this Anabaptist approach to exile holds any water, it means that exile is, at least in this age, our default setting, and that the collapse of Christendom provides us an opportunity to see more clearly who we are and to proclaim the gospel in a way that is impossible when we see our role in society as, in some way, underwriting the claims of the nation-state.[58] As with the exiles in Babylon, our own exilic status 'challenges the virtual capitulation to the normative status of nationalism as the only viable context for Christian theology and Christian social existence'.[59]

In struggling to come to terms with our post-Christian moment, and in endeavouring to exorcise ourselves of Constantinianism, segments of the Western church will need to find new ecclesiological models from which to learn. While it is certainly valuable to learn from others in a Western context, we must avoid the temptation to limit the scope of our learning to the West, lest we model ourselves on those who are probing the same questions that we are. The growth of the church in regions where Christianity has, historically-speaking, never been dominant, provides exciting (and humbling) opportunities for such learning.

In their recent book, *The Radical Muslim and Mennonite*, Agus Suyanto and Paulus Hartono tell the story of their Mennonite community building bridges with militant Islamic groups in Solo, Indonesia over the last twenty years. Such bridge-building, a response to local enmities that have simmered since colonial missionary days,[60] arose out of traditional Mennonite convictions of peacebuilding and reconciliation, and was made possible only by the faithfulness of the peace witness and practice of the Mennonite community over the course of its existence. The Mennonite

---

57   Smith-Christopher, *Biblical Theology of Exile*, 194.
58   Hauerwas and Willimon, *Resident Aliens*, 39.
59   Smith-Christopher, *Biblical Theology of Exile*, 8.
60   For an overview of Muslim-Christian relations in Indonesia, see Suyanto and Hartono, *Radical Muslim and Mennonite*, 27–30.

community in Solo, living as it does in a country where over 87 percent of people practice Islam, sought not only to build relationships with moderate Muslims, but actively sought friendship with the paramilitary Islamic group, the Hizbullah Front.

This friendship began slowly after Rev Paulus Hartono was invited to mediate between the Hizbullah Front and another moderate Muslim group in a dispute over access to radio bandwidth frequencies—an exemplary image of Yoder's picture of God's diasporic people using their skills in the service of the welfare of the wider culture. Hartono, a Christian, Chinese and pastor, was for the Hizbullah Front the epitome of an 'infidel'.[61] But through persistent love and communication, Hartono developed an unlikely friendship with the Hizbullah Front's commander, Yanni Rusmanto. This led them and their respective groups to serve together in various humanitarian projects, including in Aceh in the aftermath of the 2004 tsunami. The trust that was built here led Hizbullah Front members to attend conflict transformation training run by the Mennonite church. More recently, beginning in early 2014, the Mennonites initiated a joint project with Hizbullah to repair the run-down houses of Hizbullah Front's family members living in Solo's slums. This occurred despite the fact that Hizbullah had long been involved in shutting down churches. All of this is but a glimpse of the larger story articulated in *The Radical Muslim and Mennonite*, but it nonetheless reflects the powerful witness of a minority community, committed to the truth and practices of its own tradition, working for the *shalom* of the wider culture, including its enemies, even despite danger, enmity, and, at times, persecution.

Interestingly, in the twenty years since Hartono and the Mennonites initiated relationships with Islamic fronts, the Mennonite church in Solo has grown tenfold.[62] Perhaps even more interestingly, when reflecting on

---

61 Suyanto and Hartono, *Radical Muslim and Mennonite*, 65.
62 Suyanto and Hartono, *Radical Muslim and Mennonite*, 107.

the lessons for the church that their story provokes, the authors first turn their attention to the need for self-transformation.[63] Speaking about the wider global situation of the church, they claim that:

> *In this increasingly post-Christian world, it is important more than ever for followers of Christ to learn how to engage with other communities of faith in a way that is authentic, peaceful, and full of integrity, especially if followers are met with hostility.*[64]

The ecclesiological wisdom here is beyond adequate analysis in this context, except to say two things. First, embracing its marginal, 'not-at-home' status affords the church the opportunity to be more faithful to what it is. Indeed, if the Mennonites in Solo had been socially dominant—they are far more marginal than we will ever be in our lifetimes—they would never have been able to achieve the peaceful gains that they have. Second, the need for an exilic community to be faithful in its internal life together in no way detracts from the need for that exilic community to be faithful to the work of seeking the wholeness of the host culture in which they find themselves. Anabaptists are frequently accused of sectarianism, and in some cases this is fair, but from a neo-Anabaptist perspective the teaching of 'separation' refers only to nonconformity with the dominant culture, non-alliance with a state,[65] and to the practice of a faithful Christian presence. Separation does not mean abandoning the world, but rather it is the distinctiveness necessary to reveal the 'peace that surpasses all understanding' and true human existence to a world entangled in sin and violence. Such revelation occurs through, among other things, nonconformity and truth telling, as

---

63 Suyanto and Hartono, *Radical Muslim and Mennonite*, 96.
64 Suyanto and Hartono, *Radical Muslim and Mennonite*, 104.
65 Nancey Murphy describes free church polity—the separation of church and state—as 'the rejection of institutional longing for alliance with the power of the state'. Murphy, 'Traditions, Practices', 91. This obviously applies beyond Anabaptism, but well describes the Anabaptist insistence on proactively being separated from the state, rather than simply accepting it as the historical reality now upon us in the form of post-Christendom.

well as loving, indiscriminate service. We are, mercifully, ensnared by the reality—always true for the church since its inception but contrary to the grain of modern epistemology—that our only truly convincing *apologia* is the form of Christ recognisable in the church in the entirety of its existence.

Final Thoughts

Beyond the ecclesiological dimensions of exile, some additional comments are necessary. Chief among them is that this rendering of the theme of exile is only possible by way of a robust Christology and eschatology. Though the christological and eschatological bases of exilic theology have been relegated to this essay's backdrop, it is at least worth stating explicitly that the lordship of Christ, and an eye toward creation's *telos*, must ever be present in our missiological musings on this post-Christian age, lest we fall into one or more of the related traps of sectarianism, accommodationism, or triumphalism. Each of these postures is, in one way or another, a failure to adequately discern and embrace the character and substance of our confession that 'Jesus is Lord' and our steadfast hope that God is uniting all things in Christ. It is only by way of this confession and hope that we might properly embody the model of living in exile that I have attempted to describe, a model that seeks, like Jesus, neither to abandon, become, or control the world, but rather to seek the world's wholeness while maintaining the separation necessary to offer a credible witness to what wholeness entails.

Second, the language of exile, though appropriate if read correctly, is fraught with problems. Apart from the contested nature of this language, certain abuses of it (supersessionism, for example), make it less than desirable. Moreover, the theological use of exilic language might lead to confusion with literal forms of exile. When we say the church is in exile, we should not mean to say that its experience is akin to those sixty-five million displaced persons in the world today, nor those numerous indigenous peoples who have been dispossessed of their lands through colonialism. Nor should we even mean to say the church's experience is like that of Israel. By equating the church's exile, a form of grace, with physical exilic experiences in our world, we risk trivialising such experiences or, worse, assigning to them divine causation. Such would be a particularly distasteful kind of indifference.

For such reasons, I suggest a move away from the language of exile to that of diaspora. This is not because the language of diaspora is perfect, but because it is less susceptible to confusion and misuse. In a positive sense, diaspora conjures in the popular imagination images not of divine punishment, but of movement. It captures the reality that the church is not at home in the world as it is, as well as the missiological dimension of our movement—we have been sent out among the nations as strangers.

The church is in diaspora because God has called us to be a people who inhabit a kingdom that is not of this world. We have all manner of historical examples on which to model ourselves: the early church, the Benedictines, the Radical Reformers, Indonesian Mennonites—the list could go on. But, following Yoder, our positive model of diaspora is perhaps best embodied by Judaism. The experience of the Babylonian exiles was 'normative rather than exceptional, and permanent rather than temporary'.[66] For Yoder,

> *diaspora existence is centrally characterized by: the synagogue, 'a decentralized, self-sustaining, non-sacerdotal community life form'; the Torah, 'a text around the reading and exposition of which the community is defined'; and the rabbinate, 'a non-sacerdotal, non-hierarchical, non-violent leadership elite whose power is not civil but intellectual, validated by their identification with the Torah'.*[67]

---

66   Colucciello, 'Epistemological Violence', 288.
67   Colucciello, 'Epistemological Violence', 288.

DIASPORA AS MEANS OF GRACE

It is no exaggeration to say that the church's repudiation of Judaism made conceivable the heresy of Constantinianism. Maybe, then, the most diasporic thing we can do is to remember, and to embrace again who we are, knowing that a people flooded by the radical grace of the God of Jesus Christ belong neither hidden in an ark, nor drifting in the seemingly unstoppable torrent upon which it floats.

3

NO PLACE FOR EXILE[1]

KATE HARRISON BRENNAN

In public life, Christians are seeking answers to fundamental questions: Where are we? Who are we? What's happening? How should we respond? Of late, the most prominent response has uncritically adopted the position of exile for the contemporary church, as if this were an imaginative option open for us today, when it is not. Prominent Christian leaders, some church institutions and a good number of local churches in developed countries are adopting an exilic mindset, while still enjoying a privileged position in society. This led David Starling to muse in an article published last year in the Christian newspaper, Eternity, that 'exile, it seems is the flavour of the year'.[2] The seriousness with which this framing had been adopted was reflected in one of the numerous examples Starling cited: a post by Steven McAlpine, in which McAlpine argued that his readers needed to brace themselves for 'Exile Stage Two'.[3]

At its worst, *exile* is invoked to characterise what is perceived as the decline in the status and social location of Christians in Western societies as the result of God's judgement on our communal departures from

---

[1] This chapter was first published as an article. See Brennan, 'No Place for Exile'.

religious life. This interpretation sees those departures of modernity as one continuous breakdown of a 'covenant' with God—as apostasy.

In this volume, various views are presented that suggest Christians should make sense of their place in the world through the framework of exile. Steven McAlpine, in chapter 1, argues that there is a 'coming apocalyptic exile'.[4] Matt Anslow, in chapter 2, argues an alternative position that, as a diaspora, we can draw on 'exile' as a positive theological theme.[5] Michael Frost, in chapter 12, argues that we live in an 'increasingly antagonistic secular society',[6] and that, in order for the church to do its job today, we have much to learn from Old Testament exiles.

In this chapter, however, I will argue that when Christians invoke *exile* as the way to make sense of who they are, where we are, and how we are to respond, a state of emergency is being invoked, and a rationale is created for the use of extraordinary powers. Moreover, when Christians believe that they are in exile in Western societies, contrary to the evidence of our position and power, it points to the fact that Christians are experiencing a collapse in *sense-making*. The effects, if not remedied, will be disastrous for Christian witness, and for society.

The Senses of Exile

Within the Western church, the framework of exile is ascendant in its attempt to make sense of who we are, where we are, and how we are to respond to the world. The exilic framework is being used to scaffold what Luke Bretherton describes as three of the most common ways by which churches try to make sense of the intersection between Christianity, identity and place: *co-option, competition* and *commoditisation*.[7]

---

4 McAlpine, 'Beguiling Technicolour'.
5 Anslow, 'Diaspora as Means of Grace'.
6 Frost, 'Exile'.
7 Bretherton, *Christianity and Contemporary Politics*.

But the biblical framework of exile is slippery because, as Starling has pointed out, it can be used both literally and metaphorically.[8] It thus appears to help us make sense of an ambiguous situation, without having to be clear about what we mean. Do we mean that we are literally in exile? Do we mean that we are now becoming a minority? Or do we mean that we are experiencing something similar to physical exile by being a minority that is without power, relying on the mercy of the oppressor?

When Christians try to *read* their situation as one of exile, they need to pay close attention to both social trends and biblical texts.

The key social trends being read include the decline in the proportion of those identifying as Christian in the West. In the United States, the Pew Research Center found that Christianity has declined sharply, with unaffiliated and other faiths rising.[9] NatCen's British Social Attitudes survey showed that people of no religion outnumbered Christians in England and Wales.[10] And in Australia, we are coming to terms with the latest census results, which (on top of the steady decline over the preceding thirty-five years) reported a fall from 61 percent of the population in 2011 claiming a Christian religious affiliation to 52 percent in 2016.[11]

Understanding what it means when there is a declining proportion of people within society who identify as Christian is, however, complicated by the fact that in developed countries, while Christians are becoming a minority, we still have a majority culture. While Christians in the West feel as though they are in an increasingly marginal position, Christianity is growing rapidly in the world's fastest growing region: Africa.[12] While this could counteract concern in the West, it seems that this change

---

8   Starling, 'Are Christians in Exile?'.
9   Pew Research, 'America's Changing Religious Landscape'.
10 Sherwood, 'People of No Religion'.
11 Australian Bureau of Statistics, 'Religion in Australia, 2016'. See also Zwartz, 'Christianity is Dying Out'.
12 The Economist, 'Future of the World'.

in the geographical locus of growth serves in fact to further disorient many Western Christians, and compounds the sense of loss. This sense of loss is expressed by Christians who adopt increasingly confrontational postures, condemn culture and hold what Natasha Moore has described as a sense of entitlement to special treatment.[13]

Among the key biblical texts Christians should read is the book of Jeremiah (Jeremiah's pastoral letter to the Israelites removed to exile in Babylon in 598 BC), and chapter 29, in particular. It is a rich passage that has provided inspiration for the church throughout the centuries, from the writings of Augustine to the sense of mission at Redeemer Presbyterian in New York City today.[14] Moreover, this chapter provides the launching pad for Bretherton's *Christianity and Contemporary Politics*.[15]

Yet in its everyday use in Christian communities, both leaders and lay people are reading texts such as Jeremiah 29 in oddly literal ways that account for neither biblical theology nor the genre of the book. As Walter Brueggemann has argued, Jeremiah must be understood as poetry in order to see the affective, imaginative possibilities it opens.[16] The poetry must be relished, rather than re-enacted directly.[17]

How to Make Sense

That the exilic mindset seems to be fashionably *au courant* indicates that there has been a collapse of 'sense-making', as described by Karl Weick in his sociology of organisations.[18] In Weick's analysis, organisations are in lethal danger when the individuals within them lose the ability to make

---

13 Moore, 'Churches Aren't Business'.
14 Redeemer Presbyterian Church, 'Vision and Values'.
15 Bretherton, *Christianity and Contemporary Politics*.
16 Brueggemann, *Prophetic Imagination; Book of Jeremiah;* and *Hopeful Imagination*.
17 Brueggemann, 'Prophetic Imagination'.
18 Weick, *Collapse of Sensemaking*, 628–52.

sense of the complex, ambiguous reality in which they operate, and they question their own capacity to act.

The reality in which we operate is, indeed, far more complex and ambiguous than McAlpine suggests. To take one example, in this volume, McAlpine labels the reality unfolding before us as 'the secular future', a 'glorious technicolour Oz' that is 'faith-sapping' in the 'late modern pressure' that it exerts.[19] In so doing, he misconstrues culture as something 'out there'—a land that can be evacuated because it can be distinguished from something that is purely 'Christian' and not 'culture'. Christians, we are told by McAlpine, have good reason to question their capacity to act.[20] After all, will we be able to recognise and withstand the 'pressure to conform', and find a way to breathe in the suffocating atmosphere? Will our hearts and brains be sufficient for the task?

The adoption of an exilic mindset is not only bad biblical theology. It can also be disingenuous and profoundly hazardous to the church and its mission. Christians cannot make sense of our current reality simply by superimposing the framework of exile.

However, old tools can be used in new ways to interpret our current reality. One tool that lends itself to such use is Jeremiah's pastoral letter to the Israelites. But it must be used carefully. What could happen if the contemporary church were to relish, with wisdom, the patterns of Jeremiah that Brueggemann has identified?[21] It could respond appropriately in mission and avoid a collapse in witness. More broadly, in a time in which idealists and activists seeking justice and virtue in public life feel deeply threatened by those in power, the heuristics of Jeremiah are a gift to those who need new sources for understanding their power to believe and to act in the world as it really is.

---

19 McAlpine, 'Beguiling Technicolour'.
20 McAlpine, 'Beguiling Technicolour'.
21 Brueggemann, *Book of Jeremiah*.

NO PLACE FOR EXILE

Realistically Embracing our Position[22]

The residence of the Israelites in Babylon was limited. Jeremiah's letter to the exiles makes reference to them being in exile for an additional seventy years. So God's words to them in exile were part of his plan to help them 'make do' with what they had, and to come to terms with where they were. The Israelites would not be in Babylon forever. But, as we know, measured in the span of a lifetime, it could seem like that for an individual. Life in exile could consume the experience of any one person's lifetime, and possibly the lifetimes of more than one generation. Jeremiah urges those in exile to come to grips with this reality, not to live in denial.

In a moving theological tribute to Rowan Williams, the former Archbishop of Canterbury, Stanley Hauerwas highlighted his wisdom that 'the hardest thing in the world is to be where we are'.[23] For the Israelites, it was the hardest thing in the world to be where they were in exile. And it is the hardest thing in the world for the modern church to be where it is. But that does not mean that the place in which we find ourselves is *exile*.

The similarities between where we are today, where the Israelites were, and where the church has been in past eras are multiple, but there are also important differences. The strong tendency in the church is to go even further than our general historical amnesia by adopting, directly, the identity of the Israelites. The church is tempted to inhabit an identity other than our own, and to claim a position of exile.

However, we are not in exile like the Israelites were. To be in exile means to be living in a state of being banished from your home country, usually for punitive or political reasons. There is an important sense in which to be living in exile means to have been banished from the dominion and power of your homeland.

---

22   On the need for the Israelites to have a 'realistic and intentional embrace' of the exile, see Brueggemann, *Book of Jeremiah*, 255.
23   Hauerwas, 'Living Well in Ordinary Time'.

Instead, we live on the other side of Christ's institution of the kingdom of God. In Jesus's death and resurrection, God fulfilled the promises he made to Israel and became King. With God as King, his dominion is not only coexistent with earthly dominion and power, but extends beyond it leaving no remaining wild plurality. Earthly power, politics and culture are both constrained by God's rule and given their best possibilities.

We do not, as Michael Frost has argued in his *Exiles: Living Missionally in a Post-Christian Culture,* simply live in a 'host empire of post-Christendom'.[24] It is not open to us to go back and inhabit the identity of an exiled people. Nor should we be using the terms 'diaspora' or 'minority' interchangeably with the concept of a people living in exile. They do not mean the same thing. To be a 'diaspora' is to be a people who have been dispersed beyond an original homeland. Of course, a diaspora can also be a people in exile, but it is not a necessary characteristic. But using the term 'diaspora' is not just a softer way of saying a people in exile. What is in contention is whether or not Christians have been banished from the dominion and power of our homeland. The term 'diaspora' does not have anything to say to that provocative characteristic of what it means to be 'in exile'.

Why is the church so tempted to assume the identity of a people in exile? It is because we utilise a process of pattern recognition to create our present reality. In his classic *Sensemaking in Organizations,* Weick used the example of the Mann Gulch fire disaster in which firefighters in a forest fire interpreted the fire through the pattern of their past experiences, and could not respond as a new scenario emerged.[25] However, the forest fire did not act like the fires they had experienced previously—it was a very fast-moving forest fire. One of the firemen was able to see that they were

---

24 Frost, *Exiles,* 81.
25 Weick, *Collapse of Sensemaking,* 628–52.

NO PLACE FOR EXILE

in a situation that was different from what they had ever experienced, and that they would, therefore, need to respond differently. The single fireman lit a fire ahead of the group, extinguished it, lay down in the space created by the burnt out fire, and called on all of the fire fighters to join him, to allow the fast-moving forest fire to pass over them. The other firefighters did not join him, and most of them died.

Can Christians read their current situation through the lens of what has been experienced previously? As a descent into exile? We cannot. We now stand on the other side of Christendom. That is how our present reality is best characterised—not as post-Christian or a 'secular future'.

At this point, I wish to make an aside. Just as we cannot read our current situation through the exilic framework, because as Christians, we have not been exiled from our homeland like the Jewish people were, nor should we be reading our situation through the story of 'Oz'. We are not in Kansas anymore, Toto, because we never were.

Back to what I was arguing about realistically embracing our position: with the realisation that the position of exile is no longer open to us comes grief. This grief is compounded by the fact that it is largely unacknowledged. It may present in a confrontational posture, or as Christian concern over impending chaos. At heart, however, it is a grief about a loss of ascendancy, and it is the result of us living in denial that we no longer have a majority position.

As we make sense of the rise of radical pluralism, we attempt to put on an identity that is no longer ours. Hence, the deep illogicality found in what can often be heard being bemoaned by Christian leaders at gatherings: that the church has become a victim of its own success.

We must read our situation through the poetry of Jeremiah and realise that this is not the time for victimhood. Defensive, confrontational faith, lacking in imagination, will get us nowhere. Instead, we must be schooled in the wisdom of prophets like Jeremiah to understand that new vistas can be opened if the church is to realistically embrace our position.

Intentional Ecclesial Focus

Jeremiah's letter is to exiles. They had been scattered but were now gathered, and it is through this group of exiles that Jeremiah says that the Lord God Almighty will bless the city of Babylon. God carried *them* there in order to fulfil his purpose. His will is that they would be outwardly focused, that they would 'seek the peace and prosperity of the city' and that they would pray to him for the city. The logic that is set in place is that their good is to be bound up with the good of the city. The Lord tells them if the city prospers, they too will prosper.

It is because of the time in which we find ourselves that we need to see our own situation through the frame provided by Jeremiah. In an era when there has been a loss of depth in church engagement, we need to regain an ecclesial focus and see our public engagement as something we do as church, not just as Christian individuals.

If we were to regain an ecclesial focus, we would see new ways to be more deeply engaged in society, supported by Christian organisations, in order to bring holistic ministries to those who are our neighbours. We should emphasise acting *together* as a church in local communities or in concert with other churches, rather than just as individual Christians—part of the church 'scattered'. This would, in turn, require that local churches conceive of their mission not just as tending the flock that gathers, but as tending to those who are lost.

We would also see churches regain a sense of authority that they would exercise in public, and a reduction in self-limiting beliefs manifested in a retreat from 'the secular'. In turn, this could promote an increased vibrancy in our engagement as we share the in-breaking of God's kingdom with the broader community, by bringing the gospel of Christ, in its fullness.

Enter the Journey

The Israelites were on a journey with God. God sent Jeremiah to these people. He came as a prophet to speak truth to those in exile about what lay ahead of them. The truth was that God did have a strategy, that he would restore, and that he would do that *in* and *through* their exile in Babylon. Taking this pattern and pushing it further, Luke Bretherton has suggested, following John Howard Yoder, that we could see Jeremiah as proposing that exile in Babylon was a return to the true vocation of God.[26]

Christians, however, cannot return to God's true vocation by reclaiming the position of exile, or by reclaiming the powerful position of Jerusalem (a point made by John Dickson).[27] Instead, we can and must mirror, as Bretherton suggests, the theologic of Jeremiah 29 by following the way of the cross. It is in *that* journey into exile, that we find the beginning of new life and new hope.

The way of the cross provides the most comprehensive of challenges to those who hold up the retrograde option of dwelling in exile. It challenges the exilic option as the way to maintain purity of community practices in the face of what is described as general moral degradation in society. It also challenges the assertion that exile is the only option left in the context of radical pluralism when there are real (or perceived) challenges to Christian identity and practice.

On this, Frost and I share a point of agreement. In his book, *Exiles*, Frost argues that Jesus is our standard and the example that we need to follow into a specific type of exile—dwelling on 'foreign soil', taking 'a

---

26   Bretherton, *Christianity and Contemporary Politics*, 5; Yoder, *Jewish-Christian Schism*, 161–62.

27   Shelley and Dyck, 'Church in Secular Culture'.

stance that promotes proximity between those among whom they live', going 'where Christ would go; to the poor, the marginalised, to the places of suffering', identifying 'with sinful humankind', and relinquishing 'our own desires and interests in the service of others'.[28]

However, as Christians, I think it is important that we emphasise the fact that we do not remain 'in exile', as if it were a place. We have to be on the move. Perhaps, then, it would be far better to make sense of ourselves as 'sojourners' in a strange but familiar place? Jesus did not give us the option of dwelling in self-imposed exile. We follow Jesus and the journey continues in the way of the cross: we make an offer and invitation to wider humanity to join the journey with us through prayer and service.[29] In this way, we participate in God's blessing of society.

Liberate the Imagination

The Israelites had been plucked up, torn down, almost destroyed and definitely overthrown. They had been alienated from their land and from all that they thought mattered. Their daily existence was filled with despair. And, yet, through Jeremiah, God enters their chaos and brings them new words: words that transformed their understanding of where they were, and what was possible.

The poetry of Jeremiah connected their present daily reality with a future reality. God liberated them from the belief that the possibilities of life were to be determined by Babylonian rule. And he showed them an alternative way to perceive their present situation, and how it could lead them home.

For us today, even the hopeful words of Jeremiah are not words that we should apply directly to our own lives, and to the situation of the

---

28 Frost, Exiles, 9, 54.
29 See Brueggemann, *Journey to the Common Good*.

contemporary church, as if they were a manual. As poetry, Brueggemann argues that the words are intended to be relished.[30] We need to allow the words to provide the kindling so that we can be both realistic about our present situation *and* anticipate the future—reframing the big picture of what is at stake. Unless we do so—nourishing a desire for a future that we do not yet fully inhabit—we will miss the signs of God's in-breaking kingdom; the message that we are not home yet (as the dominant culture believes we are) but are being brought home.

This poses a particular challenge for the church in the developed world, as Brueggemann has long since warned, because maintaining imagination for a homecoming forces us into the very depths of the interface between despair and hope.[31] Western Christians live within a dominant culture that denies that there are limits to resources and life, a culture that does not know how to mourn and grieve. Yet, in order to uphold an imagination for homecoming, we must be able to live with the finitude of life, embrace our own position and believe that the God of the infinite has triumphed where we are unable to go.[32]

We need to seek out meaningful models for ourselves of how to grieve, and how to live a life that is realistic about the fact that we're all preparing to go home. And we need to let these models fire our imagination so that we do not live for earthly rule.

Create Gardens in the City

The other practices of the pattern of Jeremiah were necessary preconditions for the Israelites to come to terms with their reality: that the place of exile was now the place in which God would fulfil his purposes of bringing justice and blessing through his people to the world.

---

30   Brueggemann, 'Prophetic Imagination'.
31   Brueggemann, *Reality, Grief, Hope*.
32   On homecoming, see Brueggemann, *Book of Jeremiah*, 260.

The Israelites had come to understand in the tradition of Deuteronomy that they were bound to the good of the city. In exile, they were pushed even further to see that they were bound to the good of the city of the oppressors. While once they had been commanded to build and to plant the cash crops of grain, olives and grapes (giving the alien, orphan and widow among them access and gifts), now their world is enlarged even further—the Israelites were commanded to settle down, to plant gardens and to eat what they produced. They were to 'put down roots'.

Then the Israelites were commanded to invite the most open-ended possibilities for what would happen next. They were to seek the peace and prosperity of the city to which God had carried them into exile. They were to pray to the Lord for it, because they were told that if the city prospers, they too would prosper.

The Israelites in exile were not just to tithe their cash crops, or to seek the good of their Babylonian oppressors as neighbours. Instead, they were to pray actively that the city would prosper, even before they did as a community in exile.

This is a challenge for us today—to situate ourselves firmly in local community (when the tendency is always toward the cosmopolitan) and to bind our good to the good of our neighbour and city through active investment and prayer. This has to be where we plant ourselves as individuals, families, and as the church, putting down roots for the long term, and seeking creative ways to move amid and among those who think that the city or the nation represents supreme authority.

For the Good of the City

The predominant responses from the church to the intersection between Christianity, place and identity—co-option, competition and commodification—are all attempts, Bretherton argues, to 'create a peace in the church and pursue justice for the church by prideful means'.[33] But we should seek first the peace and prosperity of the city, not the church, and do so using alternative means.

What we learn through the heuristic of Jeremiah, by allowing the words to affect our interpretation of our own reality, is that we have a God who has a history of helping his people to imagine and to pursue patterns of faithful witness.

What we experience is different from what has occurred in the past, but it is not entirely new. God has been before us, and he is with us today. He gives us the ability to make sense of our context, and commands us to learn to bless from a position of diminishing power: to love our neighbour, and work for the common good.

4

THE WEAPONS OF OUR WARFARE: CULTURE, CONFLICT AND CHARACTER IN 2 CORINTHIANS

David Starling

On a Darkling Plain

In the summer of 1851, the poet Matthew Arnold and his wife, Frances, found themselves in Dover, looking out over the beach as the tide ran out and the moon rose, meditating on the retreating tide of their own faith and the faith of those around them, and on the world it left them in. It was, as he put it in his poem, 'Dover Beach', as if they had been left stranded, standing together on the coasts of what once was Christendom, 'as on a darkling plain, Swept with confused alarms of struggle and flight, Where ignorant armies clash by night'.

It is not difficult to see connections between the picture evoked in Arnold's poem and the tumult of the times in which he wrote it—the abortive European revolutions of 1848 and the political turmoil in Britain associated with the presentation and rejection of the Chartist petition, all experienced and interpreted within the context of the 'crisis of faith' that Arnold and many of his peers were undergoing.[1] But the poem speaks to more than just its own immediate period. It has been on my mind increasingly in recent years as the culture wars have heated up in North America and our own version of them, here in Australia, has begun to grow in its intensity.[2]

As Christians we cannot possibly be indifferent to, or unaffected by, the cultural and political battles of our time between the progressive and conservative forces of our society. The social order which conservatives claim to defend and progressives would like to see adapted or dismantled is, after all, one in which the church has historically occupied a privileged place, and the beliefs and values which inform that order have been influenced, to some extent at least, by two thousand years of Christian presence within the culture. To complicate the picture somewhat, there is the additional and important fact that Christians, including some of our own evangelical Protestant forebears, have played an active role in almost all of the major social reform and civil rights movements of the last three centuries, in coalitions of various sorts with partners including the heirs of the secular enlightenment. Nor has the initiative in dismantling or modifying the old social order come solely from the political left: the forces of globalisation and market capitalism have, arguably, had at least as much of a destabilising effect on the values and structures of the old order as any of the campaigns for change that social progressives have organised. One way or another—and usually in several ways at once—we are implicated in these wars and deeply affected by them.

The challenges and temptations which a context of this sort presents for us as Christians vary depending on our social location, our

---

[1] On the 'Victorian crisis of faith', see Symondson, *Victorian Crisis*; Hempton, *Evangelical Disenchantment*; and Larsen, *Crisis of Doubt*.

[2] For description and analysis of the cultural-political background to the contemporary North American debates, see especially Hunter, *Culture Wars* and *To Change the World*.

temperament, and our politics: for some, the most tempting option will be to revise our beliefs and opinions so as to bring them into line with the values of our time, or to restrict our words and actions in the public square to causes that will retain the approval of our secular peers; for others, it will be to throw in our lot with the politicians and powerbrokers of the political right, offering them our blessing and endorsement in exchange for their promise to protect our privileges and champion our cause; and for others still it will be to retreat altogether from engagement with the wider world, keeping our heads down and our faith and politics private.

An example of that threefold temptation can be seen in the various reactions that I have seen among Australian Christians to a widely shared opinion piece by the right-wing, atheist radio host, Andrew Bolt. In the article, he catalogued a list of recent instances in which Christians had been variously picketed, threatened, misrepresented, subjected to draconian bureaucratic measures, and summonsed to appear before state tribunals to answer accusations that amounted to little more than the fact that they had argued in public forums for traditional understandings of Christian sexual morality. In response to events such as these, Bolt urged the Christians among his readership to 'prepare for persecution', 'open [their] eyes', and 'choose stronger leaders for the dark days'.[3]

Bolt's article provoked widely divergent reactions among Christian readers. A few offered nuanced responses, acknowledging the possible truth of Bolt's claim that attacks against traditional Christianity were becoming increasingly frequent but dissenting vigorously from his advice on the way in which Christians ought to respond. Most, however, reacted in a more predictable and partisan fashion, with responses that fell, broadly, into the three categories described above. Some echoed Bolt's words with loud 'amens', endorsing both his diagnosis of a 'war on religion' and

---

3   http://www.heraldsun.com.au/news/opinion/andrew-bolt/enemies-of-christianity-declaring-new-war-on-religion/news-story/043ebd5d04cf40934e983d391d5658bd

his implied prescription for the kind of 'strong leaders' that the church would need to fight back against it. Others poured scorn on the article in its entirety, arguing or implying that the only sort of Christians who encountered grief in the public square were the annoying fundamentalists who insisted on giving out Christmas cards in the school yard or writing blog posts about same-sex marriage. If we stuck to our 'core beliefs', they assured us, practising them between consenting adults in private, or if we restricted our public activism to causes that our secular critics approved of, then we had nothing to fear. And others still, I suspect, looked at their Facebook feed, sighed, and wished the whole discussion would go away.

Clearly, the times we live in involve challenges and complications that differ both in degree and in kind from what we have been used to in the recent history of the modern, Western church. If we are to navigate them faithfully, we will require both a deepened wisdom and a renewed fortitude. In the remainder of this paper, my plan is to turn, in quest for both of those things, to Paul's second letter to the Corinthians, focusing on the way in which he interprets the social context of the readers, the 'battle' that he sees them (and himself) as being caught up in, and the weapons that he encourages them to wield in that battle.

'Do not be yoked ...' (2 Cor 6:14—7:1)

In 2 Corinthians 1–7, Paul offers an extended defence of his ministry against whispered accusations that changes in his travel plans were a sign of weakness and inconsistency, and that his struggles and shameful sufferings undermined his credentials as an apostle.[4] As this section of the letter draws toward its close, in chapters 6–7, he makes a climactic appeal to the Corinthians, whose confidence in his ministry has been damaged by

---

4   For brief overviews of Paul's defence of his ministry in 2 Corinthians 1–7, see Gorman, *Cruciformity*, 202–4; Hafemann, *Paul's Message and Ministry*, 133–40; and Starling, 'We Do Not Want', 276–79.

these criticisms. His plea is that they will be fully reconciled with him in both their affections and their understanding, opening wide their hearts, taking pride in his starkly countercultural ministry, and embracing the understanding of the gospel that informs it.

At the centre of that appeal is Paul's strongly-worded and much-discussed summons to the Corinthians not to be 'yoked together with unbelievers' but instead to 'come out', 'be separate', and pursue the holiness that derives from the fear of God (6:14—7:1):

> Do not be yoked together with unbelievers. For what do righteousness and wickedness have in common? Or what fellowship can light have with darkness? What harmony is there between Christ and Belial? Or what does a believer have in common with an unbeliever? What agreement is there between the temple of God and idols? For we are the temple of the living God. As God has said:
>
> 'I will live with them
> and walk among them,
> and I will be their God,
> and they will be my people'.
> Therefore,
> 'Come out from them
> and be separate,
> says the Lord.
> Touch no unclean thing,
> and I will receive you'.
> And,
> 'I will be a Father to you,
> and you will be my sons and daughters,
> says the Lord Almighty'.
>
> Therefore, since we have these promises, dear friends, let us purify ourselves from everything that contaminates body and spirit, perfecting holiness out of reverence for God.

Given its position within the flow of the letter, it is unlikely that the passage is aimed narrowly or exclusively at the literal, physical participation of believers in meals that were eaten in the temples of the pagan gods, or in the cult prostitution that was sometimes associated with meals of that sort.[5] The more likely target of Paul's exhortation is the kind of metaphorical 'yoking' to the pagans and their gods that was informing the way in which the Corinthians assessed the ministries of Paul and his rivals, applying pagan criteria to the judging of Christian ministries. More broadly, beneath and behind that immediate and particular point of contention, Paul's warnings are directed against any pattern of thought and practice that is driven by 'worldly wisdom' (*sophia sarkikē*) rather than by 'the grace of God' (1:12).[6] 'What do righteousness and wickedness have in common?' Paul asks. 'Or what fellowship can light have with darkness?' (6:14).

'Weapons of righteousness' (2 Cor 6:7)

Behind Paul's imagery in 6:14 of an irreconcilable contrast between righteousness and wickedness, light and darkness, and closely connected with it, is the warfare metaphor that he has already implied a few verses earlier, in his depiction of himself and his fellow missionaries as soldiers, armed with 'weapons of righteousness in the right hand and in the left' (6:7).

The language Paul uses here in 2 Corinthians 6 is similar to the metaphor he uses in his letter to the Romans, where (in Rom 6:13) he urges his readers to offer themselves, with all their powers and capacities, to God as 'weapons [NIV: instruments] of righteousness'.[7] In Romans 6, the scope of the metaphor's reference is broad, embracing the role that all Christians play in the work of God to establish righteousness and justice in the world. In 2 Corinthians, it refers more narrowly to the particular role that Paul

---

5   Contra Barnett, *2 Corinthians*, 345–47, Fee, 'II Corinthians', 158–60.
6   For an argument in favour of reading 2 Cor 6:14—7:1 in this way, see Starling, 'Apistoi', 53–60.
7   Given the warfare metaphor implied in Romans 6 by the clash of powers between personified righteousness and personified sin, 'weapons' is probably a better translation of the Greek *hopla* than the NIV's 'instruments'. Cf. Jewett, *Romans*, 411; Dunn, *Romans*, 337–38.

and his fellow missionaries play in that work and warfare, but it is not without implications for the lives of his readers.[8] Within the immediate context of chapters 1–7, the account of Paul's ministry that he offers to the readers is principally apologetic in its function: in writing these things, he tells the Corinthians in 5:12, he is giving his readers 'an opportunity to take pride in us, so that you can answer those who take pride in what is seen rather than in what is in the heart'. But this is not the entirety of Paul's purpose in offering the Corinthians an account of his ministry; his hope that the Corinthians will be able to endorse his boast that 'we have conducted ourselves in the world, and especially in our relations with you, with holiness [NIV: integrity] and godly sincerity' (1:12) is matched by a corresponding hope that he will be able to make a similar boast about them (1:14; cf. 8:24; 9:2–4; 11:2–3; 12:20–21; 13:9–10).[9] Motivated by that twofold desire, Paul gives his readers a description of his ministry and the mindset that informs it, not only as a reason for the Corinthians to have confidence in him but also as an example for them to imitate themselves.

The picture in 6:7 of Paul and his fellow missionaries, armed with weapons of righteousness, should not be read in isolation from its context, at the centre of a dense and carefully composed paragraph (6:3–10) that sums up and recapitulates the portrait of Paul and his fellow workers' ministry that he has offered to his readers in 1:15—5:21:

> *We put no stumbling block in anyone's path, so that our ministry will not be discredited. Rather, as servants of God we commend ourselves in every way: in great endurance; in troubles, hardships and distresses; in beatings, imprisonments and riots; in hard work, sleepless nights and hunger; in purity, understanding, patience and kindness; in the Holy*

---

8   The remainder of this section is adapted and abridged from the longer, more detailed analysis of 2 Cor 6:7 and its surrounding context in Starling, 'Weapons of Righteousness'.

9   The translation of 1:12 departs from the NIV to read 'holiness' (hagiotēti) rather than 'integrity' (haplotēti) as original. See Thrall, '2 Corinthians 1:12', and Harris, Second Corinthians, 183, for text-critical arguments in support of this reading.

THE WEAPONS OF OUR WARFARE

> *Spirit and in sincere love; in truthful speech and in the power of God; with weapons of righteousness in the right hand and in the left; through glory and dishonor, bad report and good report; genuine, yet regarded as impostors; known, yet regarded as unknown; dying, and yet we live on; beaten, and yet not killed; sorrowful, yet always rejoicing; poor, yet making many rich; having nothing, and yet possessing everything. (2 Cor 6:3–10)*

Like the longer account in the preceding chapters, it focuses on the interrelated themes of Paul's sufferings (6:4b–5, 8–10; cf. 2:14—5:21) and his transparency and integrity (6:6–7; cf. 1:15—2:13).

The bulk of the paragraph is made up of an intricately constructed series of lists that Paul strings together in 6:4b–10, commencing with the phrase 'in great endurance', which serves as a general heading for the lists.[10] The first nine items of the list that follows (in vv. 4b–5) speak of the circumstances in the midst of which Paul and his fellow workers minister: 'in troubles, hardships and distresses; in beatings, imprisonments and riots; in hard work, sleepless nights and hunger'. The next eight (in vv. 6–7a) shift the focus to the graces, virtues and resources with which, by God's enabling, they minister in the midst of those circumstances: 'in purity, understanding, patience and kindness; in the Holy Spirit and in sincere love; in truthful speech and in the power of God'.

Verses 7b–8a contain a second, much shorter list of just three items, each introduced by the preposition *dia* (NIV: 'with' or 'through'). Like the long series of 'in …' phrases in verses 4b–7a, this list too falls into two (much shorter) sub-series. The first, in verse 7b, comprises just one item: 'with the weapons of righteousness in the right hand and the left', describing the means through which the graces and enablings listed in verses 6–7a are exercised and manifested. The second, in verse 8a, comprises two pairs of contrasting singular nouns: 'through glory and dishonour, bad report and

---

10   See especially Murray Harris's analysis and discussion in *Second Corinthians*, 465–67.

good report', focusing on the circumstances in which the weapons of verse 7b are used.

Finally, in verses 8b–10, Paul concludes the description with a series of seven more pairs of items, highlighting the contrasts between the way in which Paul and his fellow workers appear to human observers and the hidden reality of their situation, as transformed by the saving work of Christ: 'genuine, yet regarded as impostors; known, yet regarded as unknown; dying, and yet we live on; beaten, and yet not killed; sorrowful, yet always rejoicing; poor, yet making many rich; having nothing, and yet possessing everything'.

Paul's image of '[the] weapons of righteousness in the right hand and the left' (v. 7b) is thus positioned at a kind of hinge point between the graces and enablings of verses 6–7a and the contrasting pairs of responses, estimations and realities in verses 8–10.[11] That double relationship which the phrase has with what comes before it and what comes after it is crucial for interpreting and applying it.

Read in isolation, the image in 2 Corinthians 6 differs noticeably from the one in Romans 6:13, where it is the parts of believers' own bodies that are the 'weapons' in the metaphor. Here the weapons are held in the believers' hands—an image that speaks equally strongly of the active participation of believers in the war that righteousness wages against its enemies, but less directly of the self-involvement and vulnerability of believers, in their very bodies, as the weapons with which the war is waged.[12] Nevertheless, the surrounding context makes it clear that the battle Paul has in mind is not one that can be fought at (metaphorical) arm's length. The hardships listed in verses 4b–5 are all experienced bodily by Paul and his fellow workers; the graces and enablings listed in verses 6–7a are all, in one way or another, manifested in their character, speech

---

11   See Guthrie, *2 Corinthians*, 332.
12   On the vulnerability implied by Paul's image in Rom 6:13, see especially Jewett, *Romans*, 411.

and action; and the contrasting responses, estimations and realities in verses 8–10 all involve their persons and the various ways in which they are regarded.

Even within verses 7b–8a, a close connection is implied between the offensive and defensive actions in which believers exercise the 'weapons' in their right hand and in the left and the fluctuating circumstances of 'glory and dishonour ... bad report and good report' in which they find themselves. 'The "weapons" given to the apostle', as Mark Seifrid rightly stresses, 'are inseparable from the message of Christ that he bears in his own person: "through glory and dishonor, through slander and praise"'.[13]

The nature of that connection is a complex one, reflected in the chiasm that Paul creates by inverting the order of the terms within the second contrasting pair in verse 8a—'through glory [A] and dishonour [B], bad report [B1] and good report [A1]'. The implication, it seems, is that the 'bad report' Paul encounters at times—the slander and the criticism and the misrepresentation—is, at least in some instances, as much an occasion through which the gospel advances as the 'glory' and the 'good report' he receives from his friends and admirers is, potentially at least, as much a threat to his ministry as the 'dishonour' to which he is exposed.[14]

As Seifrid also (rightly) points out, Paul's references to his own active participation in the work that God's righteousness accomplishes in the world are framed by his depiction of the work of God that he 'suffers' in his fluctuating circumstances, as they are described in verses 4–7b and

---

[13] Seifrid, *Second Corinthians*, 281. Seifrid is probably drawing that connection more tightly than the text requires when he goes on to imply that the 'weapons' of offence and defence in verse 7b are the 'glory and dishonor ... slander and praise' of verse 8a.

[14] See especially 2 Cor 12:1–10. Unlike Seifrid, I am interpreting the 'glory' and 'good report' of v. 8a as references to human estimations of Paul and his fellow workers, rather than to the eschatological glory and praise given by God. See Harris, *Second Corinthians*, 478–79; Guthrie, *2 Corinthians*, 334.

verses 8b–10.[15] What Paul *does*, as an agent of God's mission, who he *is*, in his character, and what he *suffers*, in solidarity with Christ, are inseparable elements of his ministry.

'Not the weapons of the world' (2 Cor 10:4)

The picture in 6:4–10 of Paul and his fellow missionaries, viewed through human eyes, as 'impostors ... unknown ... dying ... beaten ... sorrowful ... poor, [and] ... having nothing', should not be misread as if it were an expression of resignation to the idea that their ministry in the world is ultimately powerless and ineffectual. For all his realism about the struggles and hardships of Christian ministry, Paul does not share the pessimism and heavy-heartedness of Matthew Arnold. On the contrary, as he foreshadows in chapter 6 and goes on to insist explicitly in chapters 10–13, his weak and socially marginal ministry is in fact imbued with the power of God.

At the heart of that paradox is the power of the gospel itself—the divine and utterly unworldly power of the work of the cross that Paul has resolved to make the centrepiece of his life and ministry (cf. 1 Cor 1:18—2:5). The assertion of that power, and of the unworldliness of the weapons with which it is wielded, is made most explicitly in the opening verses of 2 Corinthians 10:

> *By the humility and gentleness of Christ, I appeal to you—I, Paul, who am 'timid' when face to face with you, but 'bold' toward you when away! I beg you that when I come I may not have to be as bold as I expect to be toward some people who think that we live by the standards of this world. For though we live in the world* [en sarki ... peripatountes],

---

[15] Seifrid, *Second Corinthians*, 280–81. The quotation marks that Seifrid places around the word 'suffers' are a signal that his intended meaning is the broad, semi-technical sense of the word that embraces the whole range of experiences that Paul undergoes passively, as acted upon by God, rather than the somewhat narrower subset of those experiences which involve the enduring of pain and loss.

THE WEAPONS OF OUR WARFARE

> *we do not wage war as the world does* [ou kata sarka strateuometha]. *The weapons we fight with are not the weapons of the world* [ta gar hopla tēs strateias hēmōn ou sarkika]. *On the contrary, they have divine power to demolish strongholds. We demolish arguments and every pretension that sets itself up against the knowledge of God, and we take captive every thought to make it obedient to Christ.*

Here in 2 Corinthians 10, as earlier in the letter, Paul is referring primarily to his own work and warfare as an apostle and a messenger of the gospel. There is, of course, a broader sense in which all of the ordinary human powers and capacities of believers are to be offered up to God, in line with Paul's imagery in Romans 6, as instruments or weapons of his righteousness and justice. The scalpel of a Christian surgeon, the wisdom and influence of a Christian politician, the skills and work tools of a Christian labourer, are all to be viewed as instruments in the hands of God the creator, to be wielded for the sake of doing good in his world (cf. Rom 6:13; Prov 8:15; Col 4:23).

But the particular work on which Paul focuses here in 2 Corinthians 10—the work which he sees as being the very centre of God's re-creating and reconciling mission in the world, and the power by which God's saving righteousness is enacted and revealed—is the work that proclaims, teaches and applies the gospel of Christ. This is the work by which, according to Paul in 10:5, arrogant pretensions are overturned, and human hearts are taken captive to the obedience of Christ (10:5; cf. Rom 1:5-6, 16-17).

This is not a work that depends for its success on human powers of influence or persuasion; it is not a work that relies upon social standing or political privilege. Nor is it a work that can be reduced to strategy and technique, safely and neatly disconnected from the character of those who perform it, or their willingness to expose themselves to criticism, cost and social exclusion. On the contrary, as Paul has already emphasised in chapter 6 (and in the previous five chapters, too), it is a work which requires the gospel that is spoken and believed by Christ's servants to be embodied and demonstrated in their lives.

If we are to retain our confidence and our hope, and to have any enduring effectiveness in the changing social circumstances in which we find ourselves, we will need to arm ourselves with the same attitude. The temptation to insulate ourselves from suffering and shame by conforming to the morality and opinions of our culture, the temptation to seek protection by purchasing the support of the powerful or by imitating the kind of 'strong leadership' that they exemplify, and the temptation to hide away in a cocoon of privatised faith are all to be resisted. The way of faithfulness is the way of humble, holy, visibly countercultural strength in weakness, following in the steps of Jesus. Those who walk in that path may be weak, but they are armed with powerful weapons.

5

TO ALIENS AND STRANGERS: PREACHING THE NEW TESTAMENT AS MINORITY GROUP RHETORIC

Tim MacBride

Preaching and Minority Group Rhetoric

We're not in Kansas anymore. Neither are we preaching in Kansas anymore. No longer are Christian preachers espousing values and ethics which the dominant culture would agree with—at least in theory, if not in actual practice. No longer are ministers seen as authoritative leaders in the wider community. No longer can we preach sermons based on the assumptions of a Christian worldview, and have those assumptions go unchallenged—even by our Christian hearers. The illusion of Kansas has faded over the past few decades, and the world is now a very different place. Our minority group status should be abundantly clear.

In many ways, we are back in the land of Oz, which was once inhabited by the early church: monotheists in a pluralistic empire, small in number, marginalised by mainstream society, and committed to living out values seen variously as countercultural, or even subversive. Just like the early church, we are an occasionally persecuted, but regularly marginalised minority group.

When Christians are aware of their minority status within the wider community—whether they are in the minority simply for *being* Christian, or are already an ethnic or cultural minority with the added dynamic of Christian faith—it tends to be reflected in their preaching. Their experience of being marginalised or persecuted causes them to pay particular attention to where Scripture addresses the marginalised and persecuted, and to appropriate this message for their own context. To name but two well-known examples, we have seen this in Martin Luther King's appropriation of Exodus imagery during the civil rights struggle,[1] as well as in Latin-American liberation preaching, encapsulated so clearly by Presmanes:

> *The preacher in the Latino [sic] community struggles with the word of God to embrace the hermeneutical bias in favor of the oppressed. He or she goes to the scriptures bearing in mind the whole experience of otherness and exile of Latinos and looks for the hope and the grace being revealed in the ancient texts as well as the living texts of the Latino diaspora.*[2]

What such preaching is doing—whether deliberately or instinctively—is appropriating the minority group rhetoric inherent in Scripture itself, in order to form a new minority group rhetoric for a new context.

Christians in the majority world have been (often painfully) aware of their minority status for a long time, an awareness which has clearly informed and often formed their preaching. By contrast, believers in the West appear to have only comparatively recently become aware of

---

[1] For one such example, see 'I See the Promised Land', in King and Washington, *Testament of Hope*, esp. 281 and 286. For a detailed analysis, see Selby, *Martin Luther King*.

[2] Presmanes, 'Preaching and Culture', 14.

their minority status within the wider community.³ It therefore seems appropriate to ask how Western preaching can learn from the preaching of minorities in the way it draws on the minority group rhetoric found in Scripture, in order that it might more effectively speak into the Western church's new—or at least, newly realised—status as a minority group within a secular culture.

There is scope for this question to be asked in relation to *all* of Scripture, since it was all—at least on some level—produced in and for a minority context. For reasons of clarity and space, however, our focus will be on those New Testament writings which seem to be addressed to a minority audience *explicitly framed as a minority*, and are concerned with the group's survival in a hostile environment,⁴ most notably 1 Peter, Hebrews, 1 John and Revelation. Drawing together some of the insights from biblical scholars who have employed theories from the social sciences, we will survey the strategies employed by the writers of these texts, and at each point discuss the ways in which they might be appropriated for use in a contemporary Western context.

The Purpose of Minority Group Rhetoric⁵

Minority groups are usually under constant pressure—either overt or implicit—from the dominant culture to conform. This is particularly so in collectivist cultures (like the world of the New Testament) in which a member's sense of self and moral values are heavily dependent on the attitudes of their reference group of others—and strongly maintained

---

3   This has been evident for some time in more obviously secularised settings such as Europe and Australia, but is now also apparent even in the United States (despite many in that country still clinging to its inherited self-concept as a 'Christian nation').

4   DeSilva, *Honor, Patronage*, 50.

5   This next section is a summary of a more extended explanation found in MacBride, 'Aliens and Strangers'.

by the forces of honour and shame.[6] To survive, a minority group which deviates from the dominant culture needs to develop a way to protect itself from the shaming that comes from the wider community. In particular, it needs to articulate the reasons it is different from the rest of society, to develop strategies to insulate itself from the disapproval of the majority, and to inculcate a strong sense of belonging to the group over against the rest of society. Social scientists have often labelled this kind of discourse 'minority group rhetoric'.[7]

It should be no surprise that this kind of rhetoric is found in the writings of the New Testament. After all, they were addressed to small groups of believers who were being pressured—whether through overt persecution or more subtle marginalisation—to relinquish their allegiance to Christ and conform to the beliefs and practices of the wider community. Jewish believers faced this from their fellow Jews on account of Jesus's shameful death, his radical redefinition of Torah, and the influx of gentiles into the church.[8] Believers from a Graeco-Roman background were similarly shamed because of their non-participation in the civic religion which was central to the majority culture, and was perceived as a threat to the continuing favour of the gods and the emperor.[9] As the author of 1 Peter puts it, they lived as 'aliens and strangers' (2:11) in both a socio-economic sense,[10] as well as in a theological sense. The early church was clearly a minority group under threat, and much of the New Testament has a clear interest in persuading its readers to resist the pressure to conform.[11]

---

6   Malina, *New Testament World*, 62.
7   See Andrews, *Contemporary Rhetoric*, 59–61; Winslow, *Emergence of Deviant Minorities*, preface.
8   DeSilva, *Honor, Patronage*, 48–49.
9   See, for example, Isocrates, *Ad Dem.* 13; Plutarch, *Mor.* 1125E; a fuller discussion can be found in MacMullen, *Paganism*, 62–73.
10   Elliott, *Home for the Homeless*, 48.
11   DeSilva, *Honor, Patronage*, 50.

The first task in preaching such minority group texts is simply to draw the parallels between the first-century audience and our own. As noted above, many Christians in Western contexts do not appear to recognise the extent to which Christians are a minority, with some still believing that the West is a 'Christian society'. Our preaching, therefore, needs to encourage our audience to own the fact that they are in some ways marginalised, particularly by sections of the media and academia. This is not to argue for a return to an 'us against them' mentality, but a simple naming of the fact that the majority of society thinks our actions and worldview to be odd and out of step. It should also be noted that there is the more subtle pressure—from cultural attitudes, advertising, and the like—to buy into the majority culture's way of seeing things, even if just by default. Our audience needs to be reminded that twenty-first-century followers of Jesus are still 'aliens and strangers' in a very real sense.

Distinctive Yet Attractive

Like all pressured minority groups, the early church needed strategies to maintain its distinctiveness in order not to conform to the majority culture. Bryan Wilson, in his seminal work on religious minority groups, has shown that such groups have two options: isolation or insulation. For 'conversionist sects' like Christianity, isolation is not an option; therefore, the only way forward is insulation. This strategy creates a tension between drawing a boundary between the group and the wider society, and making that boundary permeable.[12] The distinctive values and behaviours of the group—often seen as 'shameful' by the dominant culture—are portrayed by the group in attractive terms, trying to win over outsiders by their very distinctiveness.[13] Commenting on this rhetorical strategy as it plays out in

---

12 Wilson, 'Sect Development', 12–13.
13 Elliott, *Home for the Homeless*, 108.

1 Peter, Joel Green describes group members as 'bicultural, living between two worlds, with the one a source of tension with the other'.[14]

Our preaching similarly needs to insulate against the majority culture while at the same time being attractive to it. It can also guide our hearers in determining where that balance lies in our own context. Often, Christians have done this backwards: we become distinctive where we do not need to be, and end up alienating the wider world; conversely, we slavishly copy culture in the very areas in which the gospel compels us to be different, and end up having no alternative to offer to the world. In preaching the New Testament minority group rhetoric, we can use these texts to help our audience figure out how to be 'attractively different' in our own context.

Minority Group Strategies in the New Testament

So how do the New Testament writers seek to create and maintain these strong-yet-permeable boundaries? The following discussion is a summary of what I have laid out in more detail elsewhere,[15] building on the work of pioneers like Malina, Elliott, DeSilva and others. It presents the rhetorical strategies used by minority groups in the form of answers to five key questions, and then offers some suggestions as to how the strategies might inform our preaching today.

1. Approval: Whose Opinions Do We Care About?

In any culture, but especially in a collectivist one, it is difficult for a minority group to expect its members to simply ignore the shaming of the outside

---

14 Green, *1 Peter*, 288.
15 For a more detailed discussion of these strategies and an analysis of how they are used in four of the later New Testament writings, see MacBride, 'Aliens and Strangers'. The focus here is on appropriating these strategies in our preaching of New Testament texts.

world. The group's 'court of reputation'—the collection of significant others to which members look in order to know what values and behaviours are honourable—needs to be redefined, removing those who are opposed to the group's values, and replacing them with alternative sources.[16]

We see this frequently in the New Testament. Excluded from the believer's court of reputation are both the synagogue community, which has rejected Jesus and seeks to shame his followers back into conformity (e.g. Rev 2:9), and the wider Graeco-Roman world, which does not know God and lives in ignorance (1 Pet 2:8; 4:3–5). Both these excluded groups may include family members, friends and important patrons. In their place, the New Testament writers place God firmly at the centre as the only one whose opinion truly counts (1 Pet 1:13–17; 1 John 4:4–6), and who will be the source of their ultimate vindication (1 Pet 4:7). Also included within this redefined court of reputation are God's people, who are 'the most visible and, in many senses, the most available reflection of God's estimation of the individual',[17] which is one reason the New Testament authors are keen to nurture such a community. The collection of God's people—both past and present—is both an embodiment of the alternative values of the group (Heb 10:32–24; the faithful exemplars in Heb 11), but also a place where those who are suffering acute rejection by the dominant culture can find encouragement (Heb 10:24–25; 13:1–3). In general, the New Testament writers use the characteristic strategy of deliberative rhetoric in appealing to *advantage*—urging the acceptance of the temporal disadvantage of rejection by the world in light of the eternal advantage to be had in being accepted by God and included in his people (Heb 11:26; 12:2; 1 John 2:17; the contrasted fates in Rev 14:9–13).

At its heart, weekly congregational preaching is a regular reminder of this redefined court of reputation. Its content reinforces the eternal

---

16   DeSilva, *Honor, Patronage*, 40.
17   DeSilva, *Honor, Patronage*, 58–59.

benefit of standing against the pressure from the majority, and its setting is a reminder that there are others who share this worldview. This would be all the more powerful if more were made of the fact that this is *inherent in many of the New Testament texts from which we preach.*

2. Disapproval: Whose Opinions Can We Ignore?

The negative counterpoint to the previous strategy is to reinterpret the disapproval which comes from outsiders, providing reasons it can be ignored. We have already seen how the New Testament authors portray outsiders as ignorant of group values and dishonourable in their conduct (e.g. 1 Pet 4:4),[18] who will themselves ultimately be shamed in a great 'divine reversal'.[19] Disapproval from such an ignorant and shameful group, then, is recast in a positive light, as something that should be expected; after all, it is evidence that group members are *not* like the ignorant and dishonourable outsiders (1 Pet 4:13–16; cf. Acts 5:41). In fact, the group's narrative is further reinforced when disapproval occurs, since the group has been prewarned to expect such disapproval (1 Pet 4:12; 1 John 3:13; cf. John 15:18–25).

This disapproval can also be viewed as an opportunity to display loyalty precisely because at that point it becomes costly (1 Pet 1:6–7), and gives group members the chance to imitate Jesus in his enduring the shame of the cross.[20] This is variously depicted as 'participation' in Christ's sufferings (1 Pet 4:13), as following the example of Christ in the way he 'despised' shame (Heb 12:2) by joining him 'outside the camp' (Heb 13:3), and as a symbolic 're-enactment' of Jesus's own mistreatment prior to his vindication (Rev 11:8). Disapproval should therefore be seen as honourable in that it imitates Christ.

18	DeSilva, *Honor, Patronage*, 62–63.
19	Elliott, 'Disgraced Yet Graced', 172.
20	Elliott, 'Disgraced Yet Graced', 172.

TO ALIENS AND STRANGERS

Disapproval from the dominant culture can promote conflict. However, if handled well, this can have a strengthening effect on the identity and unity of a minority group; as Coser notes, it 'contributes to the establishment and reaffirmation of the identity of the group and maintains its boundaries against the surrounding social world'.[21] More than that, however, it can also provide evangelistic opportunities by 'binding antagonists' and drawing them into interaction.[22] We see this clearly in the minority group rhetoric of 1 Peter, encouraging struggle and resistance not simply to insulate against disapproval, but 'as a necessary prerequisite for an effective missionary enterprise'.[23] That which caused the group to be shameful in the eyes of the majority produced conflict leading to dialogue, allowing the minority the opportunity to influence or even attract the wider community.

Perhaps our preaching needs to reclaim this aspect of minority group rhetoric—at least to some extent. This is not to argue for a return to the older style, circle-the-wagons approach which saw the world as an evil place to avoid at all costs, and the role of the preacher was to rail against its immorality and godlessness from a safe distance. Rather, this is a call to remember the considerable difference between the values of this world and the values of the one who called us out of this world in order to be a light to it.

One of the unintended consequences of well-intentioned 'incarnational' strategies informed by Paul's call to become 'all things to all people' (1 Cor 9:22) may have been to encourage a higher view of the surrounding culture than is warranted. Further, the pluralistic worldview assumed in much public debate pressures us—if we want to be considered participants in such debates—to at least act as if all cultures and all

---

21 Coser, *Social Conflict*, 38.
22 Coser, *Social Conflict*, 121–23.
23 Elliott, *Home for the Homeless*, 117.

religious worldviews are of equal worth, and to contain a similar degree of enlightenment. While this might be a necessary starting point when engaging in marketplace debates, the danger is that we begin to accept this as a starting point for our own identity—something which runs counter to the biblical understanding of the fallen nature of humanity and the complete 'otherness' of God's wisdom that cannot be grasped without divine help (1 Cor 2:11–14). This is not to advocate arrogance or disrespect (1 Pet 3:15), nor to adopting the *manner* of some of the more confronting anti-majority rhetoric of the New Testament (set as it is within the culture of bombastic Asiatic rhetoric delivered by a powerless, persecuted minority). However, as a means of insulating our audience against the pluralism of our own age, our preaching needs to rehearse the reasons we can ignore the world's opposition to God's values and its pressure to relinquish our characteristic beliefs and behaviours.

Furthermore, this is not purely for the sake of insulation. As noted above, conflict with the majority culture is at its heart missional. Our preaching can model how to disagree respectfully with the wider society, and to do so in a way that is attractive and invites dialogue. That is, we model how to speak of our 'attractive difference' that refuses to give unnecessary offence *and* refuses to pursue a strategy that makes us the smallest possible target. Neither error is missional.

3. Identity: Who Are We?

Much minority group rhetoric is directed to the question of group identity. The New Testament writers nurture a sense of identity firstly through the use of a common language that promotes solidarity (referring to one another in kinship terms, and the 'body' imagery of Greek politics appropriated by Paul in, for example, 1 Cor 12), as well as common rituals, such as baptism (1 Cor 10:7), and common symbols, such as the cross.

There are also frequent claims to exclusivity, expressed through terms like 'holy' and 'elect'—and a reminder that this exclusive group is bigger than their immediate context, being part of a worldwide group of similarly elect people (1 Pet 1:11; 5:13; 2 John 13) and, eventually, an eschatological multitude too numerous to count (Rev 7:9).[24] Particularly significant is the New Testament's attention to the early church's group identity in relation to the parent body from which it initially split. The majority (synagogue Judaism) is seen as being responsible for the rift, having rejected Jesus and expelled his Jewish followers from the synagogues (1 Thess 2:14–15). The Christian minority is portrayed as being in continuity with the 'true' form of the parent religion (1 Pet 2:9; Rev 2:9), and its symbols, stories, and promises are appropriated.[25]

Although the relationship between Christianity and synagogue Judaism is no longer a pressing concern in most contemporary contexts, our preaching still has a role in proclaiming our group identity. Perhaps being the 'true Israel' is of little interest to most churchgoers today; but being part of a story as old as history itself that gathers together a people from all over the world in hope of a world set right may speak to those within Western culture who are experiencing a sense of alienation, and a longing for community and purpose. The New Testament language of kinship and unity, and of shared stories and symbols, can still be powerful. This kind of New Testament preaching on *identity*—not so much individual identity but being part of a shared group identity—may well be what strikes a chord with the values of younger generations.[26]

---

24 Meeks, *First Urban Christians*, 107.
25 Elliott, 'Jewish Messianic Movement', 84–85.
26 See, for example, Greenberg and Weber, *Generation We*.

4. Practice: How Do We Live?

The next strategy we look at is probably the most obvious and well understood: God's people are called to live differently from the surrounding culture, in a way that reflects God's values. This includes living in a manner consistent with Christ's teachings, avoiding idolatry (1 John 5:21) and sexual immorality (1 Pet 4:3; Rev 2:14), and rejecting the Graeco-Roman value system which judged people on the basis of wealth, status and outward appearance (1 Cor 3:3; 1 Tim 2:8; Jas 2:1–4). Much of this is obvious and well-worn territory, and has been the subject of much Christian preaching.

Of interest, however, is that right behaviour was not promoted merely by direct commands or exhortations (such as those in, for example, 1 Pet 4; 1 John 2; Heb 13). The New Testament writers frequently employed the strategies of 'epideictic' rhetoric (one of the three genres of Graeco-Roman oratory), which sought to praise and honour those who exemplified the values and behaviours honoured by the wider society. The purpose of this was to reinforce these values among the community, and to encourage greater adherence to them through emulating those who were thus praised. Although Christ is the obvious example (1 Pet 2:21; Heb 12:2; 1 John 4:11; Rev 11:8), other such exemplars include the cloud of witnesses in Hebrews 11 and even the addressees themselves in former days (Heb 10:32–35; Rev 2:3,13), along with faithful witnesses such as Antipas (Rev 2:13), the martyrs under the altar (Rev 6:9), and the 'blameless' ones who refuse to worship the beast (Rev 14:1–5). These—and others—are examples of people who lived counterculturally in light of the eternal reward. The early church found its own examples to eulogise as a way of resisting the epideictic rhetoric of the Graeco-Roman world.

While much preaching has (rightly) focused on commanding and urging godly behaviour, perhaps this epideictic strategy of using *examples* of those who lived counterculturally—both from Scripture and from people known to us—ought to be reclaimed.[27]

5. Worldview: How Do We See the World?

Minority group survival often depends on creating and sustaining an alternative worldview from that of the dominant culture. Its rhetoric establishes a 'symbolic universe integrating values, goals, norms, patterns of belief and behaviour and supplying ultimate (divine) legitimation for the sect's self-understanding, interests, programme and strategies'.[28] Examples of this in the New Testament include: the appropriation of the story of Israel as an elect nation of priests in 1 Peter; the Johannine symbolic world of starkly-defined opposites such as light/darkness and children of God/children of the devil; and, of course, the bizarre and subversive view of the cosmos revealed to John on Patmos.

There is often an attempt to take ownership of the narrative, the lexicon, and social conventions.[29] The Christian minority's story is told not in terms of deviance from the majority culture, but in being part of a different story—such as Israel's story in 1 Peter, and God's purposes in history in Revelation. The meaning of words are reframed, so that 'Lord' refers to Jesus, not the emperor (1 Pet 2:13), and 'fear' is not anxious dread of a capricious despot but reverent respect for a sovereign creator (1 Pet 2:17).[30] The world itself is shown from a different perspective, turning the narrative upside down, so that in Revelation it is the idol worshippers of the empire who are the 'deviants' (Rev 9:20–21) and who will soon be

---

27 See further, MacBride, *New Testament as Rhetoric*, 82–84.
28 Elliott, 'Jewish Messianic Movement', 88.
29 Green, *1 Peter*, 284–88.
30 Green, *1 Peter*, 287.

destroyed unless they come into conformity with the rest of creation that exists to worship the one true God.[31]

Similarly, our preaching would do well to help our audience imagine a worldview by appropriating the symbols of our own culture and taking ownership of the narrative. Terms like 'security', 'freedom' and 'equality' are ripe for recasting in light of the gospel, in which they can be truly found only in Christ. The narratives of global terrorism, environmental catastrophe and financial meltdown can similarly be retold not as challenges which we will overcome by our own effort, but as the outworking of a world in rebellion against a sovereign creator that will only truly be defeated when he recreates his world—with us as his firstfruits.

Conclusion

Consciously reading the New Testament writings through the lens of minority group rhetoric might seem most appropriate among persecuted believers today, but to limit it to such contexts is to miss much of the point. In fact, throughout history overt persecution has often strengthened the faith and resolve of the Christian minority. A bigger danger, especially in the West, may well be the social pressure which seeks to shame the Christian minority back into conformity. This includes rejection by members of one's court of reputation, along with the steady erosion of respect for Christian belief in academic circles and in the media. In this climate, followers of Christ need preaching that appropriates the New Testament's own rhetorical strategies, teaching us how to 'despise shame', to go to our saviour outside the camp and bear the disgrace he bore, and to be confident that ultimately God will vindicate.

---

31   DeSilva, *Seeing Things John's Way*, 99.

6

STOOPING TO CONQUER: THE GENTLENESS AND GENEROSITY OF THE EARLY CHURCH

Edwina Murphy

David Wilhite, one of my colleagues in the study of early North African Christianity, has this quote from Dietrich Bonhoeffer in his email footer: 'I'm now reading Tertullian, Cyprian and others of the church fathers with great interest. In some ways they are more relevant to our time than the Reformers'.[1] Now we're not quite facing Nazi Germany, as Bonhoeffer was, but we do live in a world of competing ideologies rather than the Christian world of the Reformers. So what does the early church have to teach us about how to live in a hostile environment? How did a small group of unimpressive people change the world?

But first up, I'd like to point out that while I'll focus on the early church, when the governing authorities were largely antagonistic towards Christians, we should remember that Christendom wasn't always that much fun either, even under the Church of England. John Bunyan wrote

---

[1] Cf. Dietrich Bonhoeffer, 'To Eberhard Bethge', 29.

The Pilgrim's Progress while in a prison cell for unauthorised preaching.[2] Roman Catholics and Nonconformists like Presbyterians and Baptists were restricted from holding political office[3] and from going to Oxford and Cambridge,[4] and until 1837 the only records kept of births and deaths were of those baptised in the Church of England and those buried in its churchyards.[5] Many Christians suffered legal discrimination from the authorities, including imprisonment, so the challenges we face now are not unique, or even particularly harsh, even in modern times in the West. Having said that, let's turn our focus to the early church.

Christians as Imitators of Christ

At the heart of the early Christian project was the imitation of Christ. This applied to every area of life, but most particularly to martyrdom. As the author of *Martyrdom of Polycarp* explained: 'The martyrs we love as disciples and imitators of the Lord'.[6] In *Martyrs of Lyons*, a female slave is strikingly depicted in the image of Christ:

> *[Blandina] seemed to hang there in the form of a cross, and by her fervent prayer she aroused intense enthusiasm in those who were undergoing their ordeal, for in their torment with their physical eyes they saw in the person of their sister him who was crucified for them ... tiny, weak, and insignificant as she was, she would give inspiration to her brothers and*

---

[2] For similarities between Cyprian and Bunyan in their view of the Christian life under persecution, see Murphy, 'Cyprian', 116–30.

[3] Until the repeal of the Test and Corporations Act in 1828 and the Roman Catholic Relief Act of 1829.

[4] Subscription to the Thirty-Nine Articles was required until the mid-nineteenth century. That is why the University of Sydney was founded as a secular institution with denominational colleges.

[5] Buer, 'Civil Registration', 323.

[6] *Martyrdom of Polycarp*, 17. For a discussion of the rhetorical construction of this account, see Moss, 'Nailing Down', 117–36.

> *sisters, for she had put on Christ, that mighty and invincible athlete, and had overcome the Adversary in many contests, and through her conflict had won the crown of immortality.*[7]

The imitation of Christ leads to participation in Christ. This is also seen in the words of another female slave, Felicitas. Suffering while giving birth at eight months, she was mocked by the guard who consequently doubted her ability to withstand the beasts of the arena. Her reply? 'What I am suffering now ... I suffer by myself. But then another will be inside me who will suffer for me, just as I shall be suffering for him.'[8]

But as I said, the imitation of Christ is not limited to martyrdom. As Cyprian, bishop of Carthage in the mid-third century, wrote, 'We who desire to be Christians ought to imitate what Christ said and did'.[9] This covers our attitude towards everything from sex to money, and from how we treat friends to how we treat enemies. I am going to sum up the Christian posture under two headings: gentleness (or non-resistance) and generosity (care for those in need). But first, a waiver: Not all Christians confessed the faith under persecution. When the emperor Decius required everyone to sacrifice to the gods for the wellbeing of the empire in 250, for example, Christians did so on a large scale. They still wanted to belong to the church, however, which led to problems over the readmission of the so-called lapsed.[10] And not all Christians sold all, or even some of, their possessions and gave to the poor. Yet, enough Christians did these things to make them distinctive in the eyes of the surrounding society. The ideal was frequently taught, even if it was not always attained.

---

7   *Martyrs of Lyons*, 1.41–42. The source of the work known as *Martyrs of Lyons* is Eusebius, *Historia Ecclesia*, 5.1.3–5.2.8.

8   *Martyrdom of Perpetua and Felicitas*, 15. For a recent translation of and commentary on this work, see Heffernan, *Passion of Perpetua and Felicity*.

9   Cyprian, *Dress of Virgins*, 7.

10 See Cyprian, *Lapsed*.

Gentleness

Early Christians understood the way of Christ to be countercultural. They assumed that the Sermon on the Mount was part of Jesus's teaching on what the kingdom life looked like.[11] The emphasis on nonviolence and non-retaliation found here and elsewhere in the Gospels was, of course, exemplified by Christ himself, led as a lamb to the slaughter.[12]

As Alan Kreider has pointed out, this is rooted in patience,[13] a patience derived from the nature of God and the example of Christ. Cyprian linked patience to humility and meekness, and opposed it to the false patience of the Stoics—not only are they ignorant of the wisdom and patience of God, he claimed, but they are proud and self-satisfied.[14] Furthermore, the Christians were patient, not because of their acceptance of fate, but because of their hope: 'Patient waiting is necessary that we may fulfil what we have begun to be, and through God's help, that we may attain what we hope for and believe'.[15]

This emphasis on patience, gentleness and humility does not mean that Christians did not respond to attacks on them at all. Apologists wrote to explain Christian belief and to defend the faith. Justin Martyr, for example, writing in the mid-second century, demonstrated that just as Christ was the fulfilment of Jewish prophecy, he was likewise the fulfilment of Greek wisdom, the *logos*.[16] Justin also described Christian worship, attempting to show that Christians posed no threat to the empire, which we'll look at in

---

[11] For a summary of different perspectives on the Sermon on the Mount, see Keener, *Gospel of Matthew*, 160–62.

[12] Tertullian echoes Isa 53:7 in his discussion of Christ as an example in *Patience*, 3.

[13] For an extended discussion, see Kreider, *Patient Ferment*.

[14] Cyprian, *Advantage of Patience*, 2. Likewise, Abel is presented as a type of Christ who 'in humble and gentle patience allowed himself to be killed'. Cyprian, *Advantage of Patience*, 10.

[15] Cyprian, *Advantage of Patience*, 13.

[16] Justin Martyr, *First Apology*, 5, 46.

more detail later.[17] Even those who had ceased to be Christians, according to Pliny's letter to the emperor Trajan at the beginning of the second century, declared the innocence of their former way of life.[18] Tertullian, writing almost one hundred years later, criticised Trajan's decision in this case, which had become the standard policy for dealing with Christians, as self-contradictory: 'Christians were by no means to be sought after; but if they were brought before him, they should be punished ... It forbids them to be sought after as innocent, and it commands them to be punished as guilty. It is at once merciful and cruel; it passes by, and it punishes'.[19]

In a variation on a common apologetic theme, Cyprian wrote a spirited defence to Demetrian, perhaps a local magistrate,[20] against the allegation that the crises befalling the empire were due to Christians abandoning the worship of the gods. He refuted the charge, claiming that, firstly, the world is getting old—a classical commonplace,[21] for which Christians can hardly be blamed[22]—and secondly, these events are God's punishment on the empire for the persecution of Christians.[23] Cyprian emphasises that Christians do not defend themselves; ultimately God will take vengeance.[24] The patience and gentleness of the early church

---

17 Justin Martyr, *First Apology*, 67.
18 'They asserted, however, that the sum and substance of their fault or error had been that they were accustomed to meet on a fixed day before dawn and sing responsively a hymn to Christ as to a god, and to bind themselves by oath, not to do some crime, but not to commit fraud, theft, or adultery, not falsify their trust, nor to refuse to return a trust when called upon to do so. When this was over, it was their custom to depart and to assemble again to partake of food—but ordinary and innocent food.' Pliny the Younger, *Ep.* 10.
19 Tertullian, *Apology*, 2.
20 Sage, *Cyprian*, 276.
21 Cf. Sallust, 'omnia orta intereunt' (everything that is born must die). *Rep.* 1.5 (LCL 522:488). This is despite the presence of other themes such as the *Aeternitas* of *Roma perpetua* or *aeterna*. Marrou, 'La fin du monde antique', 80.
22 Cyprian, *To Demetrian*, 4.
23 Cyprian, *To Demetrian*, 12.
24 Cyprian, *To Demetrian*, 17.

relied on God's ultimate control of history. Cyprian does not hesitate to tell his persecutors that they will be going to hell. But even with this confrontational approach (which I'm not recommending we emulate), the work ends with a plea for his persecutors to turn to God while there is still time:

> *Because we may not hate, and we please God more by rendering no return for wrong, we exhort you while you have the power, while there yet remains to you something of life, to make satisfaction to God, and to emerge from the deep darkness of superstition into the bright light of true religion. We do not envy your comforts, nor do we conceal the divine benefits. We repay kindness for your hatred; and for the torments and penalties which are inflicted on us, we point out to you the ways of salvation. Believe and live, so that you who persecute us in time, may rejoice with us for eternity.*[25]

Gentleness is not only to characterise our relationships with those outside the church, however, but also those within. Patience, according to Cyprian, underlies all the other virtues because, in the end, faith, hope and love amount to nothing if one does not persevere in them.[26] Patience promotes unity through forgiving one another and bearing one another's burdens. It is the opposite of jealousy, through which 'the bond of the Lord's peace is broken'.[27] As Christ is the paragon of patience, it is unsurprising that Cyprian depicts the devil as the first to be impatient and jealous.[28] So shall we imitate Christ or the devil? Just in case the answer is not obvious, Cyprian uses pairs of models—Cain and Abel, Esau and Jacob, Joseph and his brothers, Saul and David—to show the necessity of patience under

---

25 Cyprian, *To Demetrian*, 25.
26 Cyprian, *Advantage of Patience*, 15.
27 Allusion to Eph 4:3. Cyprian, *Jealousy and Envy*, 6.
28 This is because God made people in his own image, drawing on Wis 2:23–25. Cyprian, *Advantage of Patience*, 19; *Jealousy and Envy*, 4.

trial and the fatal effects of yielding to jealousy and envy.[29] Since the devil seeks to destroy the church through creating division among Christians,[30] love and patience are necessary to maintain unity with our brothers and sisters, even when we disagree with them.[31]

Generosity

In the Roman Empire, giving was about status. The focus of the wealthy elites was on cultivating clients—a reciprocal means of exchange—rather than helping those who were unable to give anything in return.[32] Even the distributions of grain to the *plebs* in the first century were based on citizenship rather than need.[33] Public benefaction was ostentatious: funding buildings (with inscriptions honouring the donor), staging entertainment in the circus, and supplying gladiators and exotic beasts.[34] (Christians were, of course, sometimes involved as victims.) Gaining prestige was what it was all about.

Jewish tradition was rather different. Jesus continued the emphasis on caring for the poor, and the early community in Acts took his words seriously. But it didn't end there. Almsgiving, sharing with those in need, was central to what the early church did. We see it in the fullest early description of Christian worship in Justin Martyr's *First Apology*. He describes the elements we would expect—Scripture reading (the memoirs of the apostles and the writings of the prophets), a sermon,

---

29 Cyprian, *Jealousy and Envy*, 5; *Advantage of Patience*, 10, 19. For further discussion, see Murphy, 'Imitating the Devil'.
30 Cyprian, *Unity*, 3.
31 On this emphasis in Cyprian, see Bakke, 'Episcopal Ministry', 406.
32 Saller, *Personal Patronage*, 8.
33 Even if many of those who received it were, in fact, poor. Brown, *Poverty and Leadership*, 5.
34 Cyprian draws a contrast between seeking to please proconsuls and emperors and giving to others with God and Christ as witnesses. *Works and Almsgiving*, 21.

prayers, the Eucharist—and right in the middle of it all, giving to provide for those in need:

> *The wealthy among us help the needy and we always keep together, and for everything we have we bless the maker of all through his Son Jesus Christ, and through the Holy Spirit ... And those who are well to do, and willing, give what each thinks fit. What is collected is deposited with the president, who helps the orphans and widows and those who, through sickness or any other cause, are in need, and those who are in bonds and the strangers living among us, and in a word takes care of all who are in need.*[35]

So, assisting those in need was a core component of what Christians did when they came together. A generation later, Tertullian, when discussing the importance of Christian marriage, talks about those things that it would be difficult to do if married to an unbelieving husband. These include visiting the poor in their own meagre homes, encouraging those in prison, washing the saints' feet, providing hospitality to Christian travellers, and generally making their resources available to others.[36] In addition, unlike the modern policy of not paying ransoms, Cyprian records raising a large sum of money to redeem those captured by barbarians.[37] He uses a number of Pauline images for the motivation of the givers,[38] ending with a quote from and rewrite of Matthew 25:36:

> *Now the Lord says in His Gospel: 'I was sick and you visited me'. But His words will be accompanied by a far greater reward for our good works when He says: 'I was captive, and you redeemed me'. Again He says: 'I was in prison, and you visited me'. But it will be far more advantageous for us when He proceeds to say: 'I was held captive and in prison, I lay among*

---

35 Justin Martyr, *First Apology*, 67.
36 Tertullian, *To His Wife*, 2.4.2.
37 Cyprian, *Ep.* 62. The development of the practice of ransoming captives in early Christianity, with its background in Jewish piety, is discussed by Osiek, 'Ransom of Captives', 365–86.
38 Cyprian, *Ep.* 62.1–2. For discussion, see Murphy, 'Cyprian, Paul, and Care', 423–25.

barbarians behind bars and in chains, but you freed me from my slavery and imprisonment'; for we shall soon receive our recompense from the Lord when the day of judgment comes.[39]

The early church maintained the New Testament emphasis on giving as an evidence of faith that would be rewarded with treasure in heaven.[40]

But believers should not only care for those within their own community of faith. John Chrysostom, bishop of Constantinople, makes an impassioned plea for Christians of his day to imitate the early church in their generosity, imagining how it would radically transform the city.[41] Pontius, Cyprian's biographer, records how the bishop encouraged his flock in the midst of a plague to give not only to Christians, but non-Christians as well, alluding to Matthew 5:44-45: 'Your heavenly Father causes the sun to rise on the good and the evil, and causes the rain to fall on the just and the unjust'.[42] Cyprian himself uses this same text to encourage generosity to unbelievers—Christians should imitate their heavenly father and not hold back from helping.[43] In *The Rise of Christianity*, the sociologist Rodney Stark credits this sacrificial care as the means by which many non-Christians survived the plague and entered the church.[44] Christian care for the poor may even have been too successful, as Origen refers to those who 'pretend to be Christians for material gain'.[45]

Generosity means looking for the welfare of the other rather than the self. Michael Frost says that these days, there is nothing surprising

---

[39] Cyprian, *Ep.* 62.3.1.
[40] Cf. Matt 19:21, Luke 12:33.
[41] Chrysostom, *Homilies on Acts*, 11.
[42] Pontius, *Life of Cyprian*, 9.
[43] Matt 5:45 in Cyprian, *Works and Almsgiving*, 25. Cyprian also uses Matt 5:45-46 to demonstrate that Christians should pray for unbelievers that they might become heavenly rather than earthly (*Lord's Prayer*, 17) and to support the testimony, 'Even our enemies must be loved' (*To Quirinus*, 3.49).
[44] Stark, *Rise of Christianity*, 73-94.
[45] Origen, *Against Celsus*, 1.67.

about a Christian organisation giving, and so it has little impact.[46] That may be so. (And a lot of Christian organisations these days are funded by the government and staffed largely by non-Christians anyway.) But giving should not simply for that reason be disregarded as a powerful means of imitating Christ and revealing him to the world. (And, in fact, such generosity and hospitality are expressed in Frost's practices of 'Bless' and 'Eat'.[47]) First, Jesus commanded us to care for the poor and not to worry about our food or clothing.[48] Second, generosity changes us. It shifts us from a scarcity mentality to one of abundance. It frees us from the bondage of wealth and liberates us to follow Jesus. Instead of being consumed by desire for what others have, we share what we do have with those in need, which protects from the danger of envy, something the early Christians talked about a lot more than we do. I love what John Chrysostom says on this point:

> *Now consider this, and be rid of the disease of envy. Even if you are unwilling to set your neighbour free, at least set yourself free from these countless evils. Why do you carry war into your own thoughts? Why fill your soul with trouble? Why work up a storm? Why turn things upside down? How will you be able, in this state of mind, to ask forgiveness of sins?*[49]

Generosity and reciprocal giving create community and unity rather than the divisiveness of conflict. And people will notice. According to Tertullian, non-Christians exclaimed, 'See how they love each other'.[50]

---

46 Frost, *Surprise the World*, 13.
47 Frost, *Surprise the World*, 29–55.
48 Matt 6:25–34.
49 Chrysostom, *Homily 7 on Romans* 3.9–18.
50 Tertullian, *Apology*, 39.7. Cf. John 13:34–35.

Conclusion

As Chrysostom said, 'Now love is not speaking empty words to people, but taking care of them, and putting itself forward by works—relieving poverty, helping the sick, rescuing those in danger, standing by those who are in difficulty, weeping with those who weep, and rejoicing with those who rejoice'.[51] That kind of love takes effort; it involves sacrifice. The early Christians were able to persevere in being gentle and generous because they had hope for the future and set their heart not on earthly, but on heavenly rewards. This did not mean, however, that they were 'so heavenly minded they were of no earthly good'. Instead, it freed them to behave in countercultural ways which did, in fact, change the world. As C. S. Lewis said regarding hope:

> *A continual looking forward to the eternal world is not (as some modern people think) a form of escapism or wishful thinking, but one of the things a Christian is meant to do. It does not mean that we are to leave the present world as it is. If you read history you will find that the Christians who did most for the present world were just those who thought most of the next. The Apostles themselves, who set on foot the conversion of the Roman Empire, the great men who built up the Middle Ages, the English Evangelicals who abolished the Slave Trade, all left their mark on Earth, precisely because their minds were occupied with Heaven.*[52]

There are, of course, differences between the circumstances of the early church and ours. The early church faced the challenge of being new in a world that valued what was ancient—novelty was suspect. Now the church (in the West, at least), faces the challenge of being old in a world that values what is new. Christianity has been so successful that many of its

---

51 Chrysostom, *Homily 7 on Romans* 3.9–18.
52 Lewis, *Mere Christianity*, 134.

truths—that all people are created equal and have the right to life, liberty and the pursuit of happiness—have become self-evident.

But I think the qualities of gentleness and generosity still have something to contribute. We are living in an anxious age. Christians seem just as prone to it as everyone else—in some ways more so, as we see society changing around us. If we have confidence in God, though, if we entrust ourselves to him, we will radiate something different. As Cyprian wrote in the midst of barbarian attacks, natural disasters, plagues and persecution:

> *There flourishes with us the strength of hope and firmness of faith, and in the midst of the very ruins of a collapsing world our mind is lifted up and our courage is unshaken, and never is our patience unhappy, and our soul is always secure in its God, just as the Holy Spirit says and exhorts through the prophet, strengthening the firmness of our hope and faith by his heavenly voice.*[53]

There is tremendous freedom in living with confidence in the future, as citizens of the heavenly city.[54] And there is tremendous impact in following Christ in his gentleness and generosity. As Cyprian said, 'New-created and newborn of the Spirit by the mercy of God, let us imitate what we shall one day be'.[55]

---

53   Cyprian, *To Demetrian*, 20.
54   Augustine, *City of God*, 15.1.
55   Cyprian, *Lord's Prayer*, 36.

7

WHY WE NEED THE WORLD: MUSINGS FROM THE INTERFACE OF THEOLOGY AND EDUCATION

D̲ave B̲enson

> *That has been fundamental right through the history of the Church, that the structural forms of the Church are determined by the secular reality, and not by the internal needs of the Church; and I think that is true to Scripture ... It is the Church of God for that place, and that is because the Church does not exist for itself but for God, and for the world that Jesus came to save.*[1]

Lost and Found: Niebuhr's Typology

My first 'Not-in-Kansas-Anymore' experience was living abroad in Canada. Having recently moved out of state school teaching and then youth work through a large Baptist church in conservative and sunny Brisbane, the shift to progressive and drizzly Vancouver was a shock to the system.

---

1   Newbigin, *Word in Season*, 53.

Such stunning natural beauty, magnificent mountains and friendly people. And yet it commingled with Dennis Oppenheim's mighty sculpture of an upturned church on the public foreshore—named 'Device to Root Out All Evil'—and the most rainbow flags per square kilometre I'd ever seen. The liberal attitude and post-Christian sentiment on most everything from drugs to sex to anti-colonial politics was disorienting. Where on earth was I? How should I make sense of, and interact with, this particular west-coast culture?

Strangely, I found my bearings in Austin, Texas, 1949. This was the unlikely setting for theologian H. Richard Niebuhr's groundbreaking series of lectures that comprised his book, *Christ and Culture*.[2] While it has been debated and dissected across decades since, it remains a lodestone for any rigorous assessment of how the church might faithfully be *in* but not *of* the world (cf. John 17:15).[3] So there I was, 2007 in Vancouver, under Regent College's green roof, studying 'Theology of Culture' with Professor John G. Stackhouse, Jr. We grappled with Niebuhr's typology, seemingly a world away in time and place from both America's Bible belt and predictable Brisbane.

Oversimplifying Niebuhr's scheme, he posits two extreme positions, and three mediating constructions to face an 'enduring problem' of the relationship between Christianity and civilisation.[4] Each provides a paradigm—a metaphor, even—for how we may construe the church's positioning relative to the two competing authorities of *Christ* and *culture*. By *culture*, Niebuhr means what individuals and institutions outside the

---

2   Niebuhr, *Christ and Culture*.

3   See Stackhouse, 'In the World', 80–81. Much of this essay is a tribute to Dr Stackhouse's teaching and frameworks, encountered while I studied at Regent College, particularly as delineated in his *Making the Best of It*, and reframed in his *Why You're Here*. My contribution is to particularise his approach for public education.

4   Niebuhr, *Christ and Culture*, 1.

church 'make' of the world, both in artefact and interpretation.[5] It's the dominant way of life marking a people.

Let me acknowledge immediately that Niebuhr's definition of culture comes in for a bruising, both from sociologists who prefer greater precision and from theologians who recognise that the church exists within culture, under Christ who is sovereign over all. Niebuhr arguably sets up a false dichotomy, perhaps even playing into a Constantinian settlement where there is an assumed partnership between church and state that is troublingly coercive in nature.[6] Even so, his categories give us a map to make sense of how we journey forward over complex terrain.[7]

At the two ends of Niebuhr's spectrum, collapsing the tension, are Christ against culture, and Christ of culture. In the former, Type I *separatists* see culture as radically against the demands of Christ, so they oppose and evacuate 'the world' as it were—*contra mundum*—to faithfully follow Christ. As a counterculture, the church simply withdraws from society, giving full reign to the monastic impulse. In the latter, Type II *accommodationists* perceive that culture is so radically Christianised that following Christ and serving culture are identical, in harmony. No tension there, just jump on board and do what the culture asks, affirming the good evident to all.

Of the three mediating positions which maintain the tension, Type III *synthesists*, holding to *Christ above culture*, acknowledge common grace at work beyond the church; they cut away sin and direct society's good toward a transcendent *telos*. Type IV *dualists*, framing *Christ and culture* as *in paradox*, recognise the real tension of living for Christ in a fallen world, doing their best to act humbly and faithfully in both this world and in God's heavenly kingdom; confession and grace must characterise any activity of

---

5 See Stackhouse, *Making*, 14–15.
6 See Ward, *Christ and Culture*, 21–22; Carter, *Rethinking Christ*.
7 See Marty, 'Foreword', xiii–xix.

Christians in the secular city. Finally, Type V *conversionists*, championing *Christ transforming culture*, work hard to reshape society according to the reign of God; they exercise influence to leverage change, anticipating the day when the kingdoms of this world become the kingdom of our Lord (Rev 11:5).

In that beautiful yet bewildering Canadian context, Niebuhr's typology gave me a powerful toolkit—a compass of sorts—to locate where I was, and from whence I came.[8] I began to reflect on this in relationship to my work in public secondary education. With *separatists*, I was tempted to despair and to retreat into Christian schooling or homeschooling, as regulations mounted barring me from even acknowledging my allegiance to Christ.[9] This withdrawal may well have been prophetic,

---

[8] Cf. Keller, *Loving the City*, 290. Keller reframes Niebuhr's five types as four models: Counterculturalist (Type I *withdrawal*), Relevance (Type II *accommodationist a*nd Type III *synthesists*), Two Kingdoms (Type IV *dualists*) and Transformationist (Type V *conversionists*). Keller helpfully analyses the strengths and weaknesses of each (208–41), noting that there seems to be a 'coming together on culture', fusing the best and defusing the worst of each model (241–43). For Keller, 'all the models are right ... and wrong' (245–48), distinguished in large part by the answer given to two hinge questions: '*Should we be pessimistic or optimistic about the possibility for cultural change? ...* [and] *Is the current culture redeemable and good, or fundamentally fallen?*' (248–49). In turn, Keller divides the four models into quadrants along two axes of optimism/pessimism concerning the degree of common grace and how active or passive the church's role should be in influencing culture (256–58). *Counterculturalists* (little common grace; passive influence) stress a prophetic stance, opposing the fallenness of the world. The Relevance model (full of common grace; active influence) stresses partnership for the common good. *Two Kingdoms* (full of common grace; passive influence) calls for faithful persistence and humble excellence. Finally, *Transformationists* (little common grace; active influence) attend to foundational beliefs behind cultural clash, stressing Christian worldview toward strategic change. Through these blended insights, shorn of triumphalism and appropriately exercised in the relevant season/time, each model has a crucial role to play; pitting these diverse spiritualities against each other is counterproductive. One without the other is prone to excess and even unfaithfulness (260–72).

[9] Since then, in my home state, Education Queensland has attempted to extend this ban to student-to-student evangelism associated with Religious Instruction, on the grounds of protecting students from potential 'harm' and maintaining a 'safe' environment. See Fowler, 'Queensland's Evangelism Ban'.

forming Christian students as a counterculture who challenge the status quo that all is good in so-called 'secular' education. Conversely, with *accommodationists*, my everyday work in physical education—cultivating healthy bodies and enjoying sport and recreation—meant that I could do my job alongside other PE teachers with no qualms, creatively delivering what I believed to be an excellent curriculum. There was a tension between Christ and culture, but most of the time it was out of sight, out of mind. With *synthesists*, I could cultivate wonder in students as to an orderly cosmos and beautifully functioning body, calling for gratitude toward some higher force. Alongside *dualists*, I recognised that disciplining students with positional power as the deputy principal demanded was in conflict with Christ's model of personal power, even as I humbly tried to honour both authorities. Finally, as a *conversionist* evangelical, I was ever hopeful that my stumbling efforts through classroom teaching and lunchtime programs bridging school and church might point students to Jesus, shaping education to reflect holistic discipleship in which all students become more truly themselves, image bearers of God.

Had you asked me in my 2007 Vancouver classroom which stance was the *right strategy*, I would have returned a confused look—as would have Niebuhr. Surely this is to miss the point. In answering how the church is to 'relate its basic loyalty to Christ with its life in the world', Niebuhr offers a typology, not a taxonomy—it's a metaphorical lay of the land, not a set of timeless directions to the city of God.[10] These are idealised responses; only a fool would settle for one strategy. You might ask whether I am a separatist, accommodationist, synthesist, dualist or conversionist, but the wiser response is to resist classification, blending insights as the culture requires and the Spirit leads. Constructs like 'world' and 'culture' include myriad elements—individuals, ideas, institutions, communities, policies, symbols, stories, language, artefacts, practices, and

---

10   Stackhouse, *Making*, 31–36. Cf. Niebuhr, *Christ and Culture*, 2.

more. It's unhelpful to lump this together as an integrated whole calling for a single response.[11] Niebuhr's most strident critics, perhaps missing this fundamental distinction between typology and taxonomy, made the point for him. As John Howard Yoder submitted:

> *Some elements of culture the church categorically rejects (pornography, tyranny, cultic idolatry). Other dimensions of culture it accepts within clear limits (economic production, commerce, the graphic arts, paying taxes for peacetime civil government). To still other dimensions of culture Christian faith gives a new motivation and coherence (agriculture, family life, literacy, conflict resolution, empowerment). Still others it strips of their claims to possess autonomous truth and value, and uses them as vehicles of communication (philosophy, language, Old Testament ritual, music). Still other forms of culture are created by the Christian churches (hospitals, service of the poor, generalized education, egalitarianism, abolitionism, feminism).*[12]

Perhaps we face the same danger in framing this symposium. When speaking of '*the* role of the church in an increasingly post-Christian West'—'are we activist exiles or quaint keepers of an ancient flame? Are we to lean into culture and insist on our right to act as chaplains to a fading Christendom, or should we withdraw and exercise the "Benedict option"?—we are

---

11 Hunter, *Change the World*, 18–47. Cf. Stackhouse, *Making*, 14–18.
12 Yoder, 'Richard Niebuhr', 69.

tempted to reply with a single dominant metaphor guiding the entire church, responding to the whole world as an undifferentiated entity.[13]

Singular Strategies: BenOp

This problem is particularly apparent when we turn to Rod Dreher's highly influential manifesto, *The Benedict Option*.[14] One would hope that this 'most discussed and most important religious book of the decade' might offer a nuanced 'strategy for Christians in a post-Christian nation', as its subtitle

---

13 This problem afflicts even excellent volumes with which I largely agree, such as Frost, *Exiles*. Drawing heavily on Brueggemann, *Cadences of Home*, Frost rightly recognises parallels between Israel's exile and that of the modern church from culture; he poses this powerful metaphor as dominant for our missional spirituality today (8-10, 27). In the flow of redemptive history, Frost acknowledges that through Jesus, the literal exile is over and 'we indeed have found our way home ... in the presence of our gracious, loving, forgiving God' (326-27). And through this imagery we are helpfully called to action as a people of the promise, for the sake of the world: to be authentic, to serve a cause greater than ourselves, to create missional community and work righteously, being generous and practising hospitality (82). Amen and Amen! And yet, leaning so heavily on this singular metaphor amplifies the motif of being a *counter*culture, aligned with Anabaptist sensibilities prone to prophetic denunciation and 'dangerous criticism' (ix, 18-21). It arguably downplays, even undermines, the righteous use of remaining church power that celebrates common grace and upbuilds culture toward a common good. Seeing ourselves as exclusively 'exiles on foreign soil' (9) distorts Jesus's own mission as one of 'ultimate exile' (29), rather than the true light entering his own created world, albeit unrecognised (John 1), and in turn sending his disciples out into the whole world—blessed to be a blessing—where every step onto formerly foreign soil becomes a sign of God's already-but-not-yet kingdom breaking in (Matt 28:18-20). The dangerous example of Daniel is a brilliant analogue for 'those who *feel* like exiles in a post-Christendom era' (17, 27; emphasis mine). Daniel, Jeremiah and our other prophetic forebears may even be the most informative examples for educators seeking the *shalom* of the city through a faithful intermingling of cross-cultural wisdom (cf. Shortt, 'Daniel'). Nevertheless, unless we are prepared to posit Christendom as the promised land—something Frost clearly rejects with his strident criticism of the Constantinian settlement (4-8)—we must enrich our imaginary for cultural engagement with a more complete biblical theology of diverse metaphors alongside that of exile.

14 Dreher, *Benedict Option*.

suggests.[15] Facing an increasingly hostile culture, how should the church respond? There is much in BenOp, as it's often abridged, that I love—stuff my home church is presently putting into practice to build a deeper identity resistant to corrosive secularism and consumerism in which our society swims. I've also put Dreher's advice to work in my theological and classical education classrooms. Unfortunately, when it comes to schooling outside of the Christian confines, we find gems like this:

> *Because public education in America is neither rightly ordered, nor religiously informed, nor able to form an imagination devoted to Western civilization, it is time for all Christians to pull their children out of the public school system.*[16]

Dreher offers no qualifications or caveats. He simply urges—en masse, evacuate! Perhaps Dreher would argue differently in the Australian context, though I suspect not. After a two-page interlude, lamenting the rise of LGBT activists in the school, and a secular slide in sexual activity, drug use and mainstreaming of anti-Christian, especially left-leaning ideology in the curriculum, he surmises the following:

> *This kind of thing is why more and more Christian parents are concluding that they cannot afford to keep their children in public schools. Some tell themselves that their children need to remain there to be 'salt and light' to the other kids. As popular culture continues its downward slide, however, this rationale begins to sound like a rationalization. It brings to mind a father who tosses his child into a whitewater river in hopes that she'll save another drowning child.*[17]

These are striking metaphors, to be sure. But they all fit within a single strategy and uniform imagination: Withdraw! Retreat 'while there is still

---

15 Brooks, 'Benedict Option'.
16 Dreher, *Benedict Option*, 155.
17 Dreher, *Benedict Option*, 157.

WHY WE NEED THE WORLD

time'![18] Jamie Smith, in his review, contrasts this cloistered response with 'The Augustinian Call' to remain at your post, using your gifts for the common good:

> The Benedict Option *begins with a flood and ends with an earthquake. In between is an instruction manual for building an ark and a map that will get you to the hills. That's not my impression; it's Dreher's point.*
>
> *In the first trope, the Benedict Option is offered as a way 'to quit piling up sandbags and to build an ark in which to shelter until the water recedes and we can put our feet on dry land again'. Instead of 'wasting energy and resources fighting unwinnable political battles', the Benedict Option offers a lifeboat strategy 'that can outwit, outlast, and eventually overcome the occupation'.*
>
> *The second metaphor comes from Norcia, home to the Basilica of St. Benedict that was tragically destroyed by an earthquake in August 2016. Dreher reads it as an allegory, 'a sign to the world': 'Because they headed for the hills after the August earthquake, they survived'. Go and do likewise.*[19]

Dreher would have us secede from the worldly empire through geographical distancing in a classical education community, or at the least pursue an 'exile in place' as part of a 'vibrant counterculture', enrolling your child in the best Christian school money can buy.[20] This sounds like self-interested protectionism, concern for the survival of the church as the world drowns, whilst Niebuhr's typology whirs quietly in the background. Psychologising his strategy, Dreher sounds like a depressed Type 5 conversionist, lamenting the cultural slide from the medieval ages where Christianity fulfilled pagan hopes (Type 3 synthesist) and became the Christ of culture (Type 2 accommodationist). As the paradox (Type 4 dualist) of living in an

---

18   Dreher, *Benedict Option*, 3.
19   Smith, 'Benedict Option?'
20   Dreher, *Benedict Option*, 18, 158–75.

increasingly post-Christendom society grows, and the optimism of a fully transformed society disappears, Dreher is calling for a strategic retreat (Type 1 separatist) to get our bearings and to protect the barely faithful remnant. Perhaps, then, after this new 'dark age', the church as a light on the hill will descend back into the valley of culture and guide a stumbling society back to God.

After years spent researching the place of sacred texts in secular education, I can see this same psychology at work in evangelical sorties to impact state schools. Almost all of our energy has been expended reminding the state that we have a colonial settlement privileging Christian religious instruction for an hour a week, which we protect at all costs against comparative religion, ethics classes and other educational alternatives. We fight to ensure Christian chaplains—rather than secular youth workers—retain a funded place in the establishment, and rally when our right to evangelise is threatened. I'm not saying these crusades are inconsequential or unfounded.[21] They are 'goods' we're protecting. But they nostalgically hearken back to a pre-secular utopia where we had say and sway, at the centre of society. When the balance tips away from our favour, the rhetoric increases, and we vacillate between triumphant incursions and defeated withdrawal into exclusively Christian schooling, as though our whole mission is about getting the gospel to non-Christian kids. This blinds us to how complicit Christian culture is in a consumeristic spirituality, being 'of but not in the world'. Perhaps we should remove this therapeutic log from our own eye before exposing the problems of an exclusively this-worldly education devoid of a transcendent *telos*? We have bought into a sacred–secular dualism that as long as there is religious icing on top of the educational cake, the rest of the curricular ingredients don't matter.[22] From my reading of key documents—across eight learning areas,

---

21   See, for instance, my own efforts: James and Benson, 'School Chaplaincy'.
22   Tyson, 'Australian Evangelicals'; Blomberg, 'Curriculum Guidelines'.

seven general capabilities, and three cross-curriculum priorities—the heart of the Australian Curriculum is to form students who can 'make sense of the world' and 'work together for the common good'.²³ Is this not a shared concern with the Christian religion and biblical revelation? If so, then why are we almost solely concerned with a relatively minor extracurricular dimension that, if removed, would leave an otherwise secular curriculum? And yet, in principle at least, I have found this whole curriculum permeable to faith-based perspectives. The Australian Curriculum is open to transcendent takes on the world, provided it serves each subject's stated goals and is oriented toward our shared and immanent life together, right here and now within the *saeculum*. This is a truly 'secular' education in a pluralistic context, which the church has cause to support.²⁴

For all our good work in the educational sphere, this kind of evangelical activism presents as the coin's flip side to Dreher's strategic retreat; it is tainted by self-concerned protectionism that frames education's aims by the church's agenda rather than a kenotic, cross-shaped concern for the flourishing of our neighbour. This is *Christian-centrism*, pure and simple: an excessive focus on Christianity and Christian agendas to the exclusion of others.²⁵ Take educational aims. Prominent Christian thinkers have framed education as oriented toward the end of responsive discipleship, commitment, the kingdom of God, and witness.²⁶ Theologically each purpose has merit. Yet these are Christian ends of

---

23   MCEETYA, *Melbourne Declaration*, 4, 8–9, 13. For analysis of these curricular ends, see Benson, *Schools*.
24   Sociologist Lois Lee offers a mediating definition of *secular* as 'something for which religion is not the primary reference point'—an understanding that aligns with Australia's approach to 'secular' education which aims to be non-sectarian and even-handed toward all religions and none, without slipping into 'secularism' in the sense of securing freedom *from* religion. See Lee, 'Research Note'. Cf. Benson, *Schools*, 47–55, 69–74; Stratham, 'Secular'; Stratham, *Educating for Democracy*.
25   Greider, 'Religious Pluralism', 459.
26   Cf. Goheen and Bartholomew, *Crossroads*, 170.

education for expressly Christian students, inappropriate for the public square. Is that all we can offer? What we need is a biblical vision fitting for an increasingly pluralistic student body that truly blesses 'secular' schools without demanding that they become the church.

Let me be provocative, in the prophetic tradition. Like the priest on the road to Jericho in Luke 10, we the church have been largely blind to the explicit aims of Australian public education—too busy to pay close attention, yet assuming that our conversionist agenda can simply be superimposed because we once used to call the shots. If the state won't listen, we'll simply allocate our resources elsewhere and walk on by. State schools are struggling by the side of the road, beaten down by funding cuts and political agendas, further burdened by societal, curricular and bureaucratic expectations. Confronted by widespread consumerism and a fragmentation of the common good, this institution needs support to stand. Evangelicals pass by, more concerned with what the system can offer us than how we can help. In this context, I wonder if Jesus would retell his parable, portraying secularist lobby groups as a good Samaritan who advocated for the powerless, applying the balm of a comparative and reconciliatory form of general religious education to heal society's lesions? Would he expose the hypocrisy of the 'elect' clinging to colonial privilege in state education, while en masse leaving public education injured in a ditch, en route to enrolling our children in a private religious school? This is simply conjecture. Nevertheless, Christian organisations involved in this educational space hardly appear to pause and consider our 'secular' neighbour's plight, let alone sacrificially attend to their stated needs.

Strategic Missteps: Our 'Secular' Educational Mission

I grant that this reading of both *The Benedict Option* and conservative Christian interaction with public education is harsh. This strategy, in some regards, is well motivated. Dreher, for instance, does tie the strength of the church to the fate of the culture. 'We cannot give the world what we do not have.'[27] His primary concern—a point echoed even by liberals[28]—is that the church has lost its distinctiveness, like salt that has lost its savour (Matt 5:13).[29] Our young people mirror the moralistic therapeutic deism (MTD) of the wider culture, wherein we essentially worship ourselves, projected onto a distant God who just wants us to be good and feel good.[30] Yes, this must be addressed. There is no good news in Australian statistics, for instance, that two in five young people have 'no religious identification', for of the rest, it would seem that perhaps only ten percent regularly attend church services, and even fewer bow the knee to Christ's lordship as something more than an individualistic self-help scheme.[31] The point being, we are to be radically different *for* the sake of the world; if we fail at protecting our faith-based identity in this post-Christendom context, then we also fail the world. With this, I agree. Even while my concern is public education, let me clearly affirm the work of fellow symposium presenters

---

27 Dreher, *Benedict Option*, 19.
28 Thorngate, 'Deep Roots, Open Doors'.
29 Cf. Messmore, 'Not Of the World'. Messmore wisely asks two counterbalancing questions, directed respectively to communities more prone to be *salt* (agents of preservation and change in society) or *light* (a radically distinct community showing a different way of life): '[H]ow can Christians expect to offer their neighbours a different way of thinking and loving if they fully immerse themselves in their neighbours' ways of speaking and acting? ... [and] how will those who live according to a different worldview be able to see the church's distinct witness as intelligible and attractive?'
30 Dreher, *Benedict Option*, 10–12; Smith and Denton, *Soul Searching*, 162, 171; cf. Mason, Singleton and Webber, *Generation Y*, 75–82, 203–7, 311.
31 Australian Bureau of Statistics, 'Religion in Australia'. Cf. McCrindle, 'Faith and Belief'. For commentary on the 2016 Australian Census and MTD, see McAlpine, '51 Percent'.

like Professor James Dalziel, as they strive to form solid Christian schooling that truly blesses the world.

My concern is twofold. Firstly, after studying the questionable data and constructs underlying the classic secularisation thesis, it's easy to settle for simplistic analysis that supports an alarmist reading of a cultural slide away from faith: that we must act now in dramatic fashion for a final salvage effort before escaping divine judgement on Sodom.[32] Unfortunately, buying into this narrative becomes a self-fulfilling prophecy that accelerates the shift—which is hardly a loving response to the surrounding culture apparently lost in the dark. It further distances the church from the surrounding society, in an us-versus-them zero-sum game.[33] Certainly, the percentage of Australians associated with a religious institution is on the decline, and those with no religious identification are on the rise. I concede that there has been greater opposition to the church's involvement in established activities like religious instruction in public education and chaplaincy in state schools.[34] Additionally, there is considerable contest over the interpretation of the word 'secular' in state schools, ranging from hard secularism that seeks freedom from religion, through pluralists calling for evenhanded treatment of all faiths and none, to 'secular' authorities having the power to privilege Christian faith above others if it is educationally and socially justifiable.[35] In this context, it's easy to interpret any opposition as persecution, justifying parents pulling their children out of public education, and teachers following the narrow path of private Christian schooling. In reality, however, this 'persecution complex' is misplaced; by and large it is better understood as the renegotiation of colonial Christian privilege in pursuit of a more equitable power dynamic

---

32 Benson, *Sacred Texts*, 130–226.
33 See Catto, 'Accurate Diagnosis?'; Ward, 'Where We Are'.
34 See, for instance, Stevenson, 'Faith in Schools'.
35 Benson, *Schools*, 48–51. Cf. Byrne, *Religion*, 31, 208–9; Maddox, *Taking God to School*, loc. 3873, Kindle.

serving partnership in our post-Christendom pluralistic society.[36] And if we follow Jesus in valuing reciprocity, doing to our neighbour as we would have them do to us, then this is a righteous shift, even if it's not in our favour.[37] The hypersensitive may find this justification enough to abandon 'the world', but I'm not convinced Jesus is at the head of the pack.

My second and more significant concern, however, is that of ill-defined *mission*. Operating out of this dominant motif of prophetic critique and following the pendulum swing of cultural incursion reversing into *contemptus mundi*, we lack a larger cause to keep these problematic tendencies in check. Dreher wisely draws from Alasdair MacIntyre's trenchant analysis that we are now living *After Virtue*, where ethical arguments on hot-button topics like same sex-marriage and non-binary gender theory in 'Safe Schools' campaigns have become incommensurable, reduced to emotional outbursts masquerading as logic.[38] Surely it would be good for the world were a new Benedict to arise and reinvigorate the church with rich practices and deep formation as a community of blessing that could reconcile polarised parties.[39] Nevertheless, before advocating a monastic retreat for the entire church in the West, shunning secular education as a whole, it would be wise to revisit the heart of MacIntyre's proposal. The way forward requires that we first go back to the primary question of *telos*. What on earth are we here for? Toward where do we head? In his most quoted passage, MacIntyre asserts: 'I can only answer the question "What am I to do?" if I can answer the prior question "Of what story or stories do I find myself a part?"'[40] Lest we major on the minors or adopt an incomplete agenda that creates more problems than

---

36 Inazu, 'Benedict Option'; Campbell, 'Persecution Complex'.
37 Volf, 'Exclusion or Saturation?'; Campbell, 'Benedict Option?' Cf. Maclure and Taylor, *Secularism and Freedom*, 20.
38 Dreher, *Benedict Option*, 2–3, 16–19, 108–9. Cf. Jones, 'Safe Schools Coalition'.
39 For my efforts in this space, see our house church community at https://christspieces.org/.
40 MacIntyre, *After Virtue*, 216.

it solves, both Christian mission and secular schooling require a clearly defined purpose. Education requires a larger story that captures the heart and mind of students and orients them in the world. Indeed, without a sense of who we are and where we're going, educational aims become arbitrary.[41] So, what are we as Christians here for, and how does this relate to the ends of secular education?

A Better Story: The Journey Toward Shalom

Niebuhr's typology exposes the weakness of adopting a singular metaphor such as Christ against culture to determine a strategy for engaging 'the world'. Beyond separatism, we do well to see how the accommodationist, synthesist, dualist and conversionist might also be faithful in this pivotal moment. However, Niebuhr fails to tie these superficially contradictory strategies into a coherent whole. He lacks a larger story, grounding our mission and guiding our action.[42] With Chris Wright, I contend that 'The Bible renders to us the story of God's mission through God's people in their engagement with God's world for the sake of God's whole creation'.[43] We must tell this story afresh at pivotal times when we're tempted to abandon the world and simply focus on the church, whether out of frustration that we've lost the cultural war, or out of guilt that we've unjustly pushed our pluralistic society around for too long.

In the final section of this chapter, then, I want to sketch a biblical theology for cultural engagement that might illuminate a more coherent and complete way to serve public education. I will sketch the six act story

---

41 Noddings, 'Aims of Education'; Postman, *End of Education*, x–xi, 7.
42 On this critique, and offering constructive narrative theologies in Niebuhr's stead, see Keller, *Loving*, 250–58, 274–93 (Andy Crouch's structuring of cultural engagement around the 'image story—image bearing, image breaking, image restoring, and image revealing' is especially helpful, 274–88); Carson, *Christ and Culture*, 31–65.
43 Wright, *Mission of God*, 22.

of creation, the fall, Israel, Jesus, the church, and new creation, binding diverse Niebuhrian stances together in the one metaphor of education as 'the journey toward *shalom*'.[44] Following Nicholas Wolterstorff and other leading philosophical theologians and educators, the duty and delight of 'holistic flourishing' is rightly understood as the *telos* toward which our collective story heads:

> *[S]halom is delight in all one's relationships: with God, neighbor, nature, and self. Shalom unites the fulfillment of culture with the liberation of justice. Life in the city of God is a life committed to struggling for shalom and to appreciating the flickers of shalom that already brighten our existence. Christian education is education for shalom.*[45]

Following John Stackhouse's framework, our abiding human mission is captured by the creation commandments—'to love God and our neighbours as ourselves as we cultivate the world'. This is further served by the church's particular redemption commandments in response to sin—to especially love fellow believers as an example for the world, and to cultivate faithfulness to Christ through evangelism and discipleship.[46] How might we reconceive cultural interaction when located within this narrative? In each of the six stages of this educational journey, God would have us learn about and make sense of the world in which we live; and God calls us to join him in working for a truly common good. In so doing, the divine pedagogue draws—rather than coerces—us from infancy in the garden to maturity in the new Jerusalem, by way of the paradoxical cross.

---

44 For a fuller framing of this educational model, and retelling of the biblical story, see Benson, *Schools*, 76–117.
45 Wolterstorff, *Educating for Life*, 79, emphasis his. See also Wolterstorff, *Educating for Shalom*.
46 Stackhouse, *Making*, 205–20. Cf. Benson, 'Shalom and Sustainability'.

Within 'God's Curriculum'[47] we find an implicit rationale to resist any single Niebuhrian stance, especially our present penchant to evacuate the culture and secular education where Christians strike out on their own adventure apart from our neighbours. In short, this biblical story offers one coherent metaphor with six modes of cultural engagement, collectively making a powerful case for *why we need the world*.

Where to start, then? Well, in the beginning, of course.

I. CREATION: Garden Together/Direct

Stage one: creation, where the cosmos is designed for good. We were infants in Eden, making shalom as we learned about the duty and delight of work, called to cultivate God's garden. In Andy Crouch's exposition, humans are groundlings planted on Earth to bring out the latent potential in all of creation like a patient gardener; and we're invited to paint something fresh that changes the horizon of how we see and move on the planet like a gifted artist.[48] Something has gone horribly wrong when the primary posture of 'culture keeping' and 'culture making' is displaced by an occasional gesture that is occasionally appropriate, such as condemning, critiquing, copying, or uncritically consuming culture.[49] In Niebuhrian terms, this is Christ above culture. Like the original goodness of secular reality, the public school synthesist looks for what can be affirmed in subject matter as the ground we till and the base from which we wonder

---

[47] Most of the framing of the biblical story that follows comes from Benson, 'God's Curriculum'. The language of 'designed for good, damaged by evil, restored for better, sent together to heal' (with my addition of 'chosen to bless' and 'God sets everything right') comes from Choung, *True Story*.

[48] Crouch, *Culture Making*, 78-98. Cf. Brown, 'Gardener and Groundling'.

[49] Crouch, *Culture Making*, 96-98.

at the world; we direct what is truly good below toward its source above, infusing this secular Australian Curriculum with a transcendent telos.

Why, then, does the church need the world? Following the narrative logic, irrespective of religious affiliation or none, all humans are fellow image bearers with a role to play. Working side-by-side in public schools, rather than only watering parallel religious institutions, helps us understand the diverse visions of and for the planet that our neighbours have; we can then add our energy to their rightly ordered efforts. Awareness of each other's plans for this world God has formed is part of learning to *garden together*, cultivating what serves the common good of all creatures.[50]

II. FALL: Expose Error/Challenge

With the move to stage two, the fall, all creation is damaged by evil. As toddlers we believed a lie in the garden, and threw a tantrum at Babel, breaking *shalom*; God focused our attention on the promise and peril of knowledge, calling us to repent over the prideful towers we build. This is Christ against culture. The separatist adopts a prophetic stance, identifying idolatry and what must be denounced. For some, this may necessitate an 'exile in place' or even geographic distancing from sinful distortion to retain our identity as faithful witnesses, forming classical education schools as *The Benedict Option* wisely suggests.[51] This may well have the greatest formative power to counteract moralistic therapeutic deism, functioning as a light on a hill and a countercultural model to the wider establishment of quality pedagogy centred on God. At the same time, I pray that many Christians remain within the secular education system, speaking truth to power as we *challenge* the illusion of autonomous

---

50 The rationale for why we need the world parallels Benson, 'Uncommon Good', 22–24.
51 Dreher, *Benedict Option*, 145–50.

individuals who can know and do apart from trust in something beyond oneself, especially the giver of life.

We need the world to *expose error*. These distortions, however, lie on both sides of the monastic walls. Only together can we learn to confess our sin and embrace the dynamics of trust. *The fall* reveals our God-given 'freedom' to choose a lie, and our shared tendency to deceive and be deceived. Exposure to a competing take on life's *telos*, in the course of one's studies, may thus jolt the community of God out of complacency, ignorance, pride and self-interested readings that enshrine unjust privilege and further deform the world. This won't happen when we are holed up in an echo chamber.

III. ISRAEL: Seek Wisdom/Partner

With stage three, Israel is chosen to bless the world. To fix the fall, the divine pedagogue concentrated on the few as a means to rescue the many. The children of Abraham, as wanderers seeking shalom, learned about obedience to the way of wisdom, called to bless from the humble pilgrim tent. We are thus oriented by a vision of flourishing. The narrative of Israel has often been ignored in the church's self-understanding. It's a winding tale hard to summarise, for it addresses a nation of slaves selected to model godly rule. Like the people of God today, their education required that they remember their identity located in the conservative stories of the elders, at the same time as hearing a progressive gospel vision of prophets pointing toward a just future; at this nexus they would discover inspired solutions to present-day problems.[52] Israel as God's peculiar people was called to be prophet, priest, king, healer and liberator.[53] Their identity, into which we are grafted, at once fuses the Niebuhrian types and resists

---

52   Brueggemann, *Creative Word*, 75. Cf. Thorngate, 'Deep Roots, Open Doors'.
53   Van Engen, *God's Missionary People*, 119–27.

a single stance in relation to the world: 'For everything there is a season, and a time for every purpose under heaven' (Eccl 3:1, ASV).[54] They were chosen for the good of their neighbour, at times even directing and leading righteous change. Their mission was thus predicated on some degree of *partnership* with the Other. Total separation was a cause for lament. Protectionism in the face of opposition and preservation of their distinct identity was a means relative to the end of total peace for all.

We need the world to *live well*, seeking wisdom to read and respond to life's patterns for the common good.[55] Like Israel, our election to seek the *shalom* of the city—even while in cultural captivity—requires an expansive wisdom such as pursued by Joseph in Egypt and Daniel in Babylon.[56] It is open to multiple perspectives and truth wherever it may be found, especially in the cries of minorities easiest to ignore.[57] Being informed as wise peacemakers in a divided world demands meaningful 'coalition building' across diverse canonical and secular wisdom traditions, such as genuine partnership between Christian and state schools. As the British educational philosopher Trevor Cooling argues, 'the culture [must be] one of collegiality, listening carefully to each other's views, taking account of differences, and looking for ways of working together in the cause of the common good and community cohesion'.[58]

IV. JESUS: Redeem Life/Sacrifice

Onwards, then, to stage four: Jesus, where humanity is restored for better. The elect, like every other nation, were blown off course by their selfish desire. So, the Teacher stepped in as the true Israelite to anchor

---

54   Cf. Keller, *Loving*, 263–66.
55   Cf. Strom, *Lead with Wisdom*.
56   Jer 29:1–14; Dan 1:4; Cooling, *Supporting Christians*, 10–22.
57   Ford, *Shaping Theology*, 65–66. Cf. Ford, *Christian Wisdom*, 14–51.
58   Cooling, *Christian Vision*, 161.

their identity, fulfil their call, and embody our *telos*. Through Jesus's example, instruction, sacrifice and resurrection, God was saving *shalom*. As adolescents with a real choice to make, we learned about reciprocity, called to love on the mountain of Calvary. This is Christ and culture in paradox. Dualists acknowledge, and even submit, to Caesar's authority as derived from God. Our kingdom is not *from* this world, but it is certainly *for* this world.[59] It is not coercively dropped from heaven on an unwilling people, demanding their conformity or threatening to walk away. Rather, it is characterised by incarnation—a love that humbly moves into the neighbourhood, its community and schools, and mixes with its messiness. A tough love that disarms evil through *sacrifice*. As E. Stanley Jones notes, in reference to Jesus's baptism, 'He would be a savior from within—not from above, apart from, separated'.[60]

We need the world because our mission is to *redeem life*—the life of individuals through evangelism, to be sure, but we also participate in redeeming the life of secular institutions like your local public school. 'For God so loved the *cosmos*'—this good creational order developed by fallen humanity where cultural wheat and tares inextricably intermingle—'that he gave his only Son ... [not] to condemn the world, but to save the

---

59 Cf. John 18:28–40.
60 Jones, *Unshakable Kingdom*, 112. Cf. Frost, *Exiles*, 54–56; John 1 (Message paraphrase).

world through him' (John 3:16–17, NIV).⁶¹ We are saved *for*, not *from*, this world; our mission of *shalom* and salvation, under the total lordship of Christ over all, will not permit an exclusively exilic stance. Rather, our vocation is to listen to and radically love our neighbour, irrespective of creed. We are people of the Golden Rule, eschewing unjust colonial privilege, and working for reciprocity and even-handedness in how diverse religious, spiritual and secular life stances are treated in a curriculum designed for a pluralistic educational space. Educational merit, rather than partisan preference, must drive our advocacy. This is dangerous work in a contested public sphere. So, we are called to discern how sacrificial love could break the grip of violence, laying down our rights and taking up our cross.⁶² Our hope is not in the vacillation between cultural conquest and self-righteous retreat, with a sheepish return to a post-Christendom post-apocalyptic desert when the dust has settled. Rather, located within the paradoxical story of a dying and rising Messiah, we are sent to reform the secular educational world from below as its humble servant. We enter this promised land to make disciples, respecting school principals and

---

61 See Matt 13:24–30. Cf. Edgar, *Created and Creating*, 120–23. Analysing John's use of *kosmos*, and the *contra mundum* passages that suggest 'This World, No Friend' (ch. 5, 117–26), Edgar concludes (126):

'While creation is originally good, and not to be eschewed, a malignancy has been introduced. When God mercifully decided to redeem his people, he did not take them out of the world. Nor did he identify the creation as evil. Rather he placed them in the world in order to be saved and then cured them of the cancer. Avoiding the seduction of the worldly system, we nevertheless engage the world and continue to transform it. While we wait for the life to come, we do not simply evangelize, though we certainly do proclaim the gospel. We take on doing his will on earth, as it is in heaven (Mt 6:10; Rom 12:1–2). That will is comprehensive, not just so-called spiritual endeavors, but actually including the whole realm of human life: family, citizenship, farming, artistic pursuits [and, I would add, education]—in short, *culture*'.

62 For an excellent model of Christlike community work, easily adapted to secular schools, see Andrews, *Out and Out*. In contrast to monastic withdrawal (12–26), Andrews suggests five steps as the 'Logos of Christian Mysticism' (30–37): select a place to live; connect with people in that place; choose to empty ourselves for others; don't expect to be served, but to serve; and embrace the inevitable suffering involved.

education departments alike, while bearing the presence and name of our triune God.[63] Any change will be the result of 'faithful presence' and 'cultural persistence' in altruistic service, built on listening to the Other and loving action that serves the common good.[64]

V. CHURCH: Foster Wholeness/Unite

Foreshadowing our destination, we shift to stage five: the church, sent together to heal the world. Through the Spirit, God bound all people together in harmony at the table of friendship, embracing *shalom*. As emerging adults in the upper room at Pentecost, we learned about the responsibility of holiness, of Christlike character, to sustain such a community, called to reconcile in the house. This is Christ transforming culture. Conversionists approach public schools with courage and confidence in the Spirit's power, believing that change is possible. Where are the fault lines and enmity, misunderstanding and brokenness? How would Christ have us bridge these divides as a church whose primary task is to *unite* people with God, each other, and a wounded planet?

We need the world, for our mission is to foster wholeness. As the Benedict Option avers, this must begin at home. The church is a school of character, sufficiently separate to become holy and distinct from our culture's malformation.[65] Yet, this narrative ripples outwards, immersing individuals and even secular institutions in eucharistic hospitality. God's pupils include all of humanity, their myriad tongues and social imaginaries shaping the nations. The Spirit longs to remove the walls of division damaging public education and distancing people. So, we are sent to refashion the system, making the most of every opportunity,

---

63 Matt 28:18–20. Cf. Wright, *Mission*, 191–265; Stackhouse, 'View of Mission'.
64 Hunter, *Change the World*, 238–72; Stackhouse, *Making*, 7. See also Fitch, *Faithful Presence*; Frost, *Surprise the World!*
65 See Sayers, *Disappearing Church*.

as a foretaste of the unity-in-diversity that will characterise a transformed world in the fullness of time.

VI. NEW CREATION: Pre-empt Praise/Celebrate

Finally, we reach stage six: the new creation, where God sets everything right. Our *telos* is being invited into full maturity as divine image bearers, entering *shalom* in God's glorious presence. With our feet set toward the destination, we learn about hope, called to worship in the city. This vision of the new Jerusalem—not the impermanent admixture of glitter and glory as the city of Man and the city of God travel through the *saeculum*—is our education's end and final resting place.[66] No present-day school—whether public, Christian or classical—will suffice, even as each offers signs of life and a window into heaven. Proleptically, however, we can embrace the Christ of culture. Through this metaphor of the journey to *shalom*, accommodationists are invited to *celebrate* what is truly excellent, wherever it may be found.

We need the world to *pre-empt praise*. In the story of the great consummation, we look forward to fullness of life conformed to God's purposes. We will enjoy the glory of the nations in the form of the richest cultural artefacts refined through judgement, and brought into the garden-city to God's glory.[67] We can reimagine every subject, even in secular schools, as an avenue to foster holistic integration; teachers invite pilgrims through creative and reflective practices to cultivate gratitude, anticipating the song of a mixed multitude praising the Creator from whom all that is true, good and beautiful flows.

A Hopeful Posse: Questions and Character Guiding Our

---

66   Augustine, *City of God* 10.14.
67   Cf. Ps 24:1; Mouw, *When the Kings*, 21, 84, 113, 120. See also Mouw, *He Shines*.

Mission

What, then, is the role of the church in this Post-Christian world? Chaplain to the culture, activist exile, or BenOp new monastic? Separatist, accommodationist, synthesist, dualist, or conversionist?

Well, *yes*—all of the above! For 'the world' is a many and varied thing. 'Secular education' reflects the good world God formed, now deformed by sin, and informed by divine revelation that incorporates insight from multiple sources. Through Christ's sacrifice this world is reformed, further transformed by a Spirit-filled community as a foretaste of when the whole cosmos is conformed to the will of God.

It will not do to freeze occasional gestures as a fundamental posture to the world.[68] This spells the rigor mortis of the church, not a faithful response moving forward on the journey toward *shalom*.

Einstein is widely credited as advising, 'Everything should be made as simple as possible, but not simpler'. This deserves a hearty 'Amen!' when it comes to cultural engagement. Let's leave behind the cycle of conquest and withdrawal, only valuing explicitly 'Christian' activities in the public schools. We can't all bypass secular educational purposes and struggling students en route to our teaching appointment in Jericho's religious institution.

This may well be righteous for Benedict and some within the church. But it's not a universal strategy, nor our primary call. Instead, wherever we are based, let's ask at least six piercing questions:

- What partial good is evident, which I can direct to its transcendent source?

---

[68] This even applies to more nuanced reviews of Dreher's BenOp, with counterproposals tailored to specific contexts. See, for instance, Michael Bird's two-pronged 'Thessalonian Strategy' (in 'Turning the World Upside Down, Down Under') of radically loving our neighbours and simultaneously offering a 'robust challenge to the legitimacy of secular militancy'.

- What idolatry distorts life, which I must challenge, prophetically speaking truth to power?
- Where do I see the possibility of coalition building for the common good, and how may I partner?
- How has violence enslaved schools and students, and how might sacrifice break its hold over the educational system as a whole?
- How might we become a community of character capable of healing deep division? And what would it look like to unite polarised parties, nurturing integration through diversity?
- What is truly excellent in education, a sign of new creation, which we can affirm and celebrate?

In the very warp and woof of the biblical story, we discover why we need the world: to garden together, expose error, live well, redeem life, foster wholeness, and to pre-empt praise. On each front, *shalom* is our 'first and last calling' as image bearers.[69] And on this basis, we dare not abandon public education as a primary cultural institution forming the future caretakers of the cosmos for whom Christ gave his life. We invest tremendous energy and resources into defending our freedom to evangelise, and into propping up our privilege to disproportionately provide Christian religious instruction and chaplains. My hope is that we may give equal attention to secular education as a whole, seeking the flourishing of the system and students therein. Were this the case, then as happened with the state church in England back in the 1970s, we may lay down our rights and discover a novel form of comparative religious

---

69   Edgar, *Created and Creating*, 159–65. For Edgar (176–77): '*Cultural engagement is the human response to the divine call to enjoy and develop the world that God has generously given to his image-bearers.* Culture includes the symbols, the tools, the conventions, the social ties, and all else contributing to this call. Cultural activity occurs in a historical setting, and is meant to improve the human condition. Because of the fall, culture can and has become sinister. Christ's redeeming grace moves culture in the right direction, ennobles it, and allows it to extend the realm of God's *shalom*, his goodness, his justice, his love'.

education that better equips citizens in a pluralistic democracy, showing how the transcendent intersects with and animates the secular across the entire curriculum.[70]

One question remains: With all of these options for cultural engagement, which stance should we adopt and when? How do we proceed if we're not in Kansas anymore, whether confused in Vancouver or disoriented in Brisvegas? Well, we might follow Dorothy's lead by gathering together a disparate posse of people—fellow travellers on the journey to *shalom*—staying close and following the yellow brick road. In this, the BenOp guidebook is invaluable. On the way, with the humility of Dorothy and Toto's companionship, you'll discover or perhaps cultivate Scarecrow's smarts, Lion's backbone, and Tin Man's heart. Theologically framed, the church is a community of character headed toward holistic flourishing, characterised by humility, wisdom, courage and love. We get our bearings as we retell our foundational Scriptural story, faithfully improvising as the Spirit leads.[71] But we must remain fundamentally open to whatever strange characters you meet along the way, whether public school munchkins, or the good and bad wizards and witches shaping the educational landscape.

Underpinning this mission is the ability to listen—to God, our neighbours, and the created world through which God subtly speaks. 'Be quick to listen, slow to speak, and slow to get angry' (James 1:19, NLT)—for all is rarely as it first seems. In place of the colonial dynamics of triumph and defeat, I commend to you the practice of *patient dialogue* as essential when discerning how to respond.[72] What, when and how to direct, challenge, partner, sacrifice, unite and celebrate in secular education is premised upon rightly understanding the world in which we live, illuminated by its

---

70   Thomas, *Religion in Schools*, 55–68.
71   Cf. Wright, *After You Believe*, 24–6, 33, 170–73, 243; Wright, Last Word, 121–27; Hauerwas, 'Character, Narrative, and Growth'.
72   Benson, 'Uncommon Good'.

maker and informed by its diverse citizens. As opportunity allows, dwell in the schools; listen to the hopes and fears of teachers and students alike, and charitably read curriculum documents describing the *telos*. Remind your posse that 'the Church does not exist for itself but for God, and for the world that Jesus came to save'.[73] And whichever track you're on, whether public or private, may we walk together in wisdom as image bearers of the Prince of Peace.

I. GARDEN TOGETHER: *Direct* good to God

II. EXPOSE ERROR: *Challenge* idolatry & lies

III. LIVE WELL: *Partner* for common good

IV. REDEEM LIFE: *Sacrifice* to disarm evil

V. FOSTER WHOLENESS: *Unite* across dividing lines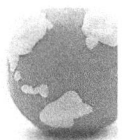

VI. PRE-EMPT PRAISE: *Celebrate* signs of God's reign

Simple & Sufficient
A Posture for Public Education

---

[73] Newbigin, *Word*, 53.

8

CHRISTIAN SCHOOL COMMUNITIES AS A TWENTY-FIRST-CENTURY BENEDICT OPTION

James Dalziel

Rod Dreher's *The Benedict Option*[1] has been the subject of considerable debate since its publication in 2016. I would summarise its overall message in two parts: (1) Conservative Christianity has lost the culture war in America, and it should expect increasing trouble for Christians in the future, and (2) Christians should focus more effort on building local Christian communities, and renewing personal and community faith practices, so as to endure the dark times ahead.

In my experience, many people place their emphasis on just one part of this message—either they focus on the loss of the culture war in (1) combined with the 'dark times ahead' at the end of (2); or they focus on the building of local Christian communities and faith renewal in (2). An external observer of recent debate could almost be forgiven for wondering if Dreher had written two different books with the same title.

It is beyond the scope of the current chapter to engage with the wider debate about the Benedict Option, particularly the culture wars issues. However, there are important truths to be distilled from the book, and from commentators who support, and oppose, the analysis of Dreher.[2]

The focus of this chapter will be on the Christian community building and faith renewal aspects of the Benedict Option as applied to Christian schooling. In particular, it will explore how Christian schools which embody an authentic Christian community can be (and already are) examples of a twenty-first-century Benedict Option, and will offer suggestions of how to further grow Christian schools as communities inspired by the Benedict Option.

Dreher on Christian Schools

Dreher has a chapter on Christian Schools (ch. 7), which is at times quite critical of existing American Christian schools. In essence, he sees two problems—first, many Christian schools are Christian in name only—they have not held on to the historic Christian faith in the face of modern secularism. The result is schools that foster a set of beliefs closer to 'Moralistic Therapeutic Deism'[3] than Christianity—that is, schools that would be uncomfortable with the exclusive claims of Jesus (e.g. John 14:6). To the extent that Dreher's critique of Christian schools is true (and no doubt it is in some contexts), it is a fundamental problem for Christian schools, and Dreher is right to be alarmed.

The second concern is the lack of focus on the civilisational heritage of the West, and hence Dreher's encouragement to Christian families to join, or form, 'Classical Christian Schools'. Where these schools combine the best of the historic Christian faith with the riches of ancient and modern Western civilisation, then this is a laudable goal.

---

2   E.g., East, 'Theologians Arguing'; Deneen, 'Moral Minority'; Beaty, 'Christians Lost'; Linker, 'Conservative Christians'; Russello, 'Sparking Renewal'; Meador, 'Reviewing Benedict Option'.

3   Smith, *Soul Searching*, 163–65.

But Dreher paints the differences between Christian schools and Classical Christian schools too starkly, and he has subsequently acknowledged that his rhetoric on this issue was too strong.[4] While the development of Classical Christian schools has much to recommend it, I would encourage these schools to work together with other faithful Christian schools to foster fellowship and shared insights in Christian education, rather than separation. For me, the most important issue for Christian schools is not just teaching Western civilisation (important as that is), but fostering Christian schools that embody authentic Christian community, not simply a 'transactional' approach to school life.

Put differently, a Classical Christian school with high scores on externally validated exams could still be weak on authentic Christian community, particularly in the lived-out practices of school life, if there is a gap between theory and practice. Equally, a new Christian school with a limited grasp of the riches of Western civilisation could still embody a deep and authentic Christian community when staff (and student and parents) live out Christian faith, hope and love with each other. At the heart of the difference is not the place of Western civilisation alone, but whether the school is viewed in 'transactional' terms, or as a Christian community.

Christian Schools: Transactional or Community?

Despite the rhetoric of many Christian school vision statements, as well as the stated hopes of some parents, schools are often viewed only transactionally. That is, parents send students to school (and typically pay for this) where teachers are expected to transmit curriculum knowledge to students; students are expected to reproduce knowledge for tests to get high marks, in order that they can get a good job after school. A Christian school may include additional Christian content, but this is typically at the

---

[4] Dreher, 'Ben Op Miscellany', lines 33–44.

edges of the school experience (such as Bible classes or chapel services). And while faithful Christian teachers may model Christian love and character in their behaviour, the real driver of student learning is getting high marks to get a good job.

While this may sound unduly harsh on some Christian schools, it can be explored with a simple test: What student activities/achievements get rewarded and recognised by the school? A balanced Christian community school will recognise and reward acts of Christian service and fellowship as well as academic achievement. The contents of report cards and end-of-year celebrations should offer a tangible answer to the extent to which achieving high marks is being balanced by recognition of Christian character in action.

A Christian school, which embodies an authentic Christian community, will seek deeper relationships with students and parents than those implied by a transactional-only view. It will nurture community life within the school, as well as reaching out into local communities (and beyond) with acts of service. It will judge new initiatives, curriculum and technology from the basis of whether or not they will grow the Christian community of the school. It will not be happy with having the right vision/mission statement if this is not lived out in practice in the school community.

A Christian community school will also tend to have a more vibrant theory of learning and student formation, because the whole person is in view, not just the 'cognitive' academic side, drawing on an understanding of every person made in the image of God (Gen 1:26–27). This will mean a richer range of learning activities, particularly those which are not easily measured for marks, and yet are important for character development (such as service activities, outdoor education, fellowship, and other 'extracurricular' activities).

It can also mean less hierarchical relationships among staff (and between staff and students), as the importance of 'servant leadership' becomes central,[5] and a shift in pedagogy towards active student learning, with the teacher not only a 'sage on the stage', but, when appropriate, a 'guide on the side'. It also encourages schools to consider their role in educating students with special learning needs, as all students are made in the image of God and equally valued by God.

A Christian community school will often seek to involve parents more closely with the school community as a way of living out Christian community together—this will go beyond occasional volunteering, and towards closer personal relationships. It may include Christian parent education, particularly for those parents who otherwise do not have contact with a traditional church.

A Christian community school will seek to help students think through how Christian faith is relevant to all subject areas, not just Bible classes—put another way, that faith is relevant to all of life, not just to private beliefs. The importance of a Christian worldview for understanding, and critiquing, the assumptions in subjects such as English, History, Geography, Science and Business is part of a well-rounded Christian educational experience.

Finally, a Christian community school should encourage a greater sense of civic and social engagement, enacted through mission and services activities. One of the underlying problems of the transactional view of schools is that school becomes 'all about me' for the student—what the student can get out of school in terms of the highest grades for personal advancement. The broader Christian community view should encourage students (and parents and teachers) to look beyond simply their own needs to the wider needs of the school community and society.

---

5   Mark 10:42–45; Greenleaf, *Servant Leadership*.

CHRISTIAN SCHOOL COMMUNITIES

All of the above is not to suggest that Christian community schools are only for Christian families—the vast majority of Christian community schools welcome families who are not of the Christian faith, as long as they understand and accept the Christian ethos of the school and the nature of the Christian community it embodies. It is not unusual for up to half of the families at Christian schools to either not hold Christian beliefs, or not be actively involved in a church on the basis of their beliefs. While the nature of authentic Christian community schools requires that all staff be active Christians in order to maintain the Christian ethos and practices of the school, the students themselves, and their families, can come from a range of backgrounds as long as they accept the ethos and practices of the school. Christian community schools see the involvement of these families as a privilege, and as an opportunity to invite families to explore the Christian beliefs of the school.

All of the above is a long way of saying that Christian schools that embody an authentic Christian community are a twenty-first-century example of the Benedict Option in action—and they have been doing it for decades, often unnoticed by churches and secular society alike. In Australia, many of the schools in Christian Schools Australia (CSA) and Christian Education National (CEN), as well as other independent Christian schools, provide living examples today of the spirit of Dreher's Benedict Option.

Viewed from this perspective, a forward-looking question is how these schools could become even more 'Benedict Option'-like by continuing to grow a Christian community that deeply shapes hearts and minds among students, parents and staff. The remainder of this chapter offers suggestions in seven areas to take the vision of the Benedict Option even further for authentic Christian community schools, based on my recent interests and discussion with Christian community schools (no doubt there are many other areas for future development).

JAMES DALZIEL

Challenging the Telos and Hidden Curriculum of Schooling

The goal or 'telos'[6] of a school can have a significant impact on whether it tends towards being only transactional or more community based. Some schools explicitly focus on academic excellence as the central purpose of education, in order for students to 'get a good job'. While academic excellence is a worthy goal when it is driven by a desire to nurture the good gifts that God gives to students, it can be at the expense of a well-rounded education of student character if it becomes an all-consuming focus of the school. Related to this, students may go on to worthy careers as doctors, nurses, lawyers, scientists, entrepreneurs, etc. (not just in Christian ministry)—but the crucial issue is the sense of calling or vocation from God, rather than simply a desire to 'get a good job', 'make a lot of money', or for some, to 'be significant'. All Christians are called to go and be 'salt and light' in the world (Matt 5:13–16), and to bring hope into a world where it is sorely needed, so the telos of a Christian community school should encourage this outward focus.

In my experience, even the most transactional schools now tend to have vision/mission statements that discuss well-rounded education, character, virtues, etc. But in practice, these elements play a minor role compared to the overwhelming focus on academic excellence (particularly in elite/grammar/older church-based schools). Given this, it is important to investigate the 'hidden curriculum' of a school in terms of well-rounded education, rather than simply looking to the words of a vision/mission statement. As in other areas, this problem reminds me of the aphorism, 'In theory there is no difference between theory and practice. In practice, there is'.[7]

---

6   Smith, *Desiring the Kingdom*, 27–34.
7   Schneier, 'Cryptography', line 37–38.

CHRISTIAN SCHOOL COMMUNITIES

While the problem of narrow-academic versus whole-person education is not unique to Christian schools, Christians should be particularly attentive to this issue, given the foundational belief of God coming in the person of Jesus—who demonstrated that words and deeds go together, and that transformation of the whole person is central to Christian discipleship. Christianity is not simply a religion of knowledge.

How does a school investigate the reality of its community life to see whether it matches up to its vision/mission statement? As noted above, the kind of recognition and rewards at a school may be illustrative of this issue (e.g. report cards, end-of-year ceremony). More broadly, the work of J. K. A. Smith on cultural liturgies is particularly relevant to this issue—what are the implied educational priorities illustrated by the daily practices of school life? What do they say about the relative importance of head, hearts and hands?

One practical step to understanding the reality of a Christian school community is to conduct interviews with thoughtful senior students (both those who hold Christian faith, and those who do not, or are unsure). The most interesting discussions that I have had with students centred on two questions: (1) Can you tell me about a few significant times for you in this school when you most felt the Christian faith to be real/compelling? (2) Can you tell me about a few significant times for you in this school when you found it most difficult to believe in the reality of the Christian faith?

With careful adaptation of wording to suit the existing beliefs of each student, these questions often reveal the best and worst aspects of a school's Christian community life 'on the ground'—and can act as an important check on mission statement rhetoric by casting light on the hidden curriculum of Christian community life in a school.

JAMES DALZIEL

Fostering Student Mission and Service

Given that love for others is at the heart of the Christian life, it should be enacted in Christian school community life. School environments that are riven with tension, hostility, feuds and ill will cry out for a greater focus on love in the daily practices of school life. This is particularly an issue where there are disputes among teachers or the school leadership—students can be remarkably perceptive of these disputes, even if they do not know the details. The lesson students can learn from these disputes is that Christians do not practice what they preach.

Opportunities for mission and service activities can be a key part of embodying the calling to love—whether within the school, in the local community, or elsewhere in the country or overseas. As schools with active mission and service programs can attest, it is often these activities that have the most life-transforming impact on students, that is to say, students experience significant 'whole person' changes that go beyond the memorising and recitation of curriculum knowledge.

For schools that provide these kinds of opportunities, they are often described as 'extracurricular'. This does a disservice to a broader whole-person educational philosophy, as it states that this kind of service learning is outside the school curriculum. It would be better to examine vision/mission statements to see whether these kinds of activities are encouraged (as they often are), and then more effectively integrate them into the broader learning program of the school—rather than treating them as an 'add on'. While these activities are usually voluntary, this does not mean they do not align with the learning goals of the school mission, and hence can be part of a broad view of curriculum. And while schools need to work within the government education structures of their society (Rom 13:1, as long as they do not conflict with the purposes of God; see Acts 5:29), if the government educational curriculum is limited in its understanding of personhood and learning, then this is an opportunity for Christian school communities to fulfil their mandated government requirements while at the same time going beyond these requirements with a wider view of whole-person learning.

Mission and service activities should not always be far away—there are usually opportunities for service with organisations, charities and businesses in the local area of the school, as well as within and across classes in the school. As building richer local community life is an important part of Dreher's Benedict Option vision, schools can act as a local community hub for engagement and service.

In practical terms, I would recommend that Christian school communities develop a service and mission program to live out love and care for others both near and far. There are many great lessons that can be learned from those schools with experience in this area, so schools that are starting out with these activities would benefit from partnerships with more experienced schools.

Encouraging Parental Involvement and Parent Christian Education

A Christian community school has significant opportunities for engaging parents more deeply in the life of the school—and this means more than simply asking parents to volunteer for odd jobs. Parents can bring expertise and experience that can enrich school life, whether in devotional activities with staff, talks for students (and staff), assistance with special projects in areas of expertise (e.g. music, arts, sport), involvement in mission and service activities, etc. Parents can be invited to spend more time at the school through provision of a parent lounge, a cafe, or both.

Christian school communities can also play a special role in helping parents better understand their primary God-given role in raising their children (Deut 6:7). Too often secular society implies, or explicitly states, that children are the responsibility of the state, not families (e.g. comments by former MSNBC host Melissa Harris-Perry),[8] and hence schools take on an inflated role in the education of children as an arm of the state. Appropriate leadership from Christian school communities can help parents gain a more accurate biblical understanding of the primary role of parents in education, and how parents and schools can work together. For an excellent resource for this and related school choice issues, see Edlin.[9]

Biblical understanding of the primary role of parents in education is not the only area where schools can provide Christian education for parents. A growing number of parents at Christian schools either have little or no understanding of the Christian faith, or even for those who hold faith, they may come from churches with little depth in their biblical teaching. While it is always desirable for churches to provide better biblical teaching, there will be practical circumstances where parents at a Christian school would greatly benefit from the school providing Christian education for parents. Schools could offer one of the many effective introductory courses on Christian faith for interested parents at a time to suit parental responsibilities.

Parental Christian education does not apply only to those with little or no understanding of Christian faith. It can also be relevant for particular topical issues where a Christian perspective may otherwise be lacking in societal discussion (or possibly in church discussion)—for example, Christian perspectives on self-harm among teenagers.

It is worth noting that for parents of teenagers, when parents encounter very difficult issues with their children, the relevant school teachers, counsellors, or leadership may be a key point of contact during

---

8 Harris-Perry, 'MSNBC'.
9 Edlin, *Thinking About Schooling*.

distressing family times—and hence the Christian school as a community can provide support far beyond that implied by the 'transactional' model—often at a time when help is greatly desired by parents. Such focal issues may provide an opportunity, if appropriate, for inviting parents to consider Christian spiritual disciplines such as prayer, forgiveness and reconciliation.

In terms of practical steps, offering opportunities for Christian parent education can add much to the richness of the Christian school community. The program should be driven by the needs and interests of parents, and schools should not be afraid to take the opportunity of offering talks/seminars on topical issues as they arise over time.

Limiting Technology Misuse

Recent years have seen the enormous impact of technology on the lives of children, especially with the rise of personal devices (phones and tablets) and 'always-on' internet. A growing body of research and commentary is noting the negative effects of this on young people, including the January 2018 concerns acknowledged by Facebook founder Mark Zuckerberg,[10] so Christian school communities need to do more to understand and respond to this problem. Despite my own research career in educational technology, I too now have grave concerns about how technology adoption is affecting young people, especially in the home.

Unfortunately, in recent decades the degree of technology adoption in schools has been seen as a marker of its 'innovation' and modern appeal. While there are good potential uses of technology in education, the wider impact of this issue is only now coming to light—particularly with the impact of school device programs that result in students overusing their devices at home (usually unintentionally). For teenagers, this is particularly

---

10   Wagner, 'Facebook'.

problematic when they use these devices unsupervised in their bedrooms (such as for homework tasks), with the potential that teenagers may also access the many unsavoury aspects of the internet under the cover of 'homework'. In addition, social media has added an unhealthy layer of 'always-on' digital social life for teenagers, as well as an obsession with idealised self-presentation to peers, which can lead to mental health issues all too frequently.

From a practical point of view, schools need to have a hard look at their marketing materials and any promotion of technology to examine whether the school is part of a wider technology problem, or whether the school is offering students constructive ways to fight back against unhealthy technology use. Overuse of devices in school, unnecessary adoption of devices for younger age groups, and school device adoption policies which lead students to an excessive use of devices at home (especially teenagers shut up in their rooms unsupervised) are all issues which need urgent attention in today's world. This is an issue that schools and parents will have to address directly and forcefully—too many billion-dollar companies have a huge investment in ensuring young people become hooked on their devices.

The days of schools trumpeting their adoption of technology are over—the future belongs to schools that teach their students how to use their technology responsibly, which in practice means less than most students want. And talks and seminars about responsible device use count for little—only activities that cause actual changes in practice matter. Ways to change practices include the use of timing restrictions at home (whether technological or human), restrictions on access to certain types of websites (using website blocking tools such as OpenDNS), restrictions on access to certain apps, and limits or bans on device use in bedrooms. In addition, parents need to take an active interest in the device use of their children—to understand how they use their devices, to provide guidance and to monitor usage for risks. My judgement is that given the digital forces arrayed against young people these days, parents need to be more proactive from a younger age, and more interventionist than in the past.

Reconnecting with Food and Healing the Land

Apart from limiting device use, one concrete way to help 'screenagers' connect with the real world is to involve them more in the food they eat, and its origins. While school vegetable gardens have been popular in some schools in recent times, there is an important reason for Christian school communities to adopt and emphasise school vegetable gardens—so that student engage with the physicality of growing food, which culminates in nourishing their own body, and the opportunity this provides for giving glory to God for the wonder and beauty of creation.

Growing food is, by definition, a slow process, and this itself is an important lesson for young people to learn in today's busy world. It can also be an opportunity to learn more about where food comes from, to visit local (and distant) farms, and to learn more about the practices used to grow food—many of which sadly are harming rather than healing the land. Yet some of the greatest work to rethink food production and healing the land has been done by Christians, such as Joel Salatin and colleagues at Polyface Farm.[11] There are great opportunities for integrated work in geography or science subjects that bring together growing food, learning more about its production, considering models like Polyface Farm, and reflecting on the meaning of good stewardship of God's creation.

So as a practical step, a school vegetable garden can be of great value if it is understood in a wider context of biblical understanding of creation and stewardship. The student who has seen a seed they planted grow into a living healthy plant will have a practical experience to help them

---

[11] Salatin, *Folks, This Ain't Normal*.

appreciate the mystery of 1 Corinthians 15, as well as enjoying nourishment from a plant they have tended.

Fostering More Onsite Community

In addition to fostering connections between Christian community schools and local community organisations, a school can foster a richer community onsite. Activities such as before- and after-school care provide a foundation for a richer engagement with parents and families that goes beyond 'babysitting'. Schools could also engage with students late on a Friday afternoon, in a style similar to church youth groups. Extending the use of the school facilities to weekends and evenings for a mixture of fun and educational activities can extend the Christian community of the school.

Going further, a school could build accommodation for staff onsite, particularly young single staff, with a focus on these staff supporting wider Christian engagement activities beyond school hours. This can include before- and after-school care, youth group activities, music/drama, as well as parent Christian education and support for other school initiatives. The purpose of the onsite accommodation is not simply subsidised rent for teachers, but also to build a richer community life within the school precinct beyond school hours.

In practical terms, the infrastructure required to implement onsite accommodation is not trivial, but it has the potential to expand the reach and depth of the Christian community at a school. In cities with high housing prices, it may be of financial benefit for young impoverished teachers while at the same time benefiting the community life of the school. The key issue is a change of thinking from seeing the school only in terms of formal school hours, to a richer, broader Christian community hub active outside of school hours.

CHRISTIAN SCHOOL COMMUNITIES

Rethinking 'Church' in the Light of the Benedict Option School

Finally, a successful Christian community school, inspired by the vision of the Benedict Option, encourages a rethinking of the theory of church. Too often church means a building, when instead it should mean people—that is, the worldwide body of Christ.

When a school is a Christian community, it can become a kind of church to those involved, particularly those with little or no contact with 'Sunday' churches, or those who have left churches unhappily. This is not to suggest that Christian schools should replace the role of a 'Sunday' church—and almost all Christian schools would encourage those connecting with Christian faith (or reconnecting) to join a local authentic Christian church. Some schools have explicit programs to encourage these connections. However, there are cases where the Christian community school is the primary, or only, point of contact for families with Christian faith. The richer the Christian community life of the school, the more these families will be touched by this experience.

Unfortunately, many churches are unaware of their local Christian schools. Given there are so many positive connections that can be made, there is much to recommend collaboration. In some contexts, the school is part of a church, and this can be both a positive and a negative situation depending on varied factors. But for Christian schools without particular church contacts, there are many benefits from building multiple church-school connections.

As a practical step, I would recommend to church leaders that they seek out Christian schools in their area and where appropriate that they explore ways of connecting and collaborating. Many Christian schools would be delighted to have more contact with local churches, and this in turn can foster a deeper Christian community in the school. There may need to be extended sharing and listening to each other, leader to leader, for this to be done in ways which build positive engagement.

Summary

The vision behind the Benedict Option can provide fruitful ways of thinking about growing Christian school communities, and how they can grow to become deep, authentic Christian communities. While there are many areas in which this vision could be developed, including Dreher's recommendation of growing Classical Christian schools, this chapter has discussed seven particular areas that would be applicable to Christian schools that have moved beyond transactional approaches towards being a Christian community school, and who wish to go further.

9

HUMILITY, EMBODIMENT AND CONTEXTUALISATION: MISSIONAL AND HOMEMAKING OPPORTUNITIES FOR THE CULTIVATION OF SHALOM BY THE CHURCH IN EXILE

Karina Kreminski

Scripture sometimes paints a picture of the church in the world as a people who are strangers in a foreign land. There is often a sense in the Bible that Christians are not meant to be quite at home in the world where we live. The practical application of this is that we are to live lives that are counter to the culture of our world. This is especially clear in 1 Peter where the readers, scattered throughout Asia Minor, are referred to as exiles and aliens, a 'diaspora' in both a literal and a metaphorical sense. If we keep this exile metaphor in mind, what is to be our contemporary posture as we relate to our world? One option is that the church withdraws from the world in a refuge mentality. The aim here would be to preserve purity and perhaps at best be an incubator of the gospel. Another option is to adopt a stance of militancy and increase our attempts to colonise our society.

The approach here is to engage in the culture wars, to 'reclaim' and 'take back' what Christians feel was once their territory. This sort of approach is in many cases driven by a longing for the return of Christendom.

An alternative to both views, and a better perspective, is to view our exile as an opportunity for careful contextualisation, cultivating the practices of humility and embodiment in order to nurture the values of *shalom* in our world. This perspective has the effect of tempering the view that this world is not our home and instead seeks to work with God to grow his reign until the return of Jesus, for a restored universe when this world will be our ultimate dwelling place.

In various parts of Scripture, we read that God's people are separate, peculiar and different from those who are not God's people. In Deuteronomy 7:6, God says to Israel: 'For you are a people holy to the Lord your God; the Lord your God has chosen you out of all the peoples on earth to be his people, his treasured possession'. What emerges from that verse is the sense that God's people are special, not because they are better than others, but simply because of God's grace shown to them. They are different, unique and counter to other cultures in the world. This theme comes through in the Gospel of John, for example, where God's people are regularly placed in contrast to 'the world', which in this Gospel has negative connotations. As Don Carson observes, 'There are no unambiguously positive occurrences' of 'the world' in John's Gospel.[1] 'Therefore when John tells us that God loves the world (3:16), far from being an endorsement of the world, it is a testimony to the character of God. God's love is to be admired not because the world is so big but

---

[1] Carson, *Gospel According to John*, 122.

HUMILITY, EMBODIMENT AND CONTEXTUALISATION

because the world is so bad'.[2] The overall sense here is that God's people, in this case the church, are different from the world.

The letter of 1 Peter develops the theme of Christians being exiles or aliens. To be in exile implies that Christians are away from their homeland. The term 'exiles' is mentioned in 1:1 and repeated in 2:11, 12. There the exhortation from the author is that Christians must live 'honourably' among the gentiles. This is important because a crucial aspect of being the people of God is being holy as God is holy (1:16); consequently, they must rid themselves of the things that might stop them from being witnesses to the world (2:1, 11, 12). We can see a similar (though not identical) concept of God's people being strangers in the world in Hebrews 11:13–16 which says, 'They confessed that they were strangers and foreigners on the earth, for people who speak in this way make it clear that they are seeking a homeland ... But as it is they desire a better country, that is, a heavenly one'.[3] It is clear that Scripture reveals that one posture and metaphor, which is appropriate for the way that we see ourselves in the world, is that of a community in exile. We do not quite fit in this world as it is currently framed—we are different, strangers, out of place and separate. To say this is not necessarily to argue that in every instance the same perspective on 'the world' is implied, as is the case in John's Gospel, but simply to point out that the *exile* metaphor for God's people in Scripture is evident.

This metaphor of not being at home or being like exiles in the world is more pertinent to the West because of our current post-Christendom context. One could argue that Christianity sat more comfortably within the context of Christendom, which privileged Christianity within the culture, merged church with state and made the assumption that the society was Christian. However, those days no longer exist. George Hunsberger in *The Church between Gospel and Culture* quotes Kennon Callahan:

---

2   Carson, *Gospel According to John*, 123.
3   Biblical quotations within this chapter are from the NRSV.

> *The day of the churched culture is over ... The day has gone when the church was generally valued by the society as important to the social and moral order and when for that reason, people tended to seek out a church for themselves. We sail today in a different kind of sea ... We are caught between a Constantinian Christendom that has ended and to which we cannot return and the culture's relegation of the church to the private realm.*[4]

The Church in the West could be experiencing acute symptoms associated with sensing that we are in an entrenched exilic posture because of our post-Christendom context. The feelings experienced by many Christians in the West are those of disorientation, grief, and, in some quarters, a longing for the return to a scenario when Christendom was prevalent, perhaps to feel that sense of comfort and familiarity with our culture again. James Thompson writes:

> *Christians now belong to a distinctly minority group. Our behavior will increasingly be considered strange to the majority of the population. This new situation presents Christians with a severe test—on the job, at school, and in our relationships with neighbours. We are now discovering the challenge of being Christians when it is not popular to be a Christian.*[5]

As a result of losing power and status in society, these exilic feeling have caused some Christians to utilise the word 'persecution' in order to describe their sense of disorientation. In 2010, the Catholic archbishop of Chicago, Cardinal Francis George, said: 'I expect to die in bed, my successor will die in prison, and his successor will die a martyr in the public square'.[6] This alarming statement was made in response to the perception that society is becoming increasingly secularised and intolerant to the Christian faith.

---

4   Hunsberger, *Gospel and Culture*, 17.
5   Thompson, *Church in Exile*, 12.
6   http://www-archive.biblesociety.org.au/news/christians-persecuted

HUMILITY, EMBODIMENT AND CONTEXTUALISATION

Perhaps mistaking a loss of power for harassment, some Christians have named persecution what is actually the experience of decreasing influence, as long-held rights and privileges are removed by a society that no longer wants to identify with Christianity.

While it may be that Christians are experiencing increased exilic symptoms because of post-Christendom, this does not mean that we should desire to return to Christendom. This is the problematic issue with the use of the *exile* metaphor, which implies a longing to return to where one has come from. If the *exile* experience is only framed in relation to Christendom, then the longing for home is to return to that context. However, the only longing for home that Christians must identify with is the desire for a new and restored heaven and earth. It is only in this sense that we can speak of the church being in exile. Helpfully, Lee Beach says:

> *Perhaps exile is the way that the people of God should understand themselves at all times in their history. Christendom, it can be argued is an anomaly that produced mixed results for the church's mission and identity. In light of this it could be that the recovery of an exilic paradigm as a means of self-definition is absolutely necessary for the church in post-modern, post-Christian times.*[7]

Therefore, an exilic metaphor is helpful for the church today, not primarily in relation to its post-Christendom experience, but as a metaphor that frames the way God's people can imagine themselves and engage in mission in our world. Here is where we come to the crucial question: What is to be our response if we accept and adopt Scripture's *exile* image in order to frame who we are and our mission on earth? What are the challenges and the benefits of using this metaphor? One response which has been analysed lengthily is the thesis presented in Rod Dreher's book *The Benedict Option: A Strategy for Christians in a Post-Christian Nation*.

---

7   Beach, *Church in Exile*, 20.

Dreher is responding to Alistair MacIntyre's notion that a time would come in the West when 'continued full participation in mainstream society was not possible for those who wanted to live a life of traditional virtue'.[8] Dreher suggests a strategy of withdrawal from society where Christians must 'develop creative, communal solutions to help us hold on to our faith and our values in a world growing ever more hostile ... We ... have to choose to make a decisive leap into a truly countercultural way of living Christianity or we ... doom our children and our children's children to assimilation'.[9]

Even though Dreher may not have intended to convey a strategy of complete withdrawal based on the fear of an increasingly secularised society, this how the 'Benedict Option' could be interpreted. If we see ourselves as exiles, is our best strategy to withdraw from the world?

Another option is to become more militant, engage in the 'culture wars' and to 'reclaim our territory', as some Christians have pronounced. This is the opposite of the Benedict Option, which advocates a passivity; instead, this is an aggressive approach. James Davison Hunter calls this posture a 'defensive against' stance.[10] The call here is for the nation to turn from its sinful ways so that the culture can be won back for Christ. The mandate is that the nation must repent and come back to faith for the evangelisation of unbelievers, and to launch a pushback or even an attack against the 'enemies' of the Christian faith. The main problem is then seen as secularisation, and the hope is that if God could be 'brought back' into public life, the church would regain its lost ground and society would hopefully return to a place of some form of Christendom.

Neither of these postures is helpful in terms of thinking about the church's missional posture as seen through an *exile* metaphor.

---

8   Dreher, *Benedict Option*, 2.
9   Dreher, *Benedict Option*, 2.
10   Hunter, *To Change the World*, 214.

HUMILITY, EMBODIMENT AND CONTEXTUALISATION

Wanting to retreat from society, or the opposite—increasing our militancy—are understandable reactions to our loss of influence and privilege, however, they both fail with respect to discerning and engaging in evangelistic and missional opportunities in our exile. Instead, the church must move towards the posture and practices of humility, embodiment of the gospel and careful contextualisation, in order to display a missional praxis which joins with God to participate in the making of our ultimate home. This is our paradoxical task in our exile; we work with God to participate in his work that will redeem this world, our place of exile, so that it will become our ultimate home.

Firstly, a practice of the church in exile must be one of humility which emulates the life of Christ and the early church. Alan Kreider in *The Patient Ferment of the Early Church* quotes Cyprian who admiringly writes this about Jesus:

> *But what wonderful equanimity in bearing with the Jews and what wonderful patience in persuading the unbelieving to accept the faith, in winning the ungrateful by kindness, in responding gently to those who contradicted him, in enduring the proud with mercy, in yielding with humility to persecutors, in wishing to win over the murderers of the prophets and those persistently rebellious against God even to the very hour of his passion and cross.*[11]

In the same way that Christ bore witness through his patience and humility in life and death, so must the church, even if it is ridiculed, stripped of its power and marginalised. We must not only see Jesus as the Lord whom we worship, but the man of humility whom we must imitate. Michael Gorman writes about how this kind of cruciformity is a mark of the Christian, and contrasts this humble attitude with empire thinking:

---

[11] Kreider, *Patient Ferment*, 27.

> *Cruciform holiness stands in marked contrast to key Roman values (which can infiltrate the body of Christ), especially those values associated with the libertine and status-seeking lifestyle of the elite, and those related to the power and domination predicated of imperial divinity. This cruciform holiness means in sum, becoming like Christ by the power of the Holy Spirit of the Father and the Son, and thus also becoming like God—for God is Christlike.*[12]

A militant and triumphalist attitude runs counter to a humble, patient and cruciform posture, which is more Christlike and representative of the early church. This is our faithful Christian witness as we embody the gospel by imitating Christ in our exile.

A second practice for missional and evangelistic witness is embodiment of the gospel. This may sound self-evident, however, evangelicalism has a tendency towards abstraction, the love of knowledge, and even Gnosticism over and above living out the gospel. Darrell Guder reminds us:

> *The centrality of the community to the gospel means that the message is never disembodied. The word must always become flesh, embodied in the life of the called community. The gospel cannot be captured adequately in propositions, or creeds or theological systems ... [T]he gospel dwells in and shapes the people who are called to be its witness. The message is inextricably linked with its messengers. If there is good news in the world, then it is demonstrably good in the way that it is lived out by the community called into its service. The early church in Jerusalem lived in such a way that they had 'the goodwill of all the people' (Acts 2:47).*[13]

---

12 Gorman, *Cruciform God*, 124.
13 Guder, *Incarnation*, 22.

HUMILITY, EMBODIMENT AND CONTEXTUALISATION

In his book, *Embodying our Faith*, Tim Morey notes the importance of the church embodying the gospel for our contemporary witness:

> *As we move deeper into a post-Christian twenty-first century, the people of God will need to rediscover the power of an embodied apologetic. By this I mean an apologetic that is based more on the weight of our actions than the strength of our arguments. This is an apologetic that is high-touch, engages people relationally, ordinarily takes place in the context of an ongoing friendship, and addresses the needs inquirers have and the questions they pose. It provides the weight to our answers that reason by itself cannot.*[14]

As Christians, we must place more emphasis on practice and fleshing out the gospel in a post-Christendom context, since this is our main witness in a context where people are highly suspicious of and have negative perceptions of the church.

Lastly, as we move towards working with God to make this world our home, our practice must be one of careful exegesis and contextualisation. As exiles who are paradoxically living in the very place that we will call our ultimate home, we must discern by listening to God's Spirit what will help us to participate in God's work to build the new heavens and earth, and also what is detrimental to that vision. This means deep listening to our culture. Often, we polarise various strategies for engagement with the world. We dichotomise countering the culture and being relevant to the culture, but careful contextualisation means that we use various strategies for embodying our faith and working with God to grow his kingdom. Being 'against the culture', 'converting the culture', 'subverting the culture', and in some sense being even 'of the culture', are simultaneously the necessary responses needed today.[15]

---

14 Tim Morey, *Embodying Our Faith*, 40.
15 Volf, *Soft Difference*, 27.

As we apply the practices of humility, embodiment and careful contextualisation, we work with God to participate in his renewing, recreating work that will make this earth where we are in exile, our home. We wait for the return of Jesus Christ, when the universe will be restored and our true home will be revealed, however today, our missional and evangelistic task is to join with God's Spirit to create our ultimate dwelling place. It is in this way that we must juxtapose another parallel image with the *exile* metaphor, that is, the 'homemaker' image. We know from Revelation 21:2 that we will not 'go up' to heaven but that God will come to us and that our new dwelling place will take the form of a city. Miroslav Volf gives a picturesque description of the way that we work with God to participate in the making of this future city:

> *What Christians end up building in the course of history does not resemble a modern city, like Brasilia, all designed and built from scratch. Instead, they are helping to build what resembles more of an ancient city with its 'maze of little streets and squares, of old and new houses, and of houses with additions from various periods; and this surrounded by a multitude of new boroughs with straight regular streets and uniform houses'.*[16]

Therefore, there is a universal God-led building plan that we are engaging in even as we live in a fallen world, which is in the process of being restored. We are homemakers in our exile. As the quote by Volf points out, there is continuity between what we see now and the new world that is to come. In the first letter to the Corinthians, the apostle Paul highlights the continuity and discontinuity between the current body we have and what we will receive at the restoration of the universe. In 1 Corinthians 15:37, Paul states that the resurrection body contains the seed of what we embody and experience now. Despite the fact that there is clearly a discontinuity between the old and new, the connection between the old

---

16   Volf, *Public Faith*, 94, quoting Ludwig Wittgenstein.

HUMILITY, EMBODIMENT AND CONTEXTUALISATION

and new is also made clear. At the end of this section, Paul implies that as a result of the coming consummation of the reign of God, we should work for the restoration of the rule of God now. Paul says, 'Therefore, my beloved, be steadfast, immovable, always excelling in the work of the Lord, because you know that in the Lord your labor is not in vain' (1 Cor 15:58).

Often Christians have a very cautious approach to engaging with the world because of a tendency towards a theologically negative view of our world. Christians can sometimes be more comfortable in claiming that this world is our place of exile, rather than accepting that the world is and will be (as redeemed and renewed by God) our ultimate home, and that we are to be homemakers in our world. This can lead to a disembodied and escapist Christian practice which focuses on a future existence, sidelining working with the Spirit now to build our new home. Craig van Gelder highlights this ambivalence within Christianity:

> *Often there seems to be a deep ambivalence about the God-world relationship. Creation is viewed either as lacking God's presence or as the mere object of missionary work. In either case, it is understood largely as being without God-given worth and agency. Most striking is the lack of imagination of the Spirit's ongoing movement within creation, especially outside the church. A more robustly Trinitarian framework invites us into a deeper, more theological view of the world and God's continuing work of creation within it.*[17]

My opinion is that this ambivalence has shaped an unhelpful interpretation of the *exile* metaphor by emphasising a countercultural posture towards the world, as opposed to a more conciliatory and less defensive view of the world which leads more naturally to engagement.

Instead of a 'defensive against' or a militant approach in our interaction with the culture, what would it look like to be a humble people

---

17   Van Gelder and Zscheile, *Missional Church*, loc. 2408, Kindle.

of God who practice embodiment and careful contextualisation in order to work with God's Spirit to make this world our home? How can we be good homemakers in our world? This is the work of living and bringing *shalom* to our world. In her book, *The Very Good Gospel: How Everything Wrong Can be Made Right*, Lisa Sharon Harper says that in Scripture, shalom means wellbeing, wholeness, the perfection of God's creation, abundance and peace. It is used as a greeting, proclaims the absence of conflicts, and can also mean the restoration of relationships, healing and peace.[18] Good relationships are a crucial part of *shalom*. Harper explains:

> *The peace of self is dependent upon the peace of the other. God created the world in a web of relationships that overflowed with forceful goodness. These relationships are far-reaching: between humanity and God, between humanity and self, between genders, between humanity and the rest of creation, within families, between ethnic groups or races, and between nations. These relationships were very good in the beginning. One word characterised them all: shalom ... Shalom is the stuff of the kingdom.*[19]

Practicing *shalom* is what it means to work with God to build his kingdom and make this world our home. As Harper says, it means working in our world to bring reconciliation between broken relationships, whether it is between individuals, classes, nations, genders or the environment.

This posture is activistic and engaged with the world, stemming from a theology that is more positive in its view about the world and an eschatological understanding that is firmly grounded in the idea that the universe is being restored now, in order to be our ultimate dwelling place.

N. T. Wright visually and strikingly portrays this image of a universe being restored:

---

18 Harper, *Very Good Gospel*, 12.
19 Harper, *Very Good Gospel*, 13.

HUMILITY, EMBODIMENT AND CONTEXTUALISATION

> *You are not oiling the wheels of a machine that's about to fall off a cliff. You are not restoring a painting that's shortly going to be thrown into the fire. You are not planting roses in a garden that's about to be dug up for a building site. You are—strange as though it may seem, almost as hard to believe as the resurrection itself—accomplishing something which will become in due course, part of God's new world. Every act of love, gratitude and kindness; every work of art or music inspired by the love of God and delight in the beauty of his creation; every minute spent teaching severely handicapped children to read or to walk; every act of care and nurture, of comfort and support, for one fellow human beings, and for that matter one's fellow non-human beings and of course every prayer, all Spirit-led teaching, every deed which spreads the gospel, builds up the church, embraces and embodies holiness rather than corruption, and makes the name of Jesus honoured in the world—all of this will find its way, through the resurrecting power of God, into the new creation which God will one day make. That is the logic of the mission of God.[20]*

This compels us to work with God now on his mission in order to transform the universe where we live.

Exile is a helpful metaphor used in Scripture to describe the posture of God's people in the world today. Nevertheless, it has sometimes been unhelpfully appropriated by the church and damaged the church's call to mission. However, if we see that being in exile means practicing disciplines which lead to shalom, the result is that we work and walk with God now as sojourners, homemakers and 'aching visionaries' who are waiting for the return of Christ:

> *So the sojourner is a homemaker, but a homemaker who is potentially on the move. And the homeland for which the sojourner yearns is not some other world, but this world redeemed and transfigured. The contrast is*

---

20 Wright, *Surprised by Hope*, 219.

> *not ontological but eschatological. Because the kingdom of God is not yet realised in its fullness, the sojourner yearns for its consummation. And that is why Christian sojourners are* aching visionaries *who bear witness to and work for a future of* shalom ... *[W]e are not immigrants or refugees, exiles or migrants, tourists, postmodern nomads. If we understand ourselves properly, then in contrast to all of them we are, in a real sense, at home. But this being at home is a posture, a way of being in the world. It is a journeying homemaking characterised by ... permanence, dwelling, memory, rest, hospitality, inhabitation, orientation and belonging.*[21]

In effect, the biblical metaphor of *exile*, when interpreted correctly and placed alongside the 'homemaker' image, ought to help us dream and imagine that this world, beautifully restored, will one day be our home. Then, as our imaginations are reoriented and aligned with God's mission, we will work for this picture of our home to become a reality today.

10
DANGEROUS MEMORIES IN THE LANDS WE NOW CALL AUSTRALIA: DO THE EXILES HEAR THE CALL TO COUNTRY TODAY?

BROOKE PRENTIS

> *My people, hear my teaching;*
> *listen to the words of my mouth.*
> *I will open my mouth with a parable;*
> *I will utter hidden things, things from of old—*
> *things we have heard and known,*
> *things our ancestors have told us.*
> *We will not hide them from their descendants;*
> *we will tell the next generation*
> *the praiseworthy deeds of the Lord,*
> *his power, and the wonders he has done.*
>
> Psalm 78:1–4[1]

---

[1] Except where otherwise indicated, biblical quotations within this chapter are from the NIV translation.

BROOKE PRENTIS

In preparation to write this paper I went on country. *Waka Waka* country. The country of my ancestors; the country where sixty-five thousand years of footprints, from my family, have been left; the country with two thousand generations of story, my family's story. The country that has had the presence of Creator Spirit since time immemorial. My country.

As I looked out across the mountains, the Bunya pines[2] and the native grasslands, as I listened to eastern whipbirds, green catbirds and kookaburras, and as I waited at sunrise for the sun to peek its head above the horizon, I remembered rightly of the Creator. I could hear the beat of the clapsticks as though in rhythm with my creation, my being. I could see the songs of creation. I could feel the stamping of feet so softly in dance on creation. I remembered rightly of the Sun, the giver of life. I felt free. Free from racism, free from injustice, free from lack of respect, lack of dignity, and lack of honour. Free from these things that I experience in society and within the Australian church. In reference to Oldenburg's model, I was in my third place.[3] Or was it indeed my first place? I had heard my call to country, and I had followed that call.

The call was from Creator God, and as I stood on the mountains, beside the living rocks, I listened to God sing to me through the wind rustling through the two hundred-year-old grasstrees in a beautiful symphony like a psalm, and he spoke like Aboriginal Elders that say, 'Care for country and country will care for you'.[4]

---

2 Bunya pines are native to Waka Waka and Gubbi Gubbi country. They are not actually a pine tree but are, in fact, part of the Araucariaceae family, with the botanical name of Araucaria bidwillii.

3 Cf. Oldenburg, *Great Good Place*.

4 Words like this and similar are often spoken by Elders during a Welcome to Country. A Welcome to Country can only be performed by an Elder of the local country where an event is taking place. This is different to an Acknowledgement of Country which can be performed by an Aboriginal or non-Aboriginal person. Proper protocol is that an Acknowledgement of Country should be performed by the most senior person in attendance at the event.

DANGEROUS MEMORIES

This song awakened memories—dangerous memories.[5] In this moment, I saw, felt, and heard the dangerous memories, that this land was *Waka Waka* country—always was, always will be, Aboriginal land—dangerous memories in the lands we *now* call Australia.

There are many dangerous memories in the lands we *now* call Australia. Aunty Jean Phillips has called to Christians for three generations, 'Come on the journey with us as Aboriginal people'. Today the call is the same, this journey is for you, my fellow exile. We are exiles for different reasons and in different circumstances—Aboriginal exile and non-Aboriginal exile. The journey today is to take a walk with me through the dangerous memories in the lands we *now* call Australia—our Creator's call to country.

The Many Meanings of Country

Country takes many meanings. Most Australians would identify only with country as Australia—an Australia birthed at Federation on January 1, 1901, a mere 118 years ago. Or an Australia, birthed at settlement—or, is that, invasion?—on January 26, 1788, a mere 231 years ago; or actually, not even technically Australia yet, but the colony of New South Wales. This Australia is bound up in an Australia Day that was not celebrated as a public holiday as a single nation of Australia until 1994.[6] This date is even confused with the date of Cook's landing.[7]

For us as Aboriginal peoples this date not only marks dispossession, disease, destruction and death, but marks our time as the beginning of our

---

[5] The use of 'dangerous memories' in this paper is a reference to the chapter title, 'Dangerous Memories', in Frost, *Exiles*.

[6] Kwan, *Celebrating Australia,* an essay commissioned by the National Australia Day Council, completed in 2007.

[7] James Cook landed in Sydney Cove on April 28/29, 1770. Arthur Phillip landed in Sydney Cove close to January 26, 1788.

exile, exiles in our own land. I describe these times as dangerous memories, taking the form of the true history of our bloodstained land in the last nearly 250 years.

Journeying into Australia's dangerous memories can take different meanings depending on whose side of history one stands, but we always hear the dominant culture's interpretation, which too easily dismisses, hides, or denies any other interpretation.

I enter these dangerous memories with trepidation: not only trepidation for the pain caused to my people and the reality of how history affects our present lives, but with trepidation that you will not listen at all, or not listen with compassion, or that you will hear with guilt and revert to the dominant culture's interpretation.

Miroslav Volf in *The End of Memory: Remembering Rightly in a Violent World*, speaks of 'dangerous truth'—this is the same as dangerous memories.[8] So often the truth telling on the side of the perpetrator or the dominant culture in Australia is a truth of an education system that is known for teaching incorrectly,[9] is a truth regurgitated by one bad experience with an Aboriginal person around the work water cooler, or is a truth of Christians who have never met an Aboriginal person but who have said to me that they will not do an Acknowledgement of Country

---

8   Volf, *End of Memory*, 56–57.

9   An Australian Curriculum was formulated following the Melbourne Declaration on Education Goals for Young Australians (MCEETYA), Ministerial Council on Education, Employment, Training and Youth Affairs, December 2008, which was a statement signed by all Australian Education Ministers. It included the following, 'As a nation, Australia values the central role of education in building a democratic, equitable and just society that is prosperous, cohesive and culturally diverse and that values Australia's Indigenous cultures as a key part of the nation's history, present and future', 04–05. Accessed at http://www.curriculum.edu.au/verve/_resources/National_Declaration_on_the_Educational_Goals_for_Young_Australians.pdf. Nearly ten years later, we are still asking for the education system to teach correctly, and asking, 'Do Our Teachers Care Enough About Indigenous Australia to Bring it Into the Classroom?', accessed December 20, 2017, https://www.sbs.com.au/nitv/article/2017/05/09/do-our-teachers-care-enough-about-indigenous-australia-bring-it-classroom.

DANGEROUS MEMORIES

because they have heard 'it's tied to the Rainbow Serpent which is a snake and that must be Satan so it is un-Christian'.[10] Volf points out that one of the problems of truth telling is 'the claim of each party to *possess* the truth, not the moral obligation of both parties to *seek* the truth'.[11]

I cannot afford to have you call dangerous memories a guilt trip, or paralyse you with fear, or be overwhelmed. Aboriginal peoples need you. Reconciliation needs you. God's kingdom needs you. The call to country I am suggesting is a call to deep listening, to relearning, and to walking together, and it starts in Volf's call to our moral obligation 'to remember truthfully, and therefore to see the truth'.[12] It is then that we can 'give others the benefit of the doubt, inhabit imaginatively the world of others, and ... endeavor to view events in question from the perspective of others, not just [our] their own'.[13]

Imagine Cook's arrival at Kurnell, and the dangerous memories of the two Aboriginal men who were fired upon against their wooden spears—seeing and feeling a gun's impact for the first time.[14] Or imagine how Bennelong might describe his dangerous memories, bound in chains

---

10   The Rainbow Serpent is a Dreaming story told across many nations from the east coast to the west coast of the lands now called Australia. The Rainbow Serpent is the Creator and in some nations is known as Biame. In nations such as the Kulin nation, the Creator is Bunjil, the eagle, and in Kaurna nation the Creator is Tjilbruke, a man who turned into an ibis.
11   Volf, *End of Memory*, 57.
12   Volf, *End of Memory*, 57.
13   Volf, *End of Memory*, 57.
14   Extract from James Cook's journal, April 29, 1770: 'We saw as we came in, several of the Natives and a few hutts;—Men, Women, and Children ... As we approached the Shore they all made off, except 2 Men ... I thought that they beckon'd to us to come ashore; but in this we were mistaken ... I fir'd a musquet between the 2, which had no other Effect than to make them retire back, where bundles of their darts lay, and one of them took up a stone and threw at us, which caused my firing a Second Musquet, and altho' the shott struck the man, it had no other effect ... (I then fired) a third shott, soon after which they both made off, but not in such haste but what we might have taken one'.

and removed from family,[15] as Arthur Phillip's prisoner, or curiosity, or the key to Phillip's survival.

Or imagine Lachlan Macquarie's 1816 Sydney and the sight of Aboriginal people being hanged from trees, decapitated, and their heads sent to England.[16] Whilst the modern-day and present-day world can remember the lynching of African Americans in 1960s United States of America, or the news of the last few years of a group, whose foundations can be found in the Middle East, holding decapitated heads; for Aboriginal peoples the sights are indelible marks on our generational memories from the lands we *now* call Australia. The dangerous memories in a present-day Australia.

Dangerous Memories, Past and Present

Dangerous memories are not only in our past, although for peoples with a memory extending sixty-five thousand years, one could argue that dangerous memories going back to 1770 are present-day memories.

Memories of an Australia that upheld the myth of *Terra Nullius*—empty land—effectively denying the existence of Aboriginal peoples until 1992 with the Mabo No. 2 decision in Australia's High Court.

Memories of an Australia where the leaders of our country come on a romanticised version of country and attend the Garma festival,[17] and then a week later tell us we don't matter in discussions about the date of Australia Day—that 'changing the date of Australia Day would be to turn our back on Australian values'.[18] Apparently our voices, the Aboriginal

---

[15] Perkins and Langton, First Australians, 15.
[16] Organ, Secret Service.
[17] The Garma festival is held annually in Arnhem land with the Yolngu peoples and is an economic forum that brings together political leaders, business leaders, academics and journalists, from across Australia and the world, and includes sharing of traditional dance and culture.
[18] Malcolm Turnbull, *Facebook*, August 16, 2017, 3:15pm.

voices and values, as part of the twenty-four million 'Australians', do not matter.

Memories of an Australia whose Prime Minister turned his back on Aboriginal peoples with the rejection of the Uluru Statement from the Heart, which was compiled by approximately three hundred Aboriginal leaders from across Australia.[19]

Australia's Exile of Aboriginal Peoples

This is an Australia that has exiled peoples and that still exiles peoples that Stan Grant described as 'older than the Pharoahs'—peoples who were 'within a generation ... ravaged'.[20]

The Australia that is 231/119 years old, I suggest, has created a colonial Jesus. This Australia, through the colonial, Western mindset of many Australian Christians, has done to Jesus exactly as Frost has described by 'imprisoning Jesus in a stained-glass cell and want only to worship him, never to follow him'.[21] This is precisely why Aboriginal peoples who identify as Christian are not sitting in the institutional church each Sunday—Aboriginal Christians are exiles from the Australian church.

The effects of the colonial Jesus, or the academic aspiration of the postcolonial Jesus are explained in Uncle Reverend Graham Paulson and Mark Brett's paper, 'Five Smooth Stones',[22] and by Aunty Reverend Denise Champion in her book, *Yarta Wandatha*.[23] Both make comparisons to Aboriginal peoples' loss of connection to culture and country by referencing Psalm 137.

---

19   Conifer, http://www.abc.net.au/news/2017-10-26/indigenous-advisory-body-proposal-rejected-by-cabinet/9087856.
20   Grant, *Talking to My Country*, 2.
21   Frost, *Exiles*, 52.
22   Paulson and Brett, *Five Smooth Stones*, 202.
23   Champion, *Yarta Wandatha*, 23.

> *By the rivers of Babylon—*
> *there we sat down and there we wept*
> *when we remembered Zion.*
> *On the willows there we hung up our harps ...*
> *How could we sing the Lord's song in a foreign land?*
> *(Ps 137:1–2, 4; NRSV)*

Aunty Denise continues: 'Remembering the old times helps people who feel forgotten or cut off. They lamented their loss and their grief. The difference for Indigenous peoples is that we have nowhere else to go. We are refugees in our own country'.[24]

Australia's true history has not been dealt with either by society or by the Australian church. I suggest that biblically, the Australian church turn to Habakkuk 2, to help remember this true history, the dangerous memories of the lands we *now* call Australia:

> *Woe to him who piles up stolen goods and makes himself wealthy by extortion! (v. 6).*

Is it not talking of the *Stolen Wages* and of the slavery of Aboriginal people in Australia?

> *Because you have plundered many nations, the peoples who are left will plunder you. For you have shed human blood; you have destroyed lands and cities and everyone in them (v. 8).*

Is it not talking of the destruction of over three hundred nations of peoples? Of the massacres and genocide and destruction of the environment, where profit and greed is valued over caring for creation?

> *Woe to him who builds his house by unjust gain, setting his nest on high to escape the clutches of ruin! (v. 9).*

---

[24] Champion, *Yarta Wandatha*, 23.

Is it not talking of the Stolen Land, including the churches and church schools built on the most spectacular pieces of land in our capital cities? That have the most amazing views and were gifted for free—not a penny paid—except for the price of Aboriginal peoples and our homes.

> *Woe to him who gives drink to his neighbors, pouring it from the wineskin till they are drunk (v. 15).*

Is it not talking of the alcohol given to Aboriginal peoples as a means of control to make us fringe dwellers of colonial Australia or given to Aboriginal people to help imprison us in present-day Australia?

> *Woe to him who builds a city with bloodshed and establishes a town by injustice! (v. 12).*

The 'stain on this nation's soul',[25] 'the blood on the wattle',[26] runs deep. Lord have mercy on Australia. I wonder how many non-Aboriginal pastors, ministers and church leaders have ever preached on the true history of Australia, using Habakkuk, and called for acknowledgement, recognition, repentance, and most importantly, friendship with Aboriginal peoples.

The Dangerous Memories of Country Before 'Australia'

It is generally accepted that there are over three hundred nations of Aboriginal peoples with over six hundred dialects of language in the lands now called Australia. The AIATSIS map of Indigenous Australia, based on the map developed by Norman B. Tindale, is the best visual representation of Aboriginal nations.[27] Yet so many 'Australians' have never seen the map, do not know an Aboriginal person, and many do not care to know.

---

25 Grant, *Closing the Gap*.
26 Elder, *Blood on the Wattle*.
27 AIATSIS map of Indigenous Australia, https://aiatsis.gov.au/explore/articles/aiatsis-map-indigenous-australia, accessed June 15, 2017.

As Aboriginal peoples, we are made to feel like strangers and refugees in a country we have known for over sixty-five thousand years.

Stan Grant describes how an Aboriginal person views this Australia: 'The past is alive in me now. Its wounds rest deep and uneasily in our soul. I am the sum of many things, but I am all history. And we are trapped in this history, all of us, and if we don't understand it we will remain chained in it ... [A]bove it all I am what you have made me. My country: Australia'.[28]

And these are our big dangerous memories—dangerous memories on a national scale. And yes 'our'—yours and mine—Aboriginal and non-Aboriginal exile. For it is in embracing the 'our' of our dangerous memories that we can hear the call to country. As Aunty Jean says, 'Your history is our history, our history is your history'.

Dangerous Memories as Dangerous Truth

Frost explains, 'For exiles trying to live faithfully within the host empire of post-Christendom, the Gospel stories are our most dangerous memories'.[29] As exiles, we can turn to what Frost calls, 'the dangerous ancient stories to judge the insipid contemporary ones'.[30] Or a step from the pages of the New Testament even further back to what Ray Aldred calls the 'gospel story proper'.[31] Or what Western theologians would refer to as starting at Genesis chapter 1. Or what Aboriginal peoples would call the Dreaming.

The dangerous memories before 1788. The dangerous memories of over sixty-five thousand years. Dangerous memories of a Creator shared in story, song and dance for over sixty-five thousand years. Dangerous memories of Jesus, a name known to Aboriginal peoples, before the white man set a foot on these shores.

---

28 Grant, *Talking to My Country*, 6.
29 Frost, *Exiles*, 51.
30 Frost, *Exiles*, 51.
31 Aldred, 'Resurrection of Story', 1.

DANGEROUS MEMORIES

This is the dangerous truth because only we as Aboriginal peoples can tell it. There is no alternate truth that exists. But it is a truth that is easily misunderstood, unacknowledged, or little interest shown in it—particularly by Christians.

The Dreaming does not just take place in the desert of Central Australia, nor in the mere existence of Aboriginal people—'Aboriginal people' in the singular, as this nation refuses to call us 'Aboriginal peoples' in the plural, recognising our vast diversity of culture, language and story.

The Dreaming is not a religion. The Dreaming is not in the past like the use of the word Dreamtime suggests. The Dreaming is not fictional. The Dreaming is all around us, in us, and with us. The Dreaming is about the Creator, caring for creation, and living in right relationship with one another. The Dreaming is the 'gospel story proper',[32] in the lands we *now* call Australia.

This is articulated so clearly by Reverend Aunty Denise Champion: 'I always say Australia is like one gigantic storybook. There's a story to every part of the land and sky and sea. When we, as *Adnyamathanha*, gather and tell our stories we always say *yarta wandatha*—"the land is speaking" ... We also say *"yarta wandatha idandadnha"*. The people are speaking as if the land is speaking. So the land is speaking to us and through us is these stories. There's a oneness there. We are not separated from the land our mother. We always talk about the land as our mother, which fits very closely with the story of Genesis of the Lord God forming humankind from the clay'.[33]

Our views on land and creation often clash between Indigenous and Western cultures and theologies in Australia. In Indigenous cultures there is no separation between human and non-human. Indigenous theology is in direct conflict with dominion theology.

---

32   Aldred, 'Resurrection of Story', 1.
33   Champion, *Yarta Wandatha*, 19.

There are close similarities with Celtic cultures as Ray Simpson explains: 'There is a language of the trees, too. A tree symbolises the centre out of which all life flows. It is a living deposit of many nutrients and is therefore a symbol of wisdom'.[34] We, as Aboriginal peoples, have known this for over sixty-five thousand years.

What It Means To Be On Country—A Third Place

On *Waka Waka* country, my country, are grasstrees and Bunya pine trees. You just have to sit or stand beside one and you feel the spirituality. They are life-giving. They are creation. They are from our Creator—yours and mine.

I know it is often difficult for non-Aboriginal peoples to feel and see and hear the Creator in Australia through creation. When we start talking about our connection to land, I see the eyes glaze over and the tuning out. But non-Aboriginal people can experience it too.

Rod Cameron explains this by retelling the story of a survey team working in the far outback. One of the men, who had previously been a sailor, became very ill and upon being offered prayer said this: 'You ask me if I believe in God. Anyone who has sailed through the Hinchinbrook must believe in God'.[35] Hinchinbrook Island off the coast of Far North Queensland is where my name, Brooke, comes from and it is indeed some of the most beautiful country in Australia.

David J. Tacey explains how he is spiritually overwhelmed by Australia's landscape by saying, 'I sometimes felt the rocky chasms and gorges would burst forth in song and praise'.[36]

The Bible, as Ray Simpson points out, 'teems with examples of people who learned about God through creation, from Noah, to Moses, to

---

34   Simpson, *Pilgrim Way*, 71.
35   Cameron, *Karingal*, 39.
36   Tacey, *Edge of the Sacred*, 20.

the psalmists, to Jeremiah, to Jesus' friends who were taught in Matthew 6:25-33 to learn from the birds and the wild flowers'.[37]

The wisdom that could be had by all Australians if the gift of the world's oldest continuing living culture was embraced and celebrated. The relationship with God that could be further enriched by every Australian if the gift of the Christian theology of the world's oldest continuing living culture was embraced, celebrated and learnt from. Paulson and Brett put it this way, 'Whether we are Indigenous or non-Indigenous … God is calling us to re-read the Bible through Aboriginal eyes'.[38]

I want now to turn to 'third places'.[39] Frost in *Exiles* uses Oldenburg's model which emphasises that healthy community needs third places, 'places of easy-going conviviality and safety'.[40] Frost suggests today's third places as 'bars, pubs, gyms, grocery stores, beauty parlors, community groups, and coffee shops'.[41] As a Christian sitting in the institutional church on a Sunday I said, 'preach it brother'. As an Aboriginal Christian feeling exiled from the church and from Australian society, I wanted something else. These were not my third places or the third places of strong and resilient Aboriginal community and communities.

For starters, when 54 percent of Aboriginal people live in poverty,[42] with the reality of the lack of closing the gap, we literally can't afford to be sitting in these third places. I also had to think of what our first and second place was. What I saw and heard was our first place is home, but that home is an overcrowded, dilapidated public housing home. Do not look

---

37 Simpson, *Pilgrim Way*, 68.
38 Paulson and Brett, *Five Smooth Stones*, 214.
39 Third places was a term coined by Ray Oldenburg in his book *The Great Good Place*, and is referred to in Frost, *Exiles*, 56–70.
40 Frost, *Exiles*, 57.
41 Frost, *Exiles*, 59.
42 The standard measure of poverty in Australia is determined as being unable to raise $2,000 within a week. Statistics from 2002–2005 can be found at https://www.lowitja.org.au/sites/default/files/docs/Beyond-Bandaids-CH5.pdf, page 79.

at this through your Australian eyes but embrace the dangerous memories of stolen wages which lasted right up until the 1970s. Our second place was not work, but Centrelink and prison. Do not look at this through your Australian eyes but embrace Beyond Blue's research of racism through their 'Stop. Think. Respect' campaign, including their finding that one in ten people, Australians, would not employ an Aboriginal person,[43] and that many of our people are sitting in jails for unpaid traffic offences. I started to get depressed—the statistics of disadvantage, real people for me, hit us, the followers of Jesus, with the amount of work to do.

And then I heard something, felt it even, a call to our third place, a call to country. I have suggested a call to deep listening, to relearning, and to walking together in the third place of Australia—the third place of being on country with First Nations custodians. This for me is hope. Hope for my people. And I wondered if the non-Aboriginal exiles would join us. Be on country with us, with the Creator. Listen to the land through the grasstrees and the kookaburras—which speak and teach. Learn from the rocks and the mountains and the rivers—many of which hold the places of the Creator's story. And walk with us, together, with First Nations leading the way. Hope for our peoples.

Walking Together Towards New Dangerous Memories

For me it's an upside-down picture. Much like the Decolonial Atlas.[44] For me it's a call to new dangerous memories, a call to country. This call to country is on every inch of this green, blue and red land and waters of Australia. It's where you live, work, worship and play.

---

[43] Accessed August 14, 2017, https://www.beyondblue.org.au/docs/default-source/research-project-files/bl1337-report---tns-discrimination-against-indigenous-australians.pdf?sfvrsn=2.

[44] 'The Decolonial Atlas: Reimagining the World', 'Australia: Aboriginal Territories and Placenames', accessed August 14, 2017, https://decolonialatlas.wordpress.com/2016/01/25/aboriginal-australia/.

DANGEROUS MEMORIES

It's in *Warrang* (Sydney) on *Dharug* country where the largest community of Aboriginal peoples in Australia reside.

It's in *Meanjin* (Brisbane) on *Turrbal* and *Yuggera* country where the second largest community of Aboriginal peoples reside in the greater Brisbane area.

It's in *Narrm* (Melbourne) on *Bunwurrung* and *Wurundjeri* country where fifty thousand non-Aboriginal people joined their Aboriginal friends, to protest injustice in front of the steps of Flinders Street Station in Melbourne.[45]

It's in *Tarndanya* (Adelaide) on *Kaurna* country where Aboriginal peoples from many nations—*Kaurna, Ngarrindjeri, Adnyamathanha, Nurrunga, Ptitinjara, Mirning, Kokatha, Anangu*—where language and culture continue to be restored, revitalised and celebrated.

It's in *Mparntwe* (Alice Springs) on *Arrente* country in Alice Springs and *Garrmlang* on *Larrakia* country in Darwin, where whilst the population is small in comparison to the Aboriginal population of Australia it is large in comparison to the non-Aboriginal people.

It's on *Ngunnawal* country in Canberra, where our national parliament meets and seems to forget about Aboriginal peoples.

And let us not forget about *Noongar* country and *lutruwita*, located in the states we now call Western Australia and Tasmania.

Creation is all around us, country is all around us, dangerous memories, and the true third place, are all around us.

Can you see it? Can you hear it? Come sit on country at the feet of Elders—learn the stories of Gariwerd, Ikara, Maiwar, Karrawirriparri.

---

[45] Davidson, 'Melbourne City Centre'.

BROOKE PRENTIS

Exiles with Open Eyes and Ears

I have said that this country, Australia, is affected by a spiritual blindness and a spiritual deafness. It's a spiritual blindness that in nineteenth-century Australia, Scottish Presbyterian theologian, Reverend James Denney, called Australia 'The Most Godless Place Under Heaven',[46] and which was repeated in 2005 by Pope Benedict XVI.[47] It's a spiritual deafness that W. E. H. Stanner called 'The Great Australian Silence'.[48]

Please don't take a mission trip to see the 'real' Aboriginal people in Alice Springs or Uluru or Cherbourg,[49] spending hundreds or thousands of dollars. For the real Aboriginal peoples are also in our capital cities. For the stories of the Creator are still known and told to the next generation, even where they are hidden under bitumen and concrete. For Jesus is knocking on the door of that overcrowded house, sitting with us in that prison, lined up outside of Centrelink waiting for the doors to open, and is marching through the streets protesting the latest injustice.

Jesus is there, but where is the church? Where are the exiles?

I'm asking you, exiles, to help lift the spiritual blindness and deafness, to remove, as Ian Breward puts it, 'the one major cultural and spiritual blind spot which impoverishes Australian Christianity—neglect of and contempt for Aboriginal religion in its primal and Christian forms'.[50]

To see country and to hear country. To walk broadly and strongly with the first peoples and the Creator, in my homeland, in your adopted homeland, and in our home together.

---

46 Breward, *Australia*, 1.
47 Collins, 'Australians Are Not Godless'.
48 Stanner, *Dreaming*, 189.
49 Cherbourg is an Aboriginal community approximately 260 kilometres north west of Brisbane. Cherbourg is on *Waka Waka* country. From 2012 to the present, a number of Christian organisations have taken trips to Cherbourg.
50 Breward, *Australia*, 93.

Aunty Reverend Denise Champion implores: 'We are being presented, both First and Second Peoples with the opportunity to follow a new path that reconciles and heals. To do that we need to be able to sing together, dance together, sit down together, eat together, learn to live together in peace and tell stories, allowing this land to speak to us and through us. Yarta Wandatha'.[51]

It's a journey, a prayer, a painting.

The Exiles Hear the Call to Country—The New Dangerous Memories in the Lands We Now Call Australia

'The Exiles Hear the Call to Country—The New Dangerous Memories in the Lands We Now Call Australia' is the title of a painting I commissioned my sister, *Waka Waka* artist, Jasmin Roberts,[52] to paint for me using my vision and words of this paper.

On the outside of the painting are contemporary dot paintings of the land and waters. This is country, as God created, abundant with life and with every provision for strength, sustenance and survival, with the role of humans, you and I, us, to care for creation.

In the centre of the painting, the big U shape, the U representing a person in Aboriginal paintings, is painted black to challenge your Western view of Jesus, and with three sets of dots in grey representing God, Holy Spirit and Jesus.

Inside the U shape, in a circle, are colourful dots. These colourful dots represent the over three hundred nations of Aboriginal peoples. This is surrounded by white dots representing the Australia of the last

---

51   Champion, *Yarta Wandatha*, 60.
52   Jasmin Roberts, *Exiles Hear the Call to Country—The New Dangerous Memories in the Lands We Now Call Australia*, 2017, acrylic on canvas, Scarborough, Queensland.

nearly 250 years. However, this is an Australia that knows and acknowledges Aboriginal peoples from over three hundred nations.

The round reddish-black circles are the dangerous memories. Painted as Songlines,[53] but in red, symbolising our bloodstained true history.

The painting represents both Aboriginal exiles and non-Aboriginal exiles. Aboriginal exiles appear as the smaller black U's—dangerous memories are in us and part of us. The non-Aboriginal exiles appear as the white dots around the smaller black U's. The non-Aboriginal exiles have now heard the call to country and have had to walk, with us, Aboriginal peoples and exiles, through the dangerous memories, with deep listening and relearning.

We, you and I, the Aboriginal exile and the non-Aboriginal exile, are now on country, the true third place of Australia, surrounded by Great Creator Spirit, sitting around the campfire of Australia, creating our new dangerous memories, an Australia built on truth, justice, love and hope, in story, song and dance.

We are living out Frost's call to the exiles in the true Australia to be 'close enough that our lives rub up against one another and that we see the incarnated Christ in our values, beliefs, and practices as expressed in cultural forms that make sense and convey impact'.[54]

We, Aboriginal and non-Aboriginal exiles are now together embracing the new dangerous memories of an Australia that acknowledges Australia as an ancient land and as one of the most God-filled places under heaven since time immemorial. A place where there are peoples created in God's image: the same people, in the same place, telling the same stories for over sixty-five thousand years of how 'God's spirit brooded like a bird

---

53 Songlines are paths that cross the lands now called Australia. Songlines are part of the Dreaming and marked routes that the Creator followed. Songlines are sung as songs, have dances associated with them, are told as stories, and are recorded in paintings.

54 Frost, *Exiles*, 55.

over the watery abyss'.[55] Over sixty-five thousand years of a continuous connection to land and waters, and a continuous connection to the Creator.

Where else will you find this in the world? Nowhere. Now that is one dangerous memory in these lands we *now* call Australia.

The Exiles' Opportunity in a New Australia

As Aboriginal and non-Aboriginal exiles, we can do what this country has failed at. Reconciliation is something we can achieve and that we have the opportunity to do so through our friendship founded on our mutual knowledge of the Creator, being led by Aboriginal Christian Leaders as we sit on country together learning from Aboriginal peoples.

Tacey reminds us, 'It is only in exile, at the edge of the known world, and in our case "down under", that the voice of revelation and guidance is heard'.[56] For exiles, being on country awakens our individual and collective consciousness,[57] a consciousness that both Tacey and Cameron refer to. A spiritual growth of expanding consciousness which allows us to grow as 'we become more aware of the length, breadth and depth of the Mystery which is in Jesus Christ'.[58] It is the exiles' opportunity to play their role in the new experience of the sacred, in the transformation of Australia—an Australia that is often blinded to the other.

It's what Aunty Denise calls a 'new path', Tacey refers to as 'transformation', Cameron calls 'a new beginning', and Frost calls 'Dangerous promises or a radical new lifestyle'. And what I, Prentis, call a 'call to country—the new dangerous memories in the lands *now* called Australia'.

55	Genesis 1:1–2, The Message.
56	Tacey, *Edge of the Sacred*, 205.
57	Tacey, *Edge of the Sacred*, 203.
58	Cameron, *Karingal*, 105.

Exile—Do you Hear the Call to Country?

The Aboriginal Exiles Lead

God is gathering together Aboriginal Christian Leaders on a scale not seen in many years. One of these ways is through the Grasstree Gathering.[59] The Grasstree Gathering is Aunty Jean Phillips's vision, to create a network of Aboriginal Christian Leaders, young and old, from all over Australia and from all denominations. The Grasstree Gathering is a grassroots Aboriginal Christian movement, led by Aboriginal Christian Leaders and for Aboriginal Christian Leaders. This network has been gaining momentum since 2012 and has over three hundred Aboriginal Christian Leaders connected from across Australia and across denominations. Sadly, many of these Aboriginal Christian Leaders are unacknowledged by the denominations to which they belong and by the wider Australian church. May the church come to acknowledge, embrace and learn from Aboriginal Christian Leaders, past, present, and future.

These are your Aboriginal exiles where the conventional church leaders say, 'there are no Aboriginal Christian Leaders', where church resources are not allocated to us, where church councils refuse to do an Acknowledgement of Country, where we do not rate a mention in the theological colleges, let alone be employed as teachers.

But as Frost puts it, in reference to all exiles, but which brings special meaning to Aboriginal exiles, 'they are on to something, and in their unorthodox practice reside the seeds of the survival of the Christian movement'.[60]

Aboriginal Christian Leaders, Aboriginal exiles as I have referred, are on to something for Jesus. A Jesus our Elders today have so faithfully followed through discrimination and disrespect. A Jesus who has walked

---

[59] www.grasstreegathering.org.au
[60] Frost, Exiles, 56.

on these ancient lands with us, Aboriginal peoples, for thousands of years. A Jesus we want the non-Aboriginal exile to know better.

And for us as Aboriginal exile and non-Aboriginal exile together, it's what Bernard J. Lee and Michael A. Cowan in their book 'Dangerous Memories' refer to as 'an Earthquake Phenomenon'.[61] Where 'all social structures—intimate ones and immense ones, civil ones and ecclesial ones—are put under requirement by the Gospel: That the world truly can be reconstructed into the People of God ... These are dangerous memories, and they are shaking some foundations'.[62] We know two are better than one, so, may we, both Aboriginal and non-Aboriginal exiles, join Creator, Holy Spirit, Jesus, and hear the call to country—the new dangerous memories in the lands we now call Australia.

---

[61] Lee and Cowan, *Dangerous Memories*, 1.
[62] Lee and Cowan, *Dangerous Memories*, 1.

11
RE-PLACING MISSION: EXILIC OPTIONS RECONSIDERED
Darrell Jackson

Introduction

Exiles With No Use for Baggage

It seems that a critical view of Christendom and of its legacy is a creedal necessity embedded deeply within the missional canon. An intentionally missional understanding of ecclesiology, missiology and ministry emerged in the work of scholars and writers, including Stuart Murray, Mike Frost and Alan Hirsch, from the mid-1990s onwards. Central to their developing understanding is a disavowal of Constantine and the era of Christendom ushered in by his embrace of Christianity as the religion of the Roman Empire.

Overlaying this work is a preferential option for the 'now'. The contemporary context is construed as a characteristically hostile environment for the high priests of Christendom, but simultaneously also those of modernity and of the Enlightenment. Set against this analytical backdrop, Frost and other missional practitioners have worked hard to reimagine communal and missional forms of discipleship free from the baggage of Christendom, modernity and the Enlightenment. Moreover, they insist that the practices and instinctive postures of Christendom, modernity and the Enlightenment are the wells from which inherited forms of the church continue to drink deeply. Intoxicated by the heady draught of privilege and protected status that these historical developments have afforded the church, buttressed by political patronage and social advantage, they argue that the institutional church is unable to comprehend or respond to a massive shift in the social, political and cultural landscape of the Western world. One of the most significant consequences of these transitions has been the relegation of the institutional church from the political and cultural centre to the cultural and political margins.

In 2006, Mike Frost, with his widely read *Exiles: Living Missionally in a Post-Christian Culture*, characterised this marginalisation as a form of exile. Indeed, he suggests that a move into exile might have to be self-imposed in some situations if an authentic gospel is to be rediscovered.

As a missiologist, I am interested to observe that an inauthentic reliance upon status and privilege has been a focus for missiological critique at least since the missiology of early missionary authors and practitioners such as Henry Venn (1796–1873),[1] Rufus Anderson (1796–1880),[2]

---

1   Venn, an Anglican CMS missionary, is regarded as the originator of the 'indigenous church' principle (self-supporting, self-governing and self-propagating).

2   Anderson was also an Anglican missionary, deeply committed to fostering indigenous expressions of church, who refused to rely on governmental sponsorship or support. He also insisted on prioritising the preaching of the gospel over civilisation, uncommon even among other missionaries of his day.

John Nevius (1829–1893)[3] and Roland Allen (1868–1947).[4] Each of these men espoused missionary forms of the indigenous church that were self-governing, self-supporting and self-propagating.

It is surprising then that most missional authors make only limited reference to the development of the work of these missionary authors within the practice of *cross-cultural* mission. Admittedly there is some use of their work as it is seen to be applicable to the missional conversation in a *Western* context, but little that can be said to represent a consistent treatment of cross-cultural mission. This is all the more surprising given the reasonably obvious observation that much of the Protestant missionary endeavour since the late eighteenth century onwards was engaged in an unresolved and ambiguous relationship with Western colonialism and the institutions of empire.

If mission was a form of exile, many missionaries in exile nevertheless appear to have been willing or unwilling accomplices in the civilising of the empire's new subjects. This tension can be clearly seen in the mission established by William Carey, the co-founder of the Baptist Missionary Society in 1792 and author of the moderate Calvinist missionary tract, *An Enquiry into the Obligation of Christians to Use Means for the Conversion of the Heathens*. Carey's mission, established in Serampore, reflects the ambiguities of the accommodation made by early Protestant missionaries to the institutions of colonial imperialism.

---

[3] Nevius was a Presbyterian missionary in China, then later in Korea, who developed the earlier work of Anderson and Venn. His development became known as the 'Nevius Plan' or the 'Nevius Method'.

[4] Roland Allen's book *Missionary Methods: St. Paul's Or Ours: A Study of the Church in the Four Provinces*, first published in 1912, continues to be read by students of mission theology.

RE-PLACING MISSION

William Carey: Missionary Exile and the Baggage of Empire

It is not difficult to portray Carey as a rather obsessed and driven individual. Smith describes him functioning 'as a metropolitan official who never traveled beyond the twelve-mile stretch between Serampore and Calcutta after 1799.' In addition to operating twenty printing presses,[5] earning money from contracts with the colonial authorities over a period of thirty years, Carey successfully solicited funds from overseas. Between 1800 and 1807 the total overseas donations to Carey's work of Bible translation amounted to £6,726, calculated at over £6.06 million in today's worth.[6]

Writing in 1873, the Secretary of State and Council of India wrote 'The labours of the foreign missionaries in India assume many forms.' He listed their duties as 'public preachers and pastors', educators, linguists and medical doctors. Primarily, however, he saw them as civilisers, 'infusing new vigour into the stereotyped life of the great populations placed under English rule ... preparing them to be in every way better men and better citizens of the great empire in which they dwell.'[7]

It *is* necessary to argue that the prodigious publishing activities of the Serampore mission were a contextualised attempt at bringing the gospel to India's peoples, particularly where illiteracy and education were felt to be an obstacle to the advance of the gospel. However, this observation underlies a potential critique of Carey; namely that he failed to adequately distinguish between the concepts and practices of colonial civilisation and those of Christian evangelisation.

The Many Faces of William Carey

In ranging views on either side, it is possible to portray Carey as entirely a man of his day, backed by a mission society, reliant upon colonial authorities, and informed by entrepreneurial endeavour. Our brief discussion in the

---

7   Sherring, 'Protestant Missions in India', 87.

preceding section offers such a portrait. Such a singular portrait does not, however, do justice to the complexities surrounding Carey and the Serampore mission. The former pastor, for example, demonstrates a social conscience with his personal embargo of the fruits of the sugar trade with the West Indies in the *Enquiry*. Carey's grasp of the gospel was broader than that of many contemporary evangelicals. It was his convictions as a social reformer that eased the manner in which he elided gospel, government, laws, arts and sciences. Carey wrote, 'Would not the spread of the gospel be the most effectual mean (sic) of their civilisation?' This relatively broad understanding of the nature of Christian mission prompts Brian Stanley[8] to suggest that the *Enquiry* should be read as an 'Enlightenment rationale'.

If this is indeed the case, then we can surmise that Carey's Enlightenment convictions allied to his understanding of the gospel gave rise to his criticisms of the colonial institutions. Carey appears to use a form of anti-Establishment rhetoric in the *Enquiry* that would have been rather obvious to the Anglican and colonial authorities in Bengal. The British East India Company had been extending British rule over India since the early 1600s. Carey pulled few punches about the fact that in England 'episcopal tyranny succeeded to popish cruelty' and that overseas, for example, 'the missions to the Spice Islands, sent by the Dutch East India Company, were soon corrupted [by] temporal gain'. In practice, Carey and the Baptist missionaries managed to cooperate more effectively with other mission societies than they did with the chaplains of the East India Company and frequently provoked the ire of the company itself.

Carey understood himself as insignificant, vulnerable and lacking support. Announcing the formation of the London Missionary Society, in 1795, reference was made to Carey being 'a preacher on the banks of the Ganges.' Such imagery evokes that of the psalmist in Psalm 138, in which the Jewish exiles hang their harps on the branches of the trees

---

8   Stanley, 'Christian Missions and the Enlightenment', 14.

and, on the banks of the Babylon, sing their laments of exile. These themes occur throughout his many letters, and it is possible to read his letters as narratives of exile.

Exiles and the Marginalisation of Cross-Cultural Mission

This brief case study of Carey's cross-cultural mission is important for my investigation of the exile theme because I am, after all, a missiologist with intercultural convictions, and this is a noticeably absent theme from the missional literature. More to the point, Carey's cross-cultural mission displays many of the characteristics of the church as a Christendom project. Michael Frost, in over three hundred pages of *Exile*, makes only scant reference to cross-cultural mission. His is a book about the church in internal exile (even 'self-imposed' exile), not a church sent into external exile. A summary of *Exiles* might imply that the missionary God is primarily active in the West, and in Western *cities* at that, in which 'third places' serve as a missional alternative to cross-cultural places. An intriguing reference to 'crossing the ocean' in mission is used only in a metaphorical sense.

Frost discusses cross-cultural mission as a form of exile with his references to the New Testament practices of the early church. He describes the 'travelling missionary community of disciples' as one with a missionary mandate to be a people on the move, exemplified in the apostle Paul's missionary journeys. As models for contemporary cross-cultural missionary practice, however, these remain relatively underexamined. *Exiles* offers only two examples of cross-cultural mission. The first is a reference to cross-cultural mission to Sudan by ethnic Sudanese from the US and, secondly, the example of the Chinese 'Back to Jerusalem' mission movement is showcased in the most extended account of cross-cultural mission in Frost's book.

In practice, his missional writing largely reflects the Western contexts in which he has ministered. The consequence of this relative absence is that cross-cultural, global mission is left to languish at the margins of the missional conversation, barely surviving there as an embarrassing relic of a bygone era when the church global was triumphant and dominant. Some legacies, it seems, are best left undiscussed.

Spatial Metaphors for Mission

Mission and the Metaphor of 'Exile'

Frost uses the metaphor of exile as a way of conceiving the orientation of the contemporary church and its mission towards a Western, post-Christian context. In doing so, Frost adopts a metaphor of location or place; a 'spatial metaphor', if you like. His metaphor makes reference to the Old Testament experiences of God's OT people in Babylon, the example of Jesus's incarnation, but also makes reference, among other sources, to the anthropology of Victor Turner and Turner's concept of 'liminality' and his application of this to 'liminal' states and 'liminal' places. This underlies Frost's intuition that exile is a transitional or temporary state, located at the intersection of the former things and those which are yet to come.

For Frost, this experience of exile is characterised by 'uncharted territory', 'critical distance from our context', 'sharing a table with the marginalised and the despised', an intentional experience of 'authentic community', the service of others, the struggle with injustice, the care of creation, a resistance to the idols of empire, and a hope-filled singing of the dangerous songs of God in the midst of a hostile empire and its people.

The use of spatial metaphors associated with mission has merit, Frost calls for the church to be re-positioned and he is not alone in doing so. The capacity of metaphor for enabling imaginative comprehension and

reinvention of missional practices cannot be underestimated. In practice, such images remain incredibly durable. Several are introduced here:
- Mission and the metaphor of 'frontier'
- Mission and the metaphor of 'margins' and 'the marketplace'
- Mission and the metaphor of 'sites of rupture'.

Each metaphor, in its own way, adds to a more adequate reimagining of mission. These things are central to the task of reimagining missiology in each new context. This concern is central to the recent work of Michael Stroope.

Exilic Option for Missiology?

Michael Stroope's 2017 book, *Transcending Mission*, represents an attempt by a Baptist theologian of mission to deconstruct the rhetoric of 'mission' and 'missionary'.[9] His primary motivation for deconstructing these terms is that 'mission' and its cognate 'missionary' are located firmly within the linguistic and conceptual domain of modernity and that, moreover, this association compromises their utility. In other words, their reliance upon the discourses of modernity leaves them fatally discredited in the face of the contemporary situations that the gospel must learn to engage in new ways. Stroope's critical stance towards both modernity and the Christendom origins of the language of 'mission' finds, as noted above, its reflection in the work of Frost and other missional authors.

Stroope's critical project gains momentum with his rejection of Bosch's delineation of the expansion of the church into six historical paradigms. Stroope collapses these six into just two periods: pre-modernity and modernity (emerging during the seventeenth century). He argues that the rhetoric of *mission* and *missionary* is firmly associated

---

9   Stroope, *Transcending Mission: The Eclipse of a Modern Tradition*. Stroope is a former missionary serving with the International Mission Board of the Southern Baptist Convention, USA, and now Professor of Missions at Truett Seminary, Baylor University.

with 'colonialization and Western imperialism' and that Protestants were initially reluctant to use it because of its introduction into Roman Catholic practice by the Jesuits. Protestants took tentative steps towards embracing this new language for Christian witness outside of Europe, with the earliest examples being the Royal Danish-Halle Mission (1704), the Moravians (1732) and, later, William Carey (1792). Stroope expresses deep reservations about the rhetoric of mission for a number of related reasons, including the inability of missiologists to arrive at a consensus definition of what they are describing. He engages just as critically with the related terms *missio Dei* and *missional*, suggesting rather that the use of missional is the most problematic of the terms and is viewed by him as ultimately an 'emblem for real, evangelical, or orthodox Christianity. As such it is the least helpful of mission-related terms'.[10]

The rhetoric of *missionary* is also problematic for him because it suffers from definitional confusion. Missiological literature offers multiple, occasionally contradictory, alternatives. On the one hand it may refer to a class of religious professional. Alternatively, it may be a term used to describe all Christians. Equally it may be used as an adjective that has, in his view, come to mean little more than Christian 'zeal or enthusiasm for any task or cause'.[11]

In the face of these challenges, Stroope believes we must discover new ways of conceiving the church's encounter with the world, identifying new language that more adequately 'expresses the church's being and activity for the time in which we live'.[12] According to him, 'The rhetorical practices that frame "What mission has been" must be honestly and courageously examined'.[13]

A first glance at Stroope's work might leave one wondering whether he has anything constructive to add to our discussion of our exilic theme. He is certainly relevant in his critical engagement with modernity and the extent to which he feels this period invests the rhetoric of mission and missionary with their colonialist and orientalist overtones. This type of argumentation is actually wholly commensurate with Frost's approach in *Exiles*, at least to the extent that Frost is also engaged critically with the ecclesial legacy of modernity.

Stroope's preference of 'pilgrim witness to the kingdom of God' in place of 'mission' is developed with explicit reference to the closely related metaphor of exile, using language such as 'dislocation', 'displacement, expulsion, and separation', and the 'homeless wanderer'. He continues that we need to see 'ourselves as we actually are—desperate exiles in need of rescue'.[14]

Stroope concludes that, biblically, followers of Jesus are called to 'live as pilgrims who give witness to the coming reign of God. They are not called *missionaries* and their life purpose is not named as *mission*. To supplant the structures of thought expressed in Scripture with the language of a modern tradition is to underestimate the power of God's kingdom to change the world through witness and pilgrims'.[15]

Some Initial Responses to Stroope

The Problematic Metaphor of 'Kingdom'

Just as *missio Dei* language has been filled with a bewildering array of competing images and orientations, the rhetoric of the kingdom of God is susceptible to partisan presentation and representation. 'Kingdom' rhetoric recalls an archaic, medieval form of sovereignty that is long outdated and uniformly criticised by postcolonial theologians. That Stroope should rely upon this form of rhetoric, without careful qualification or modification, is intriguing and less than consistent with his critical approach to 'mission'.

---

14   Stroope, *Transcending Mission*, 373.
15   Stroope, *Transcending Mission*, 376.

It seems ironic, particularly when there are post-colonial and Anabaptist theologians who offer the alternatives of 'reign' or 'realm' to translate the Greek *basilea*.

Moreover, the concept of 'kingdom' has found service at the hands of a bewildering range of Christian traditions and theologies; liberationist, charismatic, Roman Catholic, progressive, conservative, fundamentalist, mainline Protestant, and evangelical. The vision, character and program of the alleged coming 'kingdom' reflects the variety and diversity of the theological and denominational traditions engaged in staking a claim upon the concept.

The Problematic Metaphor of 'Pilgrim'

One wonders what realities this metaphor is pointing towards. Somebody who travels from NE India to work for a mission agency in Central China is not a pilgrim—at least, not in the sense that is typically accepted. A commonsense usage of the term 'pilgrim' suggests a journey from one place to another for the purposes of spiritual discovery or enlightenment, not the journey from one place to another for the sake of making disciples, for another's conversion. One wonders whether perhaps the real issue at stake for Stroope is the validity of a journey undertaken for the sake of the salvation, transformation and the discipling of others, in another place, who are not yet followers of Jesus.

The Problematic Metaphor of Witness

Stroope's use of 'witness' is offered as something that defines identity, it is who the believer is understood to be, rather than the use of 'missionary' which points to what the believer is expected to do. This is disingenuous, overlooking or ignoring the common usage and understanding of 'missionary' as something that defines who the individual believer understands themselves to be, and not merely a reference to their role or what they do.

If one were choosing to extend the same level of critique as Stroope, it would be possible to advance similar arguments to those which Stroope advances concerning the language of 'mission' and 'missionary', and to do so with the discourse of 'theology' or 'theologian'. A cursory historical review might suggest that 'theologians' and 'theology' were as devastating for the peoples of Europe as were 'missionaries' and 'mission' for the peoples of the colonised world. Moreover, 'theology' is not a biblical term and the use of the terminology of 'theology', at least in its current academic form, only appears in the fourteenth century.[16] Stroope is silent on this matter.

Re-placing Mission

In short, my response to Stroope is to affirm, with him, the need to 'displace' or 're-place' mission. My hyphenation suggests the possibility that mission can be relocated (conceptually and in practice) to another place, rather than displacing the language itself. This can be done with a genuine appreciation for Stroope's insistence that language itself profoundly shapes our capacity to comprehend and describe.[17]

Whether one uses 'exile', 'sites of rupture', 'frontier', 'margins', or 'public marketplace', these are all pointers to the sense that mission is inextricably bound up with place or 'distance'. That place might be our place or another's place, and it might be a geographical, cultural, social, or other form of 'place'.

It might be helpful and biblically more faithful to view 'witness' as the common currency of the history of the expansion of the Christian

---

16   See the note to the entry 'Theology' in the Oxford English Dictionary.
17   Stroope, *Transcending Mission*, 376.

church (following Stroope) into 'other' places. If this is so, and I am not unsympathetic to this view,[18] 'mission' can be critiqued as a form of witness that has generated and perpetuated misunderstanding and 'malpractice'. However, I am not sure that the flawed operation of 'mission' by 'missionaries' wholly invalidates it as a contextual, contemporary, and appropriate, way of referring to apostolicity and apostolic practices.[19]

As I've attempted to show, a more nuanced account of, for example, Carey's Serampore Mission, points to the ambiguities in the modern missionary endeavour, particularly in the relationship of missionaries to the colonial authorities. From the outset, the apostolic leaders and practices of the early church also had to negotiate an appropriate civil and political space in which to operate. Was the apostle Paul's appeal to Caesar little more than a pragmatic accommodation to the imperial rule, or was it an intentional journey of pilgrimage, undertaken willingly in order to advance the kingdom? There is certainly ambiguity in how we interpret Paul's decision. This same ambiguity is seen in his reliance upon imperial Roman rule, whilst, at the same time, the churches he established subvert it with their use of the imperial title 'Lord' for Jesus the Messiah.

Exilic Apostolicity

John Flett, in *Apostolicity*, points to the apostolic nature of the church as a witnessing community that must necessarily cross ethnic, cultural, linguistic and other divides (which might include the modern construct of the borders of a nation-state). This notion of apostolicity is certainly as 'biblical' as Stroope's use of 'witness' and 'kingdom of God' but it might be a preferable and more fruitful exercise to fill out the discourse of 'apostolic'

---

18 The redefinition of mission should certainly include the acknowledgement that witness belongs to everyone, for every believer, in every place, is called to a witness.

19 See the argument advanced by John Flett, for example in *Apostolicity: The Ecumenical Question in World Christian Perspective*.

and 'apostolicity' in a more concrete, comprehensive and coherent manner than one can do with 'witness'. Flett's reconceptualisation of 'apostolicity' within conciliar and evangelical Protestant discourses of mission is a huge achievement. When evangelical mission leaders and theologians met together in Cape Town in 2010, the conference statement was a radical development of earlier Lausanne mission statements. The 2010 mission conference statement, *The Cape Town Commitment*, reframed evangelical mission theology and practice with reference to the biblical commandments to 'love God' and 'love neighbour' (Matt 22:34–40).[20] A constructive theological approach to reconceiving evangelical mission would adopt the ethical imperative of 'love' as the motivation for apostolic practices that necessitate inviting others, in other places, to live lives conformed to the teaching of Jesus as a consequence of personal faith and baptism into a community of faith (Matt 28:18–20).

This leads me to a tentative conclusion that, rather than introducing the discourse of 'pilgrimage', if there is to be a re-placing of mission that retains an appropriate sense of the exilic, then it is preferable to reconceive of mission as that set of loving, apostolic practices that constitute and define the community of faith in each and every place.

12

AN ENDLESSLY CUNNING, RISKY PROCESS OF NEGOTIATION

MICHAEL FROST

In the lead up to Christmas 2017, Queensland National Party politician, Bob Katter, was filmed by Channel 7 Brisbane sending a greeting to his constituents. After naming a number of the towns and cities in his electorate, he concluded with a rousing, 'Joy to the world, the Lord has come. And we don't have to die. That's the important message'.

Maybe it was because he was caught on the spot, but in his unique way, Mr. Katter managed to conjoin lines from both *Joy to the World* and *Hark! The Herald Angels Sing* into one ham-fisted salutation, assuming 'And we don't have to die' was an allusion to 'Born that man no more may die'. Interestingly, when Channel 7 posted the link to his greeting on social media they did so with the following comment: 'Bob Katter's bizarre Christmas message—complete and uncut'. Bizarre, they called it. Admittedly, Mr. Katter's greeting might have sounded strange to a journalist or social commentator with no real understanding of the most basic tenets of the Christian faith. If you have no frame of reference for the public statements of Christian leaders or politicians, you are going to find a Christmas greeting celebrating salvation in Christ to be bizarre. But the fact that the social media manager at a major news outlet didn't even recognise the references to well-known Christmas carols in the lead up to Christmas is illustrative of the contemporary Australian religious landscape. The Christian story, along with its associated language, phraseology, allusions and themes, is completely unknown by many Australians today.

Church attendance rates continue to fall in this country. The fastest growing category in the religion section of the Australian census over the past fifty years has been 'No religion', up from just 0.8 percent in the 1960s to 30 percent in 2016. Christianity is increasingly being seen as irrelevant.

Not only are basic Christian beliefs a mystery to many, but worse, the church is seen as an insidious or malevolent force in society. After the recent revelations of the Royal Commission into Institutional Responses to Child Sexual Abuse, many of which reflected badly on all of the major denominations, as well as the perception that the church was being homophobic by resisting calls for changes in the legislation regarding marriage, the church's reputation has been greatly eroded.

German Jesuit scholar, Hans Zollner, reflected on the Royal Commission after visiting Australia recently and said that he felt Australians have completely lost trust in the church: 'There seems to be almost nil trust in what the church says. This is not true in other parts of the world. I think you are in a pretty unique situation'.[1]

In the aftermath of the same-sex marriage postal vote, won decisively by the Yes campaign, many church leaders began waging a second campaign to ensure that their religious freedoms (not to be forced to perform same-sex weddings) were preserved, which led some commentators to suggest that the church was being self-interested, a sore loser. The *Sydney Morning Herald* ran a story that read, '... if we are going to turn over some rocks in a

---

[1] Bowling, 'Australians Have Lost Trust'.

debate on religious freedom, we may see a greater need for freedom from religion, not freedom of religion'.[2]

Lyndon Bowring, Executive Chairman of CARE, said in a recent interview, 'The greatest challenge ... is the growing secularization of society, where Christianity is being increasingly squeezed out of our national life. The ultimate result of this tendency will be a society that is hostile to Christian truth and practice'.[3]

It's clear, as the title of this volume suggests, that we're not in Kansas anymore.

The Emergence of Post-Christendom

There are various terms used to describe this new era the church is currently having to navigate—the post-Christian era, the secular age, post-Constantinianism, post-Christendom. In his book, *After Christendom*, Stuart Murray defines it as 'the culture that emerges as the Christian faith loses coherence within a society that has been definitively shaped by the Christian story and as the institutions that have been developed to express Christian convictions decline in influence'.[4] Alan Roxburgh characterises the post-Christendom era as a period without a philosophical/theological centre that results in the perceived marginalisation of the church in the West.[5] This certainly describes the reality that the Australian church is facing today. But Murray also points out that many church leaders are not yet willing or able to recognise the gravity of the current situation and continue to operate as though society is still basically shaped by the Christian story. He identifies some of what he sees as the last vestiges of the Christendom mindset in the church today, including:

---

2   Hill, 'Marriage Quality'.
3   Chester and Timmis, *Everyday Church*, 20.
4   Murray, *Post-Christendom*, 11.
5   Roxburgh, *Missionary Congregation*, 12–16.

- Orientation towards maintaining (but perhaps tweaking) the status quo rather than advocating radical and disturbing change;
- Overemphasising church and internal ecclesial issues at the expense of God's mission and kingdom;
- Disgruntlement that Christian festivals (particularly Christmas and Easter) are no longer accorded the spiritual significance they once enjoyed;
- Predilection for large congregations that support a 'professional' standard of ministry and exercise influence on local power structures;
- Approaches to evangelism that rely excessively on 'come' rather than 'go' initiatives;
- Assuming churchgoing is normal social activity and that most people feel comfortable in church buildings and services;
- Attitudes towards church buildings that imply these are the focal points of God's presence.[6]

That said, Stuart Murray doesn't see this as all bad. He says we can 'celebrate the end of Christendom and the distorting influence of power, wealth and status on the Christian story'.[7] And Douglas John Hall more colourfully puts it this way:

> *If we once have the courage to give up our defence of the old facades which have nothing or very little behind them; if we cease to maintain, in public, the pretence of a universal Christendom; if we stop straining every nerve to get* everybody *baptised, to get* everybody *married in church and onto our registers (even when success means only, at bottom, a victory for tradition, custom and ancestry, not for true faith and interior conviction); if, by letting go, we visibly relieve Christianity of the burdensome*

---

6   Murray, *Post-Christendom*, 201–3.
7   Murray, *Post-Christendom*, 21.

> *impression that it accepts responsibility for everything that goes on under this Christian top-dressing, the impression that Christianity is a sort of Everyman's Religious Varnish, a folk-religion (at the same level as that of folk-costumes)—then we can be free for real missionary adventure and apostolic self-confidence.*[8]

I have echoed these views in my 2003 book, *The Shaping of Things to Come*, co-authored with Alan Hirsch:

> *Taken as a socio-political reality, Christendom has been in decline for the last 250 years, so much so that contemporary Western culture has been called by many historians (secular and Christian) as the post-Christendom culture. Society, at least in its overtly Christian manifestation, is 'over' Christendom. But this is not the case within the Western church itself. Christendom, as a paradigm of understanding, as a metanarrative, still exercises an overweening influence on our existing theological, missiological, and ecclesiological understandings in church circles. In other words, we still think of the church and its mission in terms of Christendom. While in reality we are in a post-Christendom context, the Western church still operates for the most part in a Christendom mode. Constantine, it seems, is still the emperor of our imaginations.*[9]

The point we were making in *The Shaping of Things to Come* was that this Constantinian imagination, entrenched for hundreds of years, led to mainstream churches being primarily 'attractional' in their stance towards the receptive outsider.[10] Much contemporary evangelistic enterprise is, in practice, recruitment for churches still operating with the increasingly outdated patterns of Christian expectation and church life inherited from Christendom's past. Other missional church writers also identified the

---

8   Hall, 'Metamorphosis', 67.
9   Frost and Hirsch, *Shaping of Things*, 9.
10 Frost and Hirsch, *Shaping of Things*, 18–21.

AN ENDLESSLY CUNNING, RISKY PROCESS OF NEGOTIATION

demise of Christendom as an opportunity for the church to rediscover itself as a mission movement rather than an institutional religion. In *The Missional Church*, Darrell Guder states:

> The obvious fact that what we once regarded as Christendom is now a post-Constantinian, post-Christendom, and even post-Christian mission field stands in bold contrast today with the apparent lethargy of established church traditions in addressing their situation both creatively and faithfully. Yet this helpfully highlights the need for and providential appearance of a theological revolution in missional thinking that centres the body of Christ on God's mission rather than post-Christendom's concern for the church's institutional maintenance.[11]

Marginalised or Exiled?

As we noted from Stuart Murray earlier, some Christians are adjusting to this new normal more quickly than others. While Murray, Hall and Guder see great opportunity in the newly marginal status of the church in the West, Alan Roxburgh believes that the church's self-definition as a marginalised people is unhelpful because it propels the church towards either the challenge of recovering the centre or defining a new marginal existence. He prefers that the churches 'see their current situation and reflect appropriately on how they may reconfigure their life for mission in late modernity'.[12] In this respect, he is anxious about the church's attempt to reassert its political influence as we've seen in recent US presidential elections, or to withdraw entirely to the margins, hunkering down until a new day dawns, as some proponents of the so-called Benedict Option have advocated.

---

11   Guder, *Missional Church*, 7.
12   Roxburgh, *Missionary Congregation*, 22.

In light of these sociopolitical realities, some people are suggesting the biblical metaphor of *exile* is a helpful way to understand the church's current challenge. Writers like Walter Brueggemann, Patrick Whitworth, Lee Beach, Richard John Neuhaus, and this author, have explored the possibility that we could learn from the experience of Israel's Babylonian exile to help traverse this new post-Christian territory. Foremost among those writing in this area is Old Testament scholar Walter Brueggemann, who first raised the *exile* metaphor as a way to describe the contemporary situation of the church in his book *Hopeful Imagination*. Likewise, in his book, *To Change the World*, James Davison Hunter says the church faces a situation similar to that of the Jews in Babylon 2500 years ago: 'Ours is now, emphatically, a post-Christian culture, and the community of Christian believers are now, more than ever—spiritually speaking—exiles in a land of exile'.[13]

Brueggemann makes the case that a robust biblical and practical theology rooted in both the Old Testament and New Testament visions of exile can inform the contemporary church's self-understanding and mission. In his treatment of that metaphor in *Cadences of Home*, he develops a fourfold framework for understanding the way that the Hebrew exiles sustained their faith during exile in Babylon—(a) recalling their history of release from bondage in Egypt, (b) working for the good of the foreign city, (c) offering a daring critique of the Babylonian empire, and (d) recounting the prophetic hope of freedom and the restoration of Israel.[14] In my book, *Exiles*, I used Brueggemann's framework as the outline for my examination of living in a post-Christendom world,[15] by appropriating his fourfold approach to frame the four sections of *Exiles*.[16] It was my contention

---

13 Hunter, *Change the World*, 280.
14 Brueggemann, *Cadences of Home*, 134.
15 Frost, *Exiles*, 11.
16 'Dangerous Memories', 3–80; 'Dangerous Promises', 81–202; 'Dangerous Criticism', 203–74; and 'Dangerous Songs', 275–324 in Frost, *Exiles*.

AN ENDLESSLY CUNNING, RISKY PROCESS OF NEGOTIATION

that the church could find hope and purpose in post-Christendom by embracing a number of commitments:

- Acknowledging the new reality of our situation and embracing our status as an alternative community. In Exiles, I wrote: 'I suspect that the increasing marginalisation of the Christian movement in the West is the very thing that will wake us up to the marvellously exciting, dangerous, and confronting message of Jesus. If we are exiles on foreign soil—post-Christendom, postmodern, postliterate, and so on—then maybe at last it's time to start living like exiles, as a pesky, fringe-dwelling alternative to the dominant forces of our times'.[17]
- Refocusing our attention on our history as the redeemed society of God in order to counter the idea that our currently marginal status is some kind of punishment from God.
- Finding direction in our resolve to work for the good of society, to do, as Jeremiah counselled the Hebrew exiles, and seek the peace and prosperity of the city (Jer 29:7).
- Recounting our future, convinced of the kingship of Jesus and the certainty of his return, responding in worship and joy, and being committed to being, as Lesslie Newbigin described it, 'a sign, instrument and foretaste of God's redeeming grace for the whole life of society'.[18]

All four of these commitments can be found at the heart of the so-called Newbiginian project, the agenda of missional leaders around the world to embrace the vision of Lesslie Newbigin, to practice a faithful presence in a post-Christendom world. As Newbigin himself wrote:

---

17 Frost, *Exiles*, 10.
18 Newbigin, *Pluralist Society*, 233.

> *If the gospel is to challenge the public life of our society, if Christians are to occupy the 'high ground' which they vacated in the noon time of 'modernity', it will not be by forming a Christian political party, or by aggressive propaganda campaigns. Once again it has to be said that there can be no going back to the 'Constantinian' era. It will only be by movements that begin with the local congregation in which the reality of the new creation is present, known, and experienced, and from which men and women will go into every sector of public life to claim it for Christ, to unmask the illusions which have remained hidden and to expose all areas of public life to the illumination of the gospel.*[19]

Returning to Stuart Murray, his recommended response to the challenges of post-Christendom is for the church to see itself moving along various trajectories:

- From the centre to the margins: In Christendom, the Christian story and the clergy were central to European society, occupying a structurally guaranteed position in the decision-making process, and able to contribute to the shape of society's values and mores. In post-Christendom, the church finds itself increasingly at the margins of society;
- From majority to minority: In Christendom, the majority of the European population identified as Christians, whether devoted or not. Today, in Europe and Australia, Christians are in the minority, and continuing to shrink;
- From settlers to sojourners: In Christendom, the church was thoroughly at home in a culture shaped by its story, but in post-Christendom, Christians find they are more like aliens, exiles and pilgrims in an increasingly foreign culture;

---

19   Newbigin, *Pluralist Society*, 232.

- From privilege to plurality: In Christendom, the church enjoyed the status of most-favoured religion, including government funding, tax breaks, access to schools, opportunities for launching cultural initiatives, and more. Today, many of these privileges are being removed or openly questioned;
- From control to witness: In Christendom, clergy could exert some measure of control over the culture, or at the very least voice their displeasure openly and freely. But in post-Christendom, they are having to learn how to exercise influence more relationally and sensitively, through service to others and witness;
- From maintenance to mission: In Christendom, a privileged and wealthy church found itself seeking to maintain the status quo, but in post-Christendom, the church has been rediscovering its mission within a contested environment;
- From institution to movement: In Christendom, the church had the wherewithal to operate as one of the great institutions of society. Today, while many of the vestiges of institutional religion remain, some in the church are calling for it to become again a Christian movement.[20]

No Place for Exile?

That being said, there are some who object to the use of *exile* as a metaphor for the church's current place in Western society. In her 2016 article, *No Place for Exile*, Kate Harrison Brennan dismissed the metaphor, not only as unhelpful, but as damaging:

> *When Christians believe that they are in exile in Western societies, contrary to the evidence of our position and power, it points to the fact*

---

20   Summarised from Murray, *Post-Christendom*, 11–12.

that Christians are experiencing a collapse in sense-making. The effects, if not remedied, will be disastrous for Christian witness, and for society.[21]

While acknowledging some of the similarities between Israel's experience of exile and the contemporary church's situation, Harrison Brennan believes the differences are too great for a simple use of the metaphor. She argues that, although the church is declining in size, it has shaped the majority culture in the West in a way the Israelites could never have dreamed of in Babylon. Harrison Brennan seems to believe that the adoption of an exilic self-definition makes no sense in the midst of a culture the church helped to create, and that it will lead the church to wallow in despair and lose any sense of their mission in post-Christendom. Harrison Brennan says, 'it is not only poor biblical theology, it is disingenuous and profoundly hazardous to the Church and its mission'.[22]

David Congdon, writing in the wake of the US Supreme Court's *Obergefell v. Hodges* decision to legalise same-sex marriage, a decisive moment wherein conservative evangelicals came to believe they were no longer at home in the United States, also rejects the use of the *exile* metaphor. Reacting particularly to conservatives such as Rod Dreher and Russell Moore and their use of the idea of exile-as-rejection, Congdon sounds a warning that the metaphor could lead to an unhealthy posture of separatism. In his article, *No, the American Church Isn't 'in Exile'*, he makes the point that from the beginning 'the church is not a separate community with its own culture',[23] which it then either spreads to others (imperialism) or into which others assimilate to become a distinct community (separatism). He continues,

> *The power of Christianity is found in what scholars of mission call its capacity for contextualisation, which means that the message of Christ*

---

21   Harrison Brennan, 'No Place for Exile'.
22   Harrison Brennan, 'No Place for Exile'.
23   Congdon, 'American Church'.

> can be translated into different languages, cultures, and contexts. According to Lamin Sanneh, the Gambian missiologist and professor at Yale Divinity School, the Gospel comes 'without a revealed language or a founding original culture', and therefore 'all cultural forms ... are in principle worthy of bearing the truth of Christianity'. Christians today who adopt an exilic identity have abandoned this dimension of Christianity. They are giving up on the contextualisation principle. For them, contemporary American culture is enemy territory, and the only recourse is to retreat into a separate cultural community.[24]

We shouldn't consider ourselves in exile, says Congdon, because we have no particular land or territory to be exiled *from*. For the Christian, the whole earth is a foreign land, to which we have been sent to make disciples of all nations, not to impose our home culture on them, but to incarnate the gospel within whichever host culture we find ourselves in.

While I can acknowledge the objections Congdon raises, it is important to point out that a metaphor is a figure of speech. It is not literally applicable. And, like all metaphors, that of the exile can only go some of the way in describing the church's situation today. *Exile* has been helpful in alerting church leaders to the fact that the world has changed and a new cultural reality has replaced it. But recent cultural and political shifts around the definition of marriage in both the US and Australia have led some evangelicals to use *exile* to explain their increasing marginalisation from mainstream values, and the church's need to retreat into alternate redeemed societies. However, it should also be noted that those of us writing about exile prior to 2015 (*Obergefell v. Hodges*) did not anticipate that the metaphor would be used so stridently to advocate separatism and retreat. In fact, quite the reverse. We saw the words of Jeremiah to the Hebrew exiles, as well as the examples of such exiles as Joseph, Daniel and

---

24   Congdon, 'American Church'.

Esther, as exhortations to make ourselves at home in whichever 'Babylon' we find ourselves in.

Far from using the metaphor to foster separatist communities, as Harrison Brennan and Congdon fear, we saw exiles like Joseph and Daniel as magnificent examples of how to be *in* Egypt/Babylon, but not *of* them. Like the Jewish exiles, the church today is grieving its loss of influence in society and struggling with a sense of humiliation. The ground has slipped out from under the church. She has lost her footing and needs, as Brueggemann puts it, to express an honest sadness about what was and now is not and may never again be Western civilisation.[25]

Exiles can feel like a 'motherless child', that is, abandoned, rootless, vulnerable, orphaned. Brueggemann cites such biblical material as Lamentations as expressing the honest sadness of an exilic people. But he also warns that the danger in exile is to become so preoccupied with self that one cannot step outside oneself to rethink, reimagine, and redescribe larger reality. Such self-preoccupation very rarely produces energy, courage or freedom. What exiles yearn for is an invitation to live 'freely, dangerous and tenaciously in a world where faith does not always have its own way'.[26] And here lies the root of the problem of the church today. Victimised by nostalgia and buffeted by fear, the church is focused too much on merely holding the small plot of ground it currently occupies to confidently reimagine a robust future. The result is a retreat into some fundamentalist us-versus-them model, rather than 'an endlessly cunning, risky process of negotiation'.[27]

Interestingly, the alternative metaphors offered by Harrison Brennan and by Congdon don't really differ much from the suggestions made by Walter Brueggemann or Lee Beach or myself when we were

---

25 Brueggemann, *Cadences of Home*, 4.
26 Brueggemann, *Cadences of Home*, 10.
27 Brueggemann, *Cadences of Home*, 11.

AN ENDLESSLY CUNNING, RISKY PROCESS OF NEGOTIATION

writing about exile. Referencing Jeremiah 29:7, Harrison Brennan utilises the metaphor of the *garden*, saying the church should:

> *situate ourselves firmly in local community ... and to bind our good to the good of our neighbour and city through active investment and prayer. This has to be where we plant ourselves as individuals, families and as the Church, putting down roots for the long term, and seeking creative ways to move amid and among those who think the city or the nation represents supreme authority.*[28]

Back in 2006, I could have written that line myself.

Likewise, David Congdon says:

> *The church needs to abandon talk of exile, and reclaim the possibility of being at home. Home is the cultural context within which the church already exists. Reclaiming home does not mean uncritically adopting whatever seems fashionable at the time. It means approaching cultural changes and developments with an attitude of openness and hospitality, with a readiness to embrace rather than exclude. Reclaiming home means obeying the biblical injunction to live wholly without fear or anxiety.*[29]

But this is exactly the place to which Jeremiah calls the Hebrew exiles and the advice given by many of us advocating for the use of exile. The exiles were invited to make a home for themselves, to plant gardens, on foreign soil, just as the church is called to do the same on all foreign soil, wherever God sends us. While Harrison Brennan and Congdon might take issue with the metaphor, they end up in precisely the same place that many of us have been calling the church to for decades.

---

28   Harrison Brennan, 'No Place for Exile'.
29   Congdon, 'American Church'.

MICHAEL FROST

An Endlessly Cunning, Risky Process

David Congdon calls the church to take up the 'contextualisation principle', believing any talk of exile will lead to us abandoning such a principle. But I believe that the metaphor, when understood properly, actually invites us into the 'endlessly cunning, risky process of negotiation' that Daniel was required to undertake while in exile in Babylon. Far from allowing us to wallow in self-pity, as Harrison Brennan fears, the metaphor of exile reminds us that we are a people on the move.

An illustration of this can be found in Stanley Hauerwas's book, *A Community of Character*. There he exegetes Richard Adams's charming tale about travelling rabbits, *Watership Down*.[30] Adams's much-loved book concerns Fiver, a small nervous rabbit, who develops a messianic hunch that something terrible is going to happen to their Sandleford warren. Fiver tells his brother Hazel and they try to warn their aging Chief Rabbit without success. Hazel and Fiver, marginalised as doomsayers, decide they must leave, and are joined by other rabbits with such strange names as Bigwig, Dandelion, Pipkin, Hawkbit, Blackberry, Buckthorn, Speedwell, Acorn and Silver. As they make their timely escape, their warren is destroyed by a housing developer's bulldozers. There is now no turning back.

So, the little band takes off across the countryside in search of a new home, Watership Down. As they make their escape they must court many great dangers, the likes of which rabbits never encounter. They must cross a stream, traverse a bean field and negotiate an open road. These are obstacles that rabbits must never normally approach. Everything within the DNA of a rabbit tells it to stop running, to dig deep into the cool, cool earth. Every rabbit's instinct is to hide underground. For Fiver and Hazel and their band to continue across the fox-infested open fields, they must countermand their every natural impulse. How are they to do it? The

---

30 Hauerwas, *Community of Character*, 8–16.

AN ENDLESSLY CUNNING, RISKY PROCESS OF NEGOTIATION

answer lies in a surprising quarter. The one thing that unites the band and fills them with courage are the stories they retell themselves, stories they heard as babies at their parents' knees. These stories all concern the clever rabbit folk hero El-ahrairah. The first such story told in *Watership Down* is the story of the 'Blessing of El-ahrairah'.

This story is the account of Frith, the god of the rabbits, allocating gifts to each of the species. In the story, each of the animals receives the characteristics for which we know them—the fox receives cunning, for the cat, eyes that can see in the dark, and so on. El-ahrairah is too busy dancing, eating and mating, and misses out on the best gifts. Realising that rabbits will now be at the mercy of all the other gifted creatures, Frith grants him strong hind legs for escaping and declares that all the world will be the enemy of rabbits. He declares El-ahrairah to be the prince with a thousand enemies and pronounces, 'But first they must catch you, digger, listener, runner, prince with the swift warning. Be cunning and full of tricks and your people will never be destroyed'.[31] Such a story explains to Fiver and Hazel and the others the reason for their very being. It is their creation story and El-ahrairah is their hero. This story is more than a simple explanation for why rabbits have strong hind legs; it describes the rabbits' task in life. It is not to try to make the world safe, but rather to learn to live in a dangerous world by trusting in stories, speed, wit and in each other. Says Hauerwas:

> *I suspect it is not accidental that this is the first story told by the rabbits that left Sandleford, as all new communities must remind themselves of their origin. A people are formed by a story which places their history in the texture of the world. Such stories make the world our home by providing us with the skills to negotiate the dangers in our environment in a manner appropriate to our nature.*[32]

---

31 Adams, *Watership Down*, 37.
32 Hauerwas, *Community of Character*, 15.

What keeps the rabbits running, searching for their new home? It is the stories of Elahrairah; their dangerous memories. These stories fill them with courage and provide them with answers for the dilemmas posed by life on the road. Whenever the rabbits are confronted by a challenge, they stop and rehearse the stories of their folk hero, the prince with a thousand enemies. They are, as Hauerwas refers to them, a story-formed community, and it is the stories that spur them on, driving them forward to the safety of Watership Down.

So too the Jewish exiles in Babylon and the Christian movement today. We are a story-formed community. The Christian experience is formed by the dangerous stories of our great hero. Just as the rabbits' instinct is to stop and dig, so too our very human instinct is to embrace safety, warmth and security. Our all-too-human impulses work towards being untroubled. We build houses, embrace respectability and try not to stand out. We want to escape into the cool, cool earth rather than to cut out across the open fields, courting danger and negotiating challenges. So, what will get us up and out of our safe warrens? What will continue to foster unease about being exiled in a post-Christendom world? Surely, it will be the radical stories of Jesus, the prince with a thousand enemies.

BIBLIOGRAPHY
Not In Kansas Anymore

1. The Beguiling Technicolour of Oz

Adeney, Tim. 'Predicting Benedict? A Time to Embrace and a Time to Refrain from Embracing.' https://australia.thegospelcoalition.org/article/predicting-benedict-a-time-to-embrace-and-a-time-to-refrain-from-embracing.

Butterfield, Rosaria Champagne. *Openness Unhindered: Further Thoughts of an Unlikely Convert on Sexual Identity and Union with Christ.* Pittsburgh: Crown and Covenant, 2015.

Kuehne, Dale. *Sex and the iWorld: Rethinking Relationship Beyond an Age of Individualism.* Grand Rapids: Baker Academic, 2009.

Reno, R. R. *Resurrecting the Idea of a Christian Society.* Washington: Regnery Faith, 2016. Kindle.

Sayers, Mark. *Disappearing Church: From Cultural Relevance to Gospel Resilience.* Chicago: Moody, 2016. Kindle.

Shiner, Rory. 'What Will We Wish We'd Done? A Ben-Op Thought Experiment.' https://australia.thegospelcoalition.org/article/what-will-we-wish-wed-done-a-ben-op-thought-experiment.

Smith, James K. A. *Desiring the Kingdom: Worship, Worldview and Cultural Formation.* Grand Rapids: Baker Academic, 2009.

Taleb, Nassim Nicholas. *Antifragile: Things that Gain from Disorder.* London: Penguin, 2012. Kindle.

Taylor, Charles. *A Secular Age.* Cambridge, MA: Harvard University Press, 2007. Kindle.

Volf, Miroslav. *Against the Tide: Love in a Time of Petty Dreams and Persisting Enmities.* Grand Rapids: Eerdmans, 2010.

2. Diaspora as Means of Grace: A Neo-Anabaptist('s) Perspective on the Church, 'Exile' and Post-Christian Culture

Bird, Michael F. *Crossing Over Sea and Land: Jewish Missionary Activity in the Second Temple Period.* Peabody: Hendrickson, 2010.

Brueggemann, Walter. *Cadences of Home: Preaching Among Exiles.* Louisville: Westminster John Knox, 1997.

———. *Theology of the Old Testament: Testimony, Dispute, Advocacy.* Minneapolis: Fortress, 1997.

Colucciello, Daniel. 'Epistemological Violence, Christianity, and the Secular.' In *The New Yoder*, edited by Peter Dula and Chris K. Huebner, 271–93. Cambridge: Lutterworth, 2011.

Davidson, Steed Vernyl. *Empire and Exile: Postcolonial Readings of the Book of Jeremiah.* London: T. & T. Clark, 2011.

Dreher, Rod. *The Benedict Option: A Strategy for Christians in a Post-Christian Nation.* New York: Sentinel, 2017.

Harrison Brennan, Kate. 'No Place for Exile.' *ABC Religion and Ethics*, December 16, 2016. Accessed June 21, 2017. http://www.abc.net.au/religion/articles/2016/12/16/4593491.htm.

BIBLIOGRAPHY

Hart, David Bentley. 'No Enduring City.' In *A Splendid Wickedness and Other Essays*, 216–26. Grand Rapids: Eerdmans, 2016.

Hauerwas, Stanley. 'Can Democracy Be Christian? Reflections on How (Not) To Be a Political Theologian.' *ABC Religion and Ethics*, June 24, 2014. Accessed June 21, 2017. http://www.abc.net.au/religion/articles/2014/06/24/4032239.htm.

———. 'The Servant Community: Christian Social Ethics (1983).' In *The Hauerwas Reader*, edited by John Berkman and Michael Cartwright, 371–91. Durham: Duke University Press, 2001.

Hauerwas, Stanley, and William H. Willimon. *Resident Aliens: Life in the Christian Colony*. Exp. ed. Nashville: Abingdon, 2014.

Jobes, Karen H. *1 Peter*. Baker Exegetical Commentary. Grand Rapids: Baker, 2005.

Middleton, J. Richard, and Brian J. Walsh. *Truth is Stranger Than It Used to Be: Biblical Faith in a Postmodern Age*. Downers Grove: InterVarsity, 1995.

Murphy, Nancey. 'Traditions, Practices, and the Powers.' In *Transforming the Powers: Peace, Justice, and the Domination System*, edited by Ray Gingerich and Ted Grimsrud, 84–95. Minneapolis: Fortress, 2006.

Nikolajsen, Jeppe Bach. *The Distinctive Identity of the Church: A Constructive Study of the Post-Christendom Theologies of Lesslie Newbigin and John Howard Yoder*. Eugene: Wipf & Stock, 2015.

Pitre, Brant. *Jesus, the Tribulation, and the End of the Exile: Restoration Eschatology and the Origin of the Atonement*. WUNT 2/204. Tübingen: Mohr Siebeck, 2005.

Richard, Earl J. *Reading 1 Peter, Jude, and 2 Peter: A Literary and Theological Commentary*. Macon: Smith & Helwys, 2000.

Said, Edward W. 'The Mind of Winter: Reflections on Life in Exile.' *Harper* 9 (1984): 49–55.

Senior, Donald P., and Daniel J. Harrington. *1 Peter, Jude and 2 Peter*. Sacra Pagina. Collegeville: Liturgical, 2003.

Smith-Christopher, Daniel L. *A Biblical Theology of Exile*. Minneapolis: Fortress, 2002.

———. *The Religion of the Landless: The Social Context of the Babylonian Exile*. Eugene: Wipf & Stock, 2015.

Suyanto, Agus, and Paulus Hartono. *The Radical Muslim and Mennonite: A Muslim-Christian Encounter for Peace in Indonesia*, edited by Agnes Chen. Semarang: Pustaka Muria, 2015.

Weaver, J. Denny. *Becoming Anabaptist: The Origin and Significance of Sixteenth-Century Anabaptism*. 2nd ed. Scottdale: Herald, 2005.

Wenger, John C., and C. Arnold Snyder. 'Schleitheim Confession.' *Global Anabaptist Mennonite Encyclopedia Online* (1990). Accessed June 21, 2017. http://gameo.org/index.php?title=Schleitheim_Confession&oldid=143737.

Wright, N. T. *Jesus and the Victory of God*. Minneapolis: Fortress, 1996.

———. *The New Testament and the People of God*. Minneapolis: Fortress, 1992.

Yoder, John Howard. 'Constantinian Sources of Western Social Ethics.' In *The Priestly Kingdom: Social Ethics as Gospel*, 135–47. Notre Dame: University of Notre Dame Press, 1984.

———. 'The Otherness of the Church.' In *The Royal Priesthood: Essays Ecclesiological and Ecumenical*, edited by Michael G. Cartwright, 53–64. Scottdale: Herald, 1998.

———. *The Schleitheim Confession*. Translated by John Howard Yoder. Harrisonburg: Herald, 2014.

———. 'See How They Go With Their Face to the Sun.' In *For The Nations: Essays Public and Evangelical*, 51–78. Grand Rapids; Eerdmans, 1997.

BIBLIOGRAPHY

3. No Place for Exile

Australian Bureau of Statistics. 'Religion in Australia, 2016.' http://www.abs.gov.au/ausstats/abs@.nsf/Lookup/by%20Subject/2071.0~2016~Main%20Features~Religion%20Data%20Summary~70.

Bretherton, Luke. *Christianity and Contemporary Politics: The Conditions and Possibilities of Faithful Witness*. Chichester: Wiley-Blackwell, 2010.

Brueggemann, Walter. *Hopeful Imagination: Prophetic Voices in Exile*. Fortress Press, 1986.

———. *Journey to the Common Good*. Louisville: Westminster John Knox, 2010.

———. *The Prophetic Imagination*. 2nd ed. Minneapolis: Augsburg Fortress, 2001.

———. 'The Prophetic Imagination.' *On Being with Krista Tippett*, December 19, 2013.

———. *The Theology of the Book of Jeremiah*. Cambridge: Cambridge University Press, 2007.

Frost, Michael. *Exiles: Living Missionally in a Post-Christian Culture*. Grand Rapids: Baker Books, 2006.

Harrison Brennan, Kate. 'No Place for Exile. How Christians Should (Not) Make Sense of their Place in the World.' *ABC Religion and Ethics*, December 16, 2016.

Hauerwas, Stanley. 'Living Well in Ordinary Time: A Tribute to Rowan Williams.' *ABC Religion and Ethics*, March 20, 2013. http://www.abc.net.au/religion/articles/2013/03/20/3719969.htm.

McAlpine, Steven. 'Stage Two Exile: Are You Ready for It?' *The Gospel Coalition*, June 1, 2015. https://australia.thegospelcoalition.org/article/stage-two-exile-are-you-ready-for-it.

Moore, Natasha. 'Churches Aren't Business and They Still Deserve a Tax Break.' *Sydney Morning Herald,* October 10, 2016. http://www.smh.com.au/comment/churches-arent-business-and-they-still-deserve-a-tax-break-20161007-grxntr.html.

Pew Research. 'America's Changing Religious Landscape', May 12, 2015. http://www.pewforum.org/2015/05/12/americas-changing-religious-landscape/.

Redeemer Presbyterian Church. 'Vision and Values'. https://www.redeemer.com/learn/vision_and_values.

Shelley, Marshall, and Drew Dyck. 'The Church in Secular Culture: Moving from a Stance of Admonition to Mission.' *Christianity Today,* January 2012. http://www.christianitytoday.com/pastors/2012/january-online-only/secularculture.html.

Sherwood, Harriet. 'People of No Religion Outnumber Christians in England and Wales—Study.' *The Guardian,* May 24, 2016. https://www.theguardian.com/world/2016/may/23/no-religion-outnumber-christians-england-wales-study.

Starling, David. 'Are Christians in Exile?' *Eternity News,* August 12, 2016. https://www.eternitynews.com.au/opinion/are-christians-in-exile/.

The Economist. 'The Future of the World's Most Popular Religion is African.' *The Economist,* December 25, 2015. https://www.economist.com/news/international/21684679-march-christianity-future-worlds-most-popular-religion-african?zid=315&ah=ee087c5cc3198fc82970cd65083f5281.

Weick, Karl E. 'The Collapse of Sensemaking in Organizations: The Mann Gulch Disaster.' *Administrative Science Quarterly* 38, no. 4 (1993): 628–52.

Yoder, John Howard. *The Jewish-Christian Schism Revisited.* Edited by Michael Cartwright and Peter Ochs. Grand Rapids: Eerdmans, 2003.

Zwartz, Barney. 'Christianity is Dying Out? Don't Count on It.' *The Drum*, October 5, 2015. http://www.abc.net.au/news/2015-10-05/zwartz-is-christianity-dying-out/6827658.

4. The Weapons of our Warfare: Culture, Conflict and Character in 2 Corinthians

Barnett, Paul. *The Second Epistle to the Corinthians*. NICNT. Grand Rapids: Eerdmans, 1997.

Dunn, James D. G. *Romans. 2 vols*. Dallas: Word, 1988.

Fee, Gordon D. 'II Corinthians vi.14–vii.1 and Food Offered to Idols.' *NTS* 23 (1977): 533–38.

Gorman, Michael J. *Cruciformity: Paul's Narrative Spirituality of the Cross*. Grand Rapids: Eerdmans, 2001.

Guthrie, George H. *2 Corinthians*. BECNT. Grand Rapids: Baker, 2015.

Hafemann, Scott J. *Paul's Message and Ministry in Covenant Perspective: Selected Essays*. Eugene: Cascade, 2015.

Harris, Murray J. *The Second Epistle to the Corinthians: A Commentary on the Greek Text*. NIGTC. Grand Rapids: Eerdmans, 2005.

Hempton, David. *Evangelical Disenchantment: Nine Portraits of Faith and Doubt*. New Haven: Yale University Press, 2008.

Hunter, James Davison. *Culture Wars: The Struggle to Define America*. New York: Basic Books, 1991.

———. *To Change the World: The Irony, Tragedy, and Possibility of Christianity in the Late Modern World*. New York: Oxford University Press, 2010.

Jewett, Robert. *Romans: A Commentary*. Hermeneia. Minneapolis: Fortress, 2007.

Larsen, Timothy. *Crisis of Doubt: Honest Faith in Nineteenth-Century England*. Oxford: Oxford University Press, 2006.

Seifrid, Mark A. *The Second Letter to the Corinthians*. PNTC. Grand Rapids: Eerdmans, 2014.

Starling, David I. 'The *Apistoi* of 2 Cor. 6:14: Beyond the Impasse.' *Novum Testamentum* 55 (2012): 1–17.

———. '"We Do Not Want You to Be Unaware …": Disclosure, Concealment and Suffering in 2 Cor 1–7.' *NTS* 60 (2014): 266–79.

———. '"The Weapons of Righteousness": Righteousness and Suffering in 2 Corinthians.' In *Suffering in Paul*, edited by Siu Fung Wu. Eugene: Wipf & Stock, 2019.

Symondson, Anthony. *The Victorian Crisis of Faith: Six Lectures*. London: SPCK, 1970.

Thrall, Margaret E. '2 Corinthians 1:12: *Hagiotēti* or *Haplotēti*.' In *Studies in New Testament Language and Text*, edited by J. K. Elliott, 366–72. Leiden: Brill, 1976.

5. To Aliens and Strangers: Preaching the New Testament as Minority Group Rhetoric

Andrews, Richard. *A Theory of Contemporary Rhetoric*. New York: Routledge, 2014.

Coser, Lewis A. *The Functions of Social Conflict*. Glencoe, IL: Free Press, 1956.

DeSilva, David A. *Honor, Patronage, Kinship and Purity: Unlocking New Testament Culture*. Downers Grove, IL: InterVarsity, 2000.

———. *Seeing Things John's Way: The Rhetoric of the Book of Revelation*. Louisville, KY: Westminster John Knox, 2009.

Elliott, John H. 'Disgraced Yet Graced. The Gospel According to 1 Peter in the Key of Honor and Shame.' *Biblical Theology Bulletin* 24 (1995): 166–78.

———. *A Home for the Homeless: A Social-Scientific Criticism of 1 Peter, Its Situation and Strategy*. Philadelphia, PA: Fortress Press, 1990.

BIBLIOGRAPHY

———. 'The Jewish Messianic Movement: From Faction to Sect.' In *Modelling Early Christianity: Social-Scientific Studies of the New Testament in Its Context*, edited by Philip Francis Esler, 75–95. London: Routledge, 1995.

Green, Joel B. *1 Peter*. Two Horizons New Testament Commentary. Grand Rapids, MI: Eerdmans, 2007.

Greenberg, Eric H., and Karl Weber. *Generation We: How Millennial Youth Are Taking Over America and Changing Our World Forever.* Emeryville: Pachatusan, 2008.

King, Martin Luther, and James Melvin Washington. *A Testament of Hope: The Essential Writings and Speeches of Martin Luther King, Jr.* San Francisco: Harper, 1991.

MacBride, Tim. 'Aliens and Strangers: Minority Group Rhetoric in the Later New Testament Writings.' In *Into All the World*, edited by Mark Harding and Alanna Nobbs. Grand Rapids: Eerdmans, 2017.

———. *Preaching the New Testament as Rhetoric: The Promise of Rhetorical Criticism for Expository Preaching*. ACT Monograph. Wipf & Stock, 2014.

MacMullen, Ramsay. *Paganism in the Roman Empire*. New Haven: Yale University Press, 1981.

Malina, Bruce J. *The New Testament World: Insights from Cultural Anthropology.* 3rd ed. Louisville, KY: Westminster John Knox, 2001.

Meeks, Wayne A. *The First Urban Christians: The Social World of the Apostle Paul.* New Haven, CT: Yale University Press, 1983.

Presmanes, Jorge L. 'The Juxtaposition of Dangerous Memories: Toward a Latino Theology of Preaching from the Underside of the Diaspora Experience.' In *Preaching and Culture in Latino Congregations*, edited by Kenneth G. Davis and Jorge L. Presmanes, 5–26. Chicago: Archdiocese of Chicago, 2000.

Selby, Gary S. *Martin Luther King and the Rhetoric of Freedom: The Exodus Narrative in America's Struggle for Civil Rights*. Studies in Rhetoric and Religion. Waco, TX: Baylor University Press, 2008.

Wilson, Bryan R. 'An Analysis of Sect Development.' *American Journal of Sociology* 24 (1959): 3–15.

Winslow, Robert Wallace. *The Emergence of Deviant Minorities, Social Problems and Social Change*. Social Problems Series. San Ramon, CA: Consensus, 1972.

6. Stooping to Conquer: The Gentleness and Generosity of the Early Church

Augustine. *The City of God*. In *The Nicene and Post-Nicene Fathers*, Series 1, vol. 2. Edited by Philip Schaff. Translated by Marcus Dods. 1887. Reprint, Grand Rapids: Eerdmans, 1956.

Bakke, Odd Magne. 'The Episcopal Ministry and the Unity of the Church from the Apostolic Fathers to Cyprian.' In *The Formation of the Early Church*, edited by Jostein Ådna, 379–408. Tübingen: Mohr Siebeck, 2005.

Bonhoeffer, Dietrich. 'To Eberhard Bethge, 21 November 1943.' In *Dietrich Bonhoeffer, Letters and Papers from Prison: The Enlarged Edition*, edited by Eberhard Bethge, 135. London: SCM, 1971.

Brown, Peter Robert Lamont. *Poverty and Leadership in the Later Roman Empire*. Hanover, NH: University Press of New England, 2002.

Buer, Mabel C. 'The Reformed Parliament and Civil Registration of Births and Deaths.' *Public Administration* 8 (1930): 323–34.

Cobb, L. Stephanie. *Dying to be Men: Gender and Language in Early Christian Martyr Texts*. New York: Columbia University Press, 2008.

BIBLIOGRAPHY

Cyprian. 'Epistle 62.' In *The Letters of St. Cyprian of Carthage*, vol. 3. Edited by G. W. Clarke, 95–97. Translated by G. W. Clarke. New York: Newman Press, 1986.

———. *The Good of Patience*. In *The Ante-Nicene Fathers*, vol. 5. Edited by Alexander Roberts and James Donaldson. Translated by Ernest Wallis. 1867. Reprint, Grand Rapids: Eerdmans, 1990.

———. *On Jealousy and Envy*. In *The Ante-Nicene Fathers*, vol. 5. Edited by Alexander Roberts and James Donaldson. Translated by Ernest Wallis. 1867. Reprint, Grand Rapids: Eerdmans, 1990.

———. *On the Dress of Virgins*. In *The Ante-Nicene Fathers*, vol. 5. Edited by Alexander Roberts and James Donaldson. Translated by Ernest Wallis. 1867. Reprint, Grand Rapids: Eerdmans, 1990.

———.*On the Lapsed*. In *The Ante-Nicene Fathers*, vol. 5. Edited by Alexander Roberts and James Donaldson. Translated by Ernest Wallis. 1867. Reprint, Grand Rapids: Eerdmans, 1990.

———. *On the Lord's Prayer*. In *The Ante-Nicene Fathers*, vol. 5. Edited by Alexander Roberts and James Donaldson. Translated by Ernest Wallis. 1867. Reprint, Grand Rapids: Eerdmans, 1990.

———. *On the Unity of the Catholic Church*. In *The Ante-Nicene Fathers*, vol. 5. Edited by Alexander Roberts and James Donaldson. Translated by Ernest Wallis. 1867. Reprint, Grand Rapids: Eerdmans, 1990.

———. *On Works and Alms*. In *The Ante-Nicene Fathers*, vol. 5. Edited by Alexander Roberts and James Donaldson. Translated by Ernest Wallis. 1867. Reprint, Grand Rapids: Eerdmans, 1990.

———. *Three Books of Testimonies Against the Jews (To Quirinus)*. In *The Ante-Nicene Fathers*, vol. 5. Edited by Alexander Roberts and

James Donaldson. Translated by Ernest Wallis. 1867. Reprint, Grand Rapids: Eerdmans, 1990.

———. *To Demetrian*. In *The Ante-Nicene Fathers*, vol. 5. Edited by Alexander Roberts and James Donaldson. Translated by Ernest Wallis. 1867. Reprint, Grand Rapids: Eerdmans, 1990.

Frost, Michael. *Surprise the World: The Five Habits of Highly Missional People*. Colorado Springs, CO: NavPress, 2016.

Heffernan, Thomas J. *The Passion of Perpetua and Felicity*. Oxford: Oxford University Press, 2012.

John Chrysostom. *Homilies on Acts*. In *The Nicene and Post-Nicene Fathers*, Series 1, vol. 11. Edited by Philip Schaff. Translated by J. Walker, J. Sheppard and H. Browne. 1889. Reprint, Grand Rapids: Eerdmans, 1969.

———. *Homilies on Romans*. In *The Nicene and Post-Nicene Fathers*, Series 1, vol. 11. Edited by Philip Schaff. Translated by J. B. Morris and W. H. Simcox. 1889. Reprint, Grand Rapids: Eerdmans, 1969.

Justin Martyr. *First Apology*. In *The Ante-Nicene Fathers*, vol. 1. Edited and translated by Alexander Roberts and James Donaldson. 1885. Reprint, Grand Rapids: Eerdmans, 1989.

Keener, Craig S. *The Gospel of Matthew: A Socio-Rhetorical Commentary*. Grand Rapids, MI: Eerdmans, 2009.

Kreider, Alan. *The Patient Ferment of the Early Church: The Improbable Rise of Christianity in the Roman Empire*. Grand Rapids, MI: Baker Academic, 2016.

Lewis, Clive Staples. *Mere Christianity*. 1952. Reprint, San Francisco, CA: HarperSanFrancisco, 2001.

BIBLIOGRAPHY

Marrou, Henri-Irénée. 'La fin du monde antique vue par les contemporains.' In *Christiana Tempora*, 79–85. Rome: École française de Rome, 1978.

Moss, Candida R. 'Nailing Down and Tying Up: Lessons in Intertextual Impossibility from the Martyrdom of Polycarp.' *Vigiliae Christianae* 67 (2013): 117–36.

Murphy, Edwina. 'Cyprian and The Pilgrim's Progress.' In *Beyond 400: Exploring Baptist Futures*, edited by David J. Cohen and Michael Parsons, 116–30. Eugene, OR: Pickwick Publications, 2011.

———. 'Cyprian, Paul, and Care for the Poor and Captive: Offering Sacrifices and Ransoming Temples.' *Zeitschrift für Antikes Christentum* 20 (2016): 418–36.

———. 'Imitating the Devil: Cyprian on Jealousy and Envy.' *Scrinium* 14 (2018): 75–91.

Origen. *Against Celsus*. In *The Ante-Nicene Fathers*, vol. 4. Edited by Alexander Roberts and James Donaldson. Translated by Frederick Crombie. 1885. Reprint, Grand Rapids: Eerdmans, 1989.

Osiek, Carolyn. 'The Ransom of Captives: Evolution of a Tradition.' *Harvard Theological Review* 74 (1981): 365–86.

Pliny the Younger. *Letters, Volume I: Books 1–7*. LCL 55. Translated by Betty Radice. Cambridge, MA: Harvard University Press, 1969.

Pontius. *The Life and Passion of Cyprian, Bishop and Martyr (Vita Cypriani)*. In *The Ante-Nicene Fathers*, vol. 5. Edited by Alexander Roberts and James Donaldson. Translated by Ernest Wallis. 1867. Reprint, Grand Rapids: Eerdmans, 1990.

Sage, Michael M. *Cyprian*. Philadelphia: Philadelphia Patristic Foundation, 1975.

Saller, Richard P. *Personal Patronage Under the Early Empire.* Cambridge: Cambridge University Press, 1982.

Sallust. 'Letters to Caesar.' In *Fragments of the Histories. Letters to Caesar,* edited and translated by John T. Ramsey, 475–527. LCL 522. Cambridge, MA: Harvard University Press, 2015.

Stark, Rodney. *The Rise of Christianity: How the Obscure, Marginal, Jesus Movement Became the Dominant Religious Force in the Western World.* San Francisco, CA: HarperCollins, 1997.

Tertullian. *Apology.* In *The Ante-Nicene Fathers,* vol. 3. Edited by Alexander Roberts and James Donaldson. Translated by S. Thelwall. 1885. Reprint, Grand Rapids, MI: Eerdmans, 1968.

———. *On Patience.* In *The Ante-Nicene Fathers,* vol. 3. Edited by Alexander Roberts and James Donaldson. Translated by S. Thelwall. 1885. Reprint, Grand Rapids, MI: Eerdmans, 1968.

———. *To His Wife.* In *The Ante-Nicene Fathers,* vol. 4. Edited by Alexander Roberts and James Donaldson. Translated by S. Thelwall. 1885. Reprint, Grand Rapids, MI: Eerdmans, 1989.

The Martyrdom of Perpetua and Felicitas. In *The Acts of the Christian Martyrs,* edited by Herbert Musurillo, 106–31. Oxford: Clarendon Press, 1972.

The Martyrdom of Polycarp. In *The Acts of the Christian Martyrs,* edited by Herbert Musurillo, 2–21. Oxford: Clarendon Press, 1972.

The Martyrs of Lyons. In *The Acts of the Christian Martyrs,* edited by Herbert Musurillo, 62–85. Oxford: Clarendon Press, 1972.

BIBLIOGRAPHY

7. Why We Need the World: Musings from the Interface of Theology and Education

Andrews, Dave. *Out and Out: Way-Out Community Work*. Northcote, VIC: Morning Star, 2012.

Augustine. *City of God*. Translated by Henry Bettenson. Harmondsworth: Penguin Books, 1972. Accessed August 17, 2017. http://www.sacred-texts.com/chr/ecf/102/1020285.htm.

Australian Bureau of Statistics. 'Religion in Australia: 2017 Census Data Summary.' 2071.0—Census of Population and Housing: Reflecting Australia—Stories from the Census, 2016. Accessed August 14, 2017. http://www.abs.gov.au/ausstats/abs@.nsf/Lookup/by%20Subject/2071.0~2016~Main%20Features~Religion%20Data%20Summary~25.

Benson, David. 'God's Curriculum: Re-Imagining Education as a Journey towards Shalom.' Paper presented at the Christian Schools National Policy Forum, May 22, 2017, Canberra. Accessed August 16, 2017. http://bit.ly/GodsCurriculum.

———. *Sacred Texts in Secular Education*. PhD diss., University of Queensland, 2015. Accessed August 14, 2017. http://bit.ly/SacredTextsSecularEducation.

———. *Schools, Scripture and Secularisation: A Christian Theological Argument for the Incorporation of Sacred Texts within Australian Public Education*. PhD diss., University of Queensland, 2016. Accessed August 14, 2017. http://bit.ly/SchoolsScriptureSecularisation.

———. 'Shalom and Sustainability: God's Curriculum and the Australian Curriculum Converse Over Creation and Geography.' *Australian*

Journal of Mission Studies 10, no. 2 (2016): 60–7. Accessed August 16, 2017. http://www.missionstudies.org.au/aams/201612.pdf.

———. 'Uncommon Good: Peaceable Dialogue for Partisan Times.' Annual Tinsley Lecture, Morling College, 2016. Accessed August 16, 2017. http://www.morlingcollege.com/about/why-choose-morling/tinsley-annual-lecture/.

Bird, Michael. 'Turning the World Upside Down, Down Under.' *Christianity Today*, June 14, 2017. Accessed August 17, 2017. http://www.christianitytoday.com/ct/2017/june-web-only/turning-world-upside-down-down-under.html?start=1.

Blomberg, Doug. 'Curriculum Guidelines for the Christian School.' In *No Icing on the Cake: Christian Foundations for Education in Australia*, edited by Jack Michielsen, 111–22. Melbourne: Brookes-Hall, 1980.

Brooks, David. 'The Benedict Option.' *The New York Times*, March 14, 2017. Accessed August 14, 2017. https://www.nytimes.com/2017/03/14/opinion/the-benedict-option.html?_r=0.

Brown, William P. 'The Gardener and the Groundling: The Ecology of Resurrection.' *Journal for Preachers* 32, no. 3 (2009): 33–7.

Brueggemann, Walter. *Cadences of Home: Preaching among Exiles*. Louisville, KY: Westminster John Knox, 1997.

———. *The Creative Word: Canon as a Model for Biblical Education*. Philadelphia: Fortress Press, 1982.

Byrne, Cathy J. *Religion in Secular Education: What, in Heaven's Name, Are We Teaching Our Children?* International Studies in Religion and Society. Leiden: Brill, 2014.

BIBLIOGRAPHY

Campbell, Nathan. 'Benedict Option or Golden Rule?' *St-Eutychus Blog*, April 29, 2017. Accessed August 15, 2017. http://st-eutychus.com/2017/benedict-option-or-golden-rule/.

———. 'The Persecution Complex: Real "Religious" Freedom Means Allowing Space for All Religious Agendas (Even Secular Ones).' *St-Eutychus Blog*, June 11, 2016. Accessed August 14, 2017. http://st-eutychus.com/2016/the-persecution-complex-real-religious-freedom-means-allowing-space-for-all-religious-agendas-even-secular-ones/.

Carson, D. A. *Christ and Culture Revisited*. Grand Rapids, MI: Eerdmans, 2008.

Carter, Craig A. *Rethinking Christ and Culture: A Post-Christendom Perspective*. Grand Rapids, MI: Brazos, 2007.

Catto, Rebecca. 'Accurate Diagnosis? Exploring Convergence and Divergence in Non-Western Missionary and Sociological Master Narratives of Christian Decline in Western Europe.' *Transformation* 30, no. 1 (January 2013): 31–45.

Choung, James. *True Story: A Christianity Worth Believing In*. Downers Grove, IL: IVP Books, 2008.

Cooling, Trevor. *A Christian Vision for State Education: Reflections on the Theology of Education*. London: SPCK, 1994.

———. *Supporting Christians in Education*. London: LICC, 2008.

Crouch, Andy. *Culture Making: Recovering Our Creative Call*. Downers Grove, IL: InterVarsity, 2008.

Dreher, Rod. *The Benedict Option: A Strategy for Christians in a Post-Christian Nation*. New York: Penguin, 2017.

Edgar, William. *Created and Creating: A Biblical Theology of Culture*. Downers Grove, IL: IVP Academic.

Fitch, David E. *Faithful Presence: Seven Disciplines That Shape the Church for Mission*. Downers Grove, IL: IVP, 2016.

Ford, David F. *Christian Wisdom: Desiring God and Learning in Love*. Cambridge: Cambridge University Press, 2007.

———. *Shaping Theology: Engagements in a Religious and Secular World*. Challenges in Contemporary Theology. Edited by Gareth Jones and Lewis Ayres. Malden, MA: Blackwell Publishing, 2007.

Fowler, Mark. 'Queensland's Evangelism Ban Can't Prevail Against Law.' *The Australian*, August 9, 2017. Accessed August 11, 2017. http://www.theaustralian.com.au/opinion/queenslands-christian-edict-cant-prevail-against-law/news-story/34b5f0e485aab90bc48db78834c9c985.

Frost, Michael. *Exiles: Living Missionally in a Post-Christian Culture*. Peabody, MA: Hendrickson Publishers, 2006.

———. *Surprise the World! The Five Habits of Highly Missional People*. Colorado Springs, CO: NavPress, 2016.

Goheen, Michael W., and Craig G. Bartholomew. *Living at the Crossroads: An Introduction to Christian Worldview*. Grand Rapids, MI: Baker Academic, 2008.

Greider, Kathleen J. 'Religious Pluralism and Christian-Centrism.' In *The Wiley-Blackwell Companion to Practical Theology*, edited by Bonnie J. Miller-McLemore, 452–62. Malden, MA: Wiley-Blackwell, 2012.

BIBLIOGRAPHY

Hauerwas, Stanley. 'Character, Narrative, and Growth in the Christian Life.' In *The Hauerwas Reader*, edited by John Berkman and Michael Cartwright, 221–54. Durham, NC: Duke University Press, 2005.

Hunter, James Davison. *To Change the World: The Irony, Tragedy, and Possibility of Christianity in the Late Modern World*. Oxford: Oxford University Press, 2010.

Inazu, John. 'The Benedict Option Falls Short of Real Pluralism.' *Christianity Today*, March 2, 2017. Accessed August 15, 2017. http://www.christianitytoday.com/ct/2017/february-web-only/benedict-option-should-include-muslims-too.html.

James, Peter C. J., and David Benson. 'School Chaplaincy, Secularism and Church–State Separation in a Liberal Democracy.' *University of Queensland Law Journal* 33, no. 1 (2014): 131–52. Accessed August 16, 2017. http://bit.ly/SchoolChaplaincy.

Jones, E. Stanley. *The Unshakable Kingdom and the Unchanging Person*. Bellingham, WA: McNett Press, 1972.

Jones, Timothy W. 'Safe Schools Coalition: What Is the Christian Right Afraid Of?' *The Conversation*, February 26, 2016. Accessed August 16, 2017. https://theconversation.com/safe-schools-coalition-what-is-the-christian-right-afraid-of-55296.

Keller, Tim. *Loving the City: Doing Balanced Gospel-Centred Ministry in Your City*. Grand Rapids, MI: Zondervan, 2016.

Lee, Lois. 'Research Note: Talking About a Revolution: Terminology for the New Field of Non-Religion Studies.' *Journal of Contemporary Religion* 27, no. 1 (January 2012): 129–39.

MacIntyre, Alasdair C. *After Virtue*. 3rd ed. Notre Dame, IN: University of Notre Dame Press, 2007.

Maclure, Jocelyn, and Charles Taylor. *Secularism and Freedom of Conscience*. Cambridge, MA: Harvard University Press, 2011.

Maddox, Marion. *Taking God to School: The End of Australia's Egalitarian Education?* Sydney: Allen & Unwin, 2014. Kindle.

Marty, Martin E. 'Foreword.' In *Christ and Culture*, H. Richard Niebuhr, xii–xix. New York, NY: HarperSanFrancisco, 2001.

Mason, Michael, Andrew Singleton, and Ruth Webber. *The Spirit of Generation Y: Young People's Spirituality in a Changing Australia*. Mulgrave, VIC: John Garratt, 2007.

McAlpine, Stephen. '51 Percent of Us Are Christian? Yeah, Right!' *Stephen McAlpine Blog*, June 27, 2017. Accessed August 14, 2017. https://stephenmcalpine.com/2017/06/27/51-per-cent-of-us-are-christian-yeah-right/.

McCrindle, Mark. 'Faith and Belief in Australia: A National Study on Religion, Spirituality and Worldview Trends.' Baulkham Hills, NSW: McCrindle Research Pty. Ltd., 2017. Accessed August 14, 2017. http://faithandbelief.org.au/.

MCEETYA. *Melbourne Declaration on Educational Goals for Young Australians*. E. T. Ministerial Council on Education, Producer, and Curriculum Corporation, 2008. Accessed August 16, 2017. http://www.curriculum.edu.au/verve/_resources/National_Declaration_on_the_Educational_Goals_for_Young_Australians.pdf.

BIBLIOGRAPHY

Messmore, Ryan. 'In But Not Of the World.' *The Pillar* 42 (March 29, 2017). Accessed August 15, 2017. https://www.millis.edu.au/single-post/2017/03/29/In-But-Not-Of-the-World-2-Questions.

Mouw, Richard J. *He Shines in All That's Fair: Culture and Common Grace*. Grand Rapids, MI: Eerdmans, 2001.

———. *When the Kings Come Marching In: Isaiah and the New Jerusalem*. Rev. ed. Grand Rapids, MI: Eerdmans, 2002.

Newbigin, Lesslie. *A Word in Season: Perspectives on Christian World Missions*. Grand Rapids, MI: Eerdmans, 1994.

Niebuhr, H. Richard. *Christ and Culture*. Expanded 50th anniversary ed. San Francisco: Harper, 2001.

Noddings, Nel. 'The Aims of Education.' In *The Curriculum Studies Reader*, edited by David J. Flinders and Stephen J. Thornton, 331–44. 2nd ed. New York: RoutledgeFalmer, 2004.

Postman, Neil. *The End of Education: Redefining the Value of School*. New York: Knopf, 1995.

Sayers, Mark. *Disappearing Church: From Cultural Relevance to Gospel Resilience*. Chicago: Moody, 2016.

Shortt, John G. 'Daniel: A Good Citizen of Babylon.' *EurECA Newsletter*, Autumn 2007. Accessed August 15, 2017. http://www.eureca-online.org/articles/daniel-a-good-citizen-of-babylon/.

Smith, Christian, and Melinda Lundquist Denton. *Soul Searching: The Religious and Spiritual Lives of American Teenagers*. New York: Oxford University Press, 2005.

Smith, James K. A. 'The Benedict Option or the Augustinian Call? Considering Two Ancient Options for the Contemporary Church.' *Comment*, March 16, 2017. Accessed August 14, 2017. https://www.cardus.ca/comment/article/5039/the-benedict-option-or-the-augustinian-call/.

Stackhouse, John G. Jr. 'A Bigger—and Smaller—View of Mission.' *Books and Culture* 13, no. 3 (May/June 2007). Accessed August 17, 2017. http://www.booksandculture.com/articles/2007/mayjun/11.26.html.

———. 'In the World, But ...' *Christianity Today* 46, no. 5 (April 22, 2002): 80–81. Accessed August 11, 2017. http://www.christianitytoday.com/ct/2002/april22/8.80.html.

———. *Making the Best of It: Following Christ in the Real World*. Oxford: Oxford University Press, 2008.

———. *Why You're Here: Ethics for the Real World*. Oxford: Oxford University Press, 2017.

Stratham, Audrey. *Educating for Democracy in Australian Schooling: Towards a Secular Global Age through an Inquiry into the Religious*. PhD diss., University of Divinity, Melbourne, 2014. Accessed August 16, 2017. http://repository.divinity.edu.au/1609/.

———. 'Secular: An Aspiration or a Dirty Word in Australian Education?' *The Conversation*, January 14, 2014. Accessed August 16, 2017. http://theconversation.com/secular-an-aspiration-or-a-dirty-word-in-australian-education-22004.

Stevenson, Chrys. 'Faith in Schools: The Dismantling of Australia's Secular Public Education System.' *ABC Religion and Ethics*, October 22, 2012. Accessed August 14, 2017. http://www.abc.net.au/religion/articles/2012/10/22/3615647.htm.

BIBLIOGRAPHY

Strom, Mark. *Lead with Wisdom: How Wisdom Transforms Good Leaders into Great Leaders*. Milton, QLD: Wiley, 2014.

Thomas, R. Murray. *Religion in Schools: Controversies around the World*. Westport, CT: Praeger, 2006.

Thorngate, Steve. 'Deep Roots, Open Doors: Is There a Benedict Option for Liberals?' *Christian Century* 134, no. 11 (May 24, 2017): 22–25.

Tyson, Paul. 'Australian Evangelicals: Of the World But Not In the World?' *Zadok Perspectives* 134 (Autumn 2017): 19–22.

Van Engen, Charles. *God's Missionary People: Rethinking the Purpose of the Local Church*. Grand Rapids, MI: Baker, 2001.

Volf, Miroslav. 'Exclusion or Saturation? Rethinking the Place of Religion in Public Life.' *ABC Religion and Ethics*, March 11, 2014. Accessed August 14, 2017. http://www.abc.net.au/religion/articles/2014/03/11/3960854.htm.

Ward, Graham. *Christ and Culture*. Oxford: Blackwell, 2005.

———. 'Where We Are Culturally and How the Church Might Respond.' *Colloquium* 47, no. 1 (May 2015): 3–13.

Wolterstorff, Nicholas. *Educating for Life: Reflections on Christian Teaching and Learning*. Edited by Gloria Goris Stronks and Clarence W. Joldersma. Grand Rapids, MI: Baker Academic, 2002.

———. *Educating for Shalom: Essays on Higher Education*. Edited by Clarence W. Joldersma and Gloria Goris Stronks. Grand Rapids, MI: Eerdmans, 2004.

Wright, Christopher. *The Mission of God: Unlocking the Bible's Grand Narrative*. Downers Grove, IL: IVP Academic, 2006.

Wright, N. T. *After You Believe: Why Christian Character Matters*. New York: HarperOne, 2010.

———. *The Last Word: Beyond the Bible Wars to a New Understanding of the Authority of Scripture*. New York: HarperCollins, 2005.

Yoder, John Howard. 'How H. Richard Niebuhr Reasoned: A Critique of Christ and Culture.' In *Authentic Transformation: A New Vision of Christ and Culture*, edited by Glenn H. Stassen, D. M. Yeager, and John Howard Yoder, 3–89. Nashville, TN: Abingdon, 1996.

8. Christian School Communities as a Twenty-First-Century Benedict Option

Beaty, Kathlyn. 'Christians Have Lost the Culture Wars. Should They Withdraw from the Mainstream?' https://www.washingtonpost.com/news/acts-of-faith/wp/2017/03/02/christians-have-lost-the-culture-wars-should-they-withdraw-from-the-mainstream/.

Deneen, Patrick, J. 'Moral Minority.' https://www.firstthings.com/article/2017/04/moral-minority.

Dreher, Rod. 'Ben Op Miscellany.' http://www.theamericanconservative.com/dreher/benedict-option-miscellany/.

———. *The Benedict Option: A Strategy for Christians in a Post-Christian Nation*. New York: Sentinel, 2017.

East, Brad. 'Theologians Were Arguing About the Benedict Option 35 Years Ago.' https://mereorthodoxy.com/theologians-arguing-benedict-option-35-years-ago/.

Edlin, Richard J. *Thinking About Schooling—Christians Considering Schooling Options for Their Children*. Warrawong: Edserv International, 2016.

BIBLIOGRAPHY

Greenleaf, Robert K. *Servant Leadership: A Journey Into the Nature of Legitimate Power and Greatness.* New York: Paulist Press, 2002.

Harris-Perry, Melissa. 'MSNBC Advertisement.' https://www.youtube.com/watch?v=sjczwQOnMqg.

Linker, Damon. 'Why So Many Conservative Christians Feel Like a Persecuted Minority'. http://theweek.com/articles/684365/why-many-conservative-christians-feel-like-persecuted-minority.

Meador, Jake. 'Review Rod Dreher's The Benedict Option.' https://mereorthodoxy.com/book-review-the-benedict-option-rod-dreher/.

Russello, Gerald. 'Sparking Renewal: A Review of The Benedict Option.' https://home.isi.org/sparking-renewalbr-review-benedict-option.

Salatin, Joel. *Folks, This Ain't Normal: A Farmer's Advice for Happier Hens, Healthier People, and a Better World.* New York: Center Street, 2011.

Schneier, Bruce. *'Cryptography is Harder Than it Looks.'* https://www.schneier.com/essays/archives/2016/03/cryptography_is_hard.html.

Smith, James K. A. *Desiring the Kingdom: Worship, Worldview and Cultural Formation.* Grand Rapids: Baker Academic, 2009.

9. Humility, Embodiment and Contextualisation: Missional and Homemaking Opportunities for the Cultivation of Shalom by the Church in Exile

Beach, Lee. *The Church in Exile: Living in Hope after Christendom.* Downers Grove: IVP Academic, 2015.

Bouma-Prediger, Steven, and Brian Walsh. *Beyond Homelessness: Christian Faith in a Culture of Displacement.* Grand Rapids: Eerdmans, 2008.

Carson, Don. *The Gospel According to John.* Grand Rapids: Eerdmans, 1991.

Dreher, Rod. *The Benedict Option: A Strategy for Christians in a Post-Christian Nation.* New York: Random House, 2017.

Gorman, Michael. *Inhabiting the Cruciform God: Kenosis, Justification and Theosis.* Grand Rapids: Eerdmans, 2009.

Guder, Darrell. *Incarnation and the Church's Witness.* Harrisburg: Trinity Press International, 1999.

Harper, Lisa Sharon. *The Very Good Gospel.* New York: WaterBrook, 2016.

Hunsberger, George. *The Church between Gospel and Culture.* Grand Rapids: Baker, 1996.

Hunter, James Davison. *To Change the World: The Irony, Tragedy and Possibility of Christianity in the Late Modern World.* Oxford: Oxford University Press, 2010.

Kreider, Alan. *The Patient Ferment of the Early Church.* Grand Rapids: Baker Academic, 2016.

Morey, Tim. *Embodying Our Faith: Becoming a Living, Sharing, Practicing Church.* Downers Grove: InterVarsity, 2009.

Thompson, James. *The Church in Exile: God's Counterculture in a Non-Christian World.* Abilene: Leafwood Publishers, 2010.

Van Gelder, Craig, and Dwight J. Zscheile. *The Missional Church in Perpective: Mapping Trends and Shaping the Conversation.* Grand Rapids: Baker Academic, 2011. Kindle.

Volf, Miroslav. *A Public Faith: How Followers of Christ Should Serve the Common Good.* Grand Rapids: Brazos, 2011.

———. 'Soft Difference: Theological Reflections on the Relation between Church and Culture in 1 Peter.' *Ex Auditu* 10 (1994).

Wright, N. T. *Surprised by Hope: Rethinking Heaven, the Resurrection and the Mission of the Church.* NYC: Harper One, 2008.

10. Dangerous Memories in the Lands We Now Call Australia: Do the Exiles Hear the Call to Country Today?

Aldred, Ray. 'The Resurrection of Story.' *William Carey International Development Journal* 3, no. 2 (2014): 32–38.

Breward, Ian. *Australia: 'The Most Godless Place Under Heaven'.* Melbourne: Beacon Hill Books, 1988.

Cameron, Rod. *Karingal: A Search for Australian Spirituality.* Homebush: Society of St Paul, 1995.

Champion, Denise. *Yarta Wandatha.* Salisbury: Uniting Aboriginal and Islander Christian Congress, 2014.

Collins, Paul. 'Australians Are Not Godless, They're Hungry.' *SMH*, August 23, 2005. Accessed July 6, 2017. http://www.smh.com.au/news/opinion/australians-are-not-godless-theyre-hungry/2005/08/22/1124562800483.html.

Conifer, Dan. 'Indigenous Advisory Body Rejected by PM in "Kick in the Guts" for Advocates.' *ABC News*, October 26, 2017. http://www.abc.net.au/

news/2017-10-26/indigenous-advisory-body-proposal-rejected-by-cabinet/9087856.htm.

Davidson, Helen. 'Melbourne City Centre Blocked by Protests Over Closure of Indigenous Communities—As It Happened.' *The Guardian,* October 27, 2016. Accessed June 21, 2017. https://www.theguardian.com/australia-news/live/2015/may/01/protests-at-proposed-closure-of-remote-indigenous-communities-live.

Elder, Bruce. *Blood on the Wattle: Massacres and Maltreatment of Australian Aborigines Since 1788.* Frenchs Forest: Child & Associates, 1988.

Frost, Michael. *Exiles: Living Missionally in a Post-Christian Culture.* Grand Rapids: Baker, 2006.

Grant, Stan. 'Closing the Gap: There is Something Stirring in Australia.' *NITV,* February 10, 2016. Accessed June 21, 2017. https://www.sbs.com.au/nitv/article/2016/02/10/stan-grant-closing-gap-there-something-stirring-australia.

———. *Talking to My Country.* Sydney: HarperCollins, 2016.

Kwan, Dr Elizabeth. *Celebrating Australia: A History of Australia Day.* National Australia Day Council, 2007. https://www.australiaday.org.au/storage/celebratingaustralia.pdf.

Lee, Bernard J., and Michael A. Cowan. *Dangerous Memories: House Churches and Our American Story.* New York: Sheed & Ward, 1986.

Nouwen, Henri J. M. *Making All Things New: An Invitation to the Spiritual Life.* New York: HarperCollins, 1981.

BIBLIOGRAPHY

Oldenburg, Ray. *The Great Good Place: Cafes, Coffee Shops, Community Centers, Beauty Parlors, General Stores, Bars, Hangouts, and How They Get You Through the Day.* New York: Paragon, 1989.

Organ, Michael. *Secret Service: Governor Macquarie's Aboriginal War of 1816.* Proceedings of the National Conference of the Royal Australian Historical Society, Mittagong, October 25–26, 2014.

Paulson, Graham, and Mark G. Brett. *Five Smooth Stones.* Melbourne: Whitley College, 2013.

Perkins, Rachel, and Marcia Langton, eds. *First Australians: An Illustrated History.* Carlton: Miegunyah, 2008.

Simpson, Ray. *A Pilgrim Way: New Celtic Monasticism for Everyday People.* Stowmarket: Kevin Mayhew, 2005.

Stanner, W. E. H. *The Dreaming and Other Essays.* Collingwood: Black Inc., 2009.

Tacey, David J. *Edge of the Sacred: Transformation in Australia.* Sydney: HarperCollins, 1995.

Volf, M. *The End of Memory: Remembering Rightly in a Violent World.* Grand Rapids: Eerdmans, 2006.

11. Re-placing Mission: Exilic Options Reconsidered

Alban, Donald, Robert H. Woods, and Marsha Daigle-Williamson. 'The Writings of William Carey: Journalism as Mission in a Modern Age.' *Mission Studies* 22, no. 1 (2005): 85–113.

Dowsett, Rose. *The Cape Town Commitment: Study Edition*. Peabody, MA: Hendrickson Publishers, 2012.

Flett, John. *Apostolicity: The Ecumenical Question in World Christian Perspective*. Downers Grove, IL: InterVarsity Press, 2016.

Jackson, Darrell. '"Love of God, Love of Neighbour": Is This An Evangelical Missiology of Interest to the Eastern Orthodox?' In *The Mission of God: Studies in Orthodox and Evangelical Mission*, edited by Mark Oxbrow and Tim Grass, 30–50. Oxford: Regnum Press, 2015.

Mangalwadi, Vishal, and Ruth Mangalwadi. *The Legacy of William Carey*. Wheaton, IL: Crossway Books, 1999.

Sherring, Matthew A. 'Protestant Missions in India.' *The Calcutta Review* 62 (1876): 87.

Stanley, Brian. 'Christian Missions and the Enlightenment: A Reevaluation.' In *Christian Missions and the Enlightenment*, edited by Brian Stanley, 14. Grand Rapids, MI: William B. Eerdmans Publishing Co., 2001.

Stroope, Michael W. *Transcending Mission: The Eclipse of a Modern Tradition*. Downers Grove, IL: InterVarsity Press, 2017.

12. An Endlessly Cunning, Risky Process of Negotiation

Adams, Richard. *Watership Down*. New York: Avon Books, 1972.

Bowling, Mark. 'Fr Hans Zollner: Australians Have Lost Trust in the Local Church Following Sexual Abuse Scandals.' *The Catholic Leader*, September 7, 2017. http://catholicleader.com.au/news/fr-hans-zollner-australians-have-lost-trust-in-the-local-church-following-sexual-abuse-scandals.

BIBLIOGRAPHY

Brueggemann, Walter. *Cadences of Home*. Louisville: Westminster John Knox Press, 1997.

———. *Hopeful Imagination: Prophetic Voices in Exile*. Minneapolis: Fortress Press, 1986.

Chester, Tim, and Steve Timmis. *Everyday Church: Gospel Communities on Mission*. Wheaton: Crossway, 2011.

Congdon, David. 'No, The American Church Isn't "In Exile."' *Sojourners*, April 19, 2017. https://sojo.net/articles/no-american-church-isn-t-exile.

Frost, Michael. *Exiles: Living Missionally in a Post Christian World*. Peabody: Hendrickson, 2006.

Frost, Michael, and Alan Hirsch. *The Shaping of Things to Come*. Peabody: Hendrickson, 2003.

Guder, Darrell. *Missional Church: A Vision for the Sending of the Church in North America*. Grand Rapids: Eerdmans, 1998.

Hall, Douglas John. 'Metamorphosis: From Christendom to Diaspora.' In *Confident Witness*, edited by Craig van Gelder, 67–79. Grand Rapids: Eerdmans, 1999.

Harrison Brennan, Kate. 'No Place for Exile: How Christians Should (Not) Make Sense of their Place in the World.' *ABC Religion and Ethics*, December 16, 2016. http://www.abc.net.au/religion/articles/2016/12/16/4593491.htm.

Hauerwas, Stanley. *A Community of Character: Toward a Constructive Christian Social Ethic*. Notre Dame: University of Notre Dame Press, 1981.

Hill, Crispin. 'Marriage Quality: We Need Freedom from Religion, Not Freedom of Religion.' *Sydney Morning Herald*, November 18, 2017. http://www.

smh.com.au/comment/marriage-quality-we-need-freedom-from-religion-not-freedom-of-religion-20171116-gzn7dw.html.

Hunter, James Davison. *To Change the World*. New York: Oxford University Press, 2010.

Murray, Stuart. *Post-Christendom: Church and Mission in a Strange New World*. Carlisle: Paternoster, 2004.

Newbigin, Lesslie. *The Gospel in a Pluralist Society*. 1989. Reprint, Grand Rapids: Eerdmans, 2002.

Roxburgh, Alan. *The Missionary Congregation, Leadership and Liminality*. Harrisburg: Trinity Press, 1997.

www.ingramcontent.com/pod-product-compliance
Lightning Source LLC
Chambersburg PA
CBHW051633230426
43669CB00013B/2285